HAZOR

HAZOR

The head of all those Kingdoms

JOSHUA II: 10

WITH A CHAPTER ON ISRAELITE MEGIDDO

YIGAEL YADIN
D. PHIL.

Professor of Archaeology, The Hebrew University of Jerusalem

THE SCHWEICH LECTURES
OF THE BRITISH ACADEMY
1970

LONDON
PUBLISHED FOR THE BRITISH ACADEMY
BY THE OXFORD UNIVERSITY PRESS
1972

Oxford University Press, Ely House, London W. 1

GLASGOW NEW YORK TORONTO MELBOURNE WELLINGTON
CAPE TOWN IBADAN NAIROBI DAR ES SALAAM LUSAKA ADDIS ABABA
DELHI BOMBAY CALCUTTA MADRAS KARACHI LAHORE DACCA
KUALA LUMPUR SINGAPORE HONG KONG TOKYO

ISBN 0 19 725925 1

PRINTED IN GREAT BRITAIN
AT THE UNIVERSITY PRESS, OXFORD
BY VIVIAN RIDLER
PRINTER TO THE UNIVERSITY

DEDICATED TO THE
MEMORY OF
ENG. IMMANUEL DUNAYEVSKY

PREFACE

I SHOULD like to begin by expressing my deep gratitude to the British Academy and the Schweich Committee for inviting me to deliver this distinguished series of lectures, with particular thanks to Sir Mortimer Wheeler, C.H., under whose term of office as Secretary the invitation had been extended to me, and to the present Secretary, Mr. D. F. Allen, C.B., during whose term of office the lectures were delivered and the present volume published. I should also like to thank Sir Kenneth Wheare, C.M.G., Dr. R. D. Barnett, and Sir Mortimer Wheeler for the honour they have done me in presiding over the three lectures. Special thanks are due, too, to Miss Mary Swainson for much help in editing the manuscript and preparing it for the press.

The kind hospitality extended to me by Lord Sieff of Brompton on the premises of Michael House, during my stay in London while preparing the manuscript of the present volume, was of invaluable help, as was the technical assistance rendered by the secretarial staff of Marks and Spencer and especially Miss Gail Owen.

The form of the three parts of this volume is in keeping with the titles of the three Schweich Lectures, but the contents and scope are, of course, different.

The circumstances described in the following pages, have delayed the final and summing-up volume of the Hazor Excavations as well as the text volume of *Hazor III–IV*. I therefore use this opportunity to present, for the first time, a comprehensive survey—albeit preliminary in nature—of the results of the excavations during the years 1955–8 as well as of the campaign of 1968. This provides me also with the opportunity to present the material and conclusions in a more personal manner, rather than in the 'committee report' style of the previous Hazor volumes, giving expression to the joint efforts of the Hazor staff and their various views. This may be considered, perhaps, a less objective presentation, but my sincere intention was not to blur the issues, when no unanimous views were achieved, but rather to sharpen them.

I should like to conclude this brief preface by reiterating what I deemed fit also for the conclusion of the volume itself. Nobody is more aware than I of how much is still lacking in our knowledge of the history of Hazor (which can only be remedied by further excavations) and of the possible erroneous interpretations we have given some of the facts. Yet, if I have succeeded at least in fully presenting the material we have, then the foundation for the future research and study of the history of the 'Head of all those kingdoms' has been laid.

Y. Y.

Jerusalem
Summer 1971

CONTENTS

PREFACE   *p*. vii

LIST OF PLATES   xv

LIST OF FIGURES AND PLANS   xxi

ABBREVIATIONS AND SHORT TITLES   xxiii

PART I · THE SITE AND ITS HISTORY

I. THE HISTORICAL DATA   1

    1. General   1

    2. The Egyptian Execration texts   1

    3. Hazor and Mari   2

    4. The Egyptian sources   6
       a. General   6
       b. The el-Amarna letters   7

    5. The Bible   9
       a. Joshua 11 : 10–13   9
       b. Judges 4–5   10
       c. 1 Kings 9: 15   11
       d. 2 Kings 15: 29   11

    6. Late sources   12
       a. 1 Macc. 11: 67   12
       b. Josephus, Ant. V, 199   12

II. THE SITE   13

    1. Identification, location, and general topography   13

    2. The Tell   15

    3. The Plateau   15

III. THE EXCAVATIONS   18

    1. Garstang's soundings in 1928   18
       a. The published results   18
       b. Garstang's unpublished reports in the files of the Palestine
       Archaeological Museum   19

    2. The James A. de Rothschild expedition (1955–8)   23
       a. Organization and staff   23
       b. Methods, areas, and stratigraphy   23
          1. The grids   23
          2. The excavated areas   24
          3. Loci and registration   24
       c. Publications   25

3. The 1965 soundings   25

4. The 1968 campaign   25

PART II · THE LOWER CITY

IV. NATURE, STRATIGRAPHY, DATES, AND FINDS   27

1. Introduction   27
   a. The problem   27
   b. The areas of excavation   28

2. Area C   29
   a. General   29
   b. Strata 4–3: The MB II period   29
   c. The LB periods (Strata 2, 1B, 1A) excluding the Stelae
   Temple   32
       1. LB I—Stratum 2   32
       2. LB II—Stratum 1B   32
       3. LB III—Stratum 1A   37

3. Area D   38
   a. General   38
   b. The main phases of occupation   38

4. Area F   42
   a. General   42
   b. The MB strata ⎫
   c. The LB strata ⎬ excluding the temples   43, 44

5. Area E   46

6. Area 210   47

7. Other areas in brief (H, K)   50

V. THE EARTHEN RAMPART AND FOSSE   51

1. General   51

2. Area C   52

3. Area H   53

4. The 1965 sections   54
   a. Section A–A   54
   .Section B–B   56

5. Conclusions   56

VI. THE GATES   58

1. Area K   58

2. Area P   63

3. The City's drainage-system   65

VII. THE TEMPLES   67

    1. The Stelae Temple—Area C   67
       a. Location and stratification   67
       b. The Upper Temple   69
       c. The stelae and sculpture   71
       d. The nature of the Temple   73

    2. The Orthostats Temple—Area H   75
       a. General—Location and stratification   75
       b. The MB II Temple—Stratum 3   75
       c. The LB I Temple—Stratum 2   79
       d. The LB II Temple—Stratum 1B   83
       e. The LB III Temple—Stratum 1A   87

    3. The Temples of Area F   95
       a. General   95
       b. The Double Temple of the MB II period   96
       c. The Square Temple of the LB I period   98
       d. The Open High-Place of the LB II–III   100

    4. The Long Temple—Area A—Upper City   102

    5. General conclusions   104

VIII. THE LOWER CITY—GENERAL CONCLUSIONS   106

    1. Nature, size, and population   106

    2. Date of foundation and Near Eastern chronologies   107

    3. Date of destruction and the Bible   108

PART III · THE UPPER CITY

IX. THE AREAS OF EXCAVATIONS AND THE STRATIGRAPHICAL
    EVIDENCE   110

    1. General   110

    2. Area A   112

    .Area B   114

    4. Area AB   116

    5. Area G   116

    6. Area L   117

    7. Area M   118

    8. Comparative chart of the strata of the Lower and Upper
       Cities   118

X. THE BRONZE AGE   119

    1. The Early Bronze Age   119

    2. The MB I (EB–MB)   120

3. The MB II   121

4. The LB I   125

5. The LB II–III   126

XI. THE FIRST ISRAELITE SETTLEMENTS   129

1. Stratum XII   129

2. Stratum XII and the Israelite occupation   131

3. Stratum XI   132

XII. THE SOLOMONIC PERIOD   135

1. Area A   135
   a. Stratigraphy   135
   b. The casemate-wall   136
   c. The gate   137
   d. The moat   138

2. Areas B and L   140

3. The Solomonic city layout—Area M   140

4. The sub-phases and chronology   142

XIII. HAZOR, GEZER, AND MEGIDDO IN THE TIMES OF SOLOMON
AND AHAB   147

1. General remarks   147

2. Gezer   147

3. Megiddo   150
   a. The problem and the stratigraphy   150
   b. The 1960 and 1966–7 excavations   154
   c. The 'New Palace'—6000   154
   d. The casemates   157
   e. The gates   158
   f. The water-systems   161

XIV. AHAB'S HAZOR—STRATUM VIII   165

1. The city's plan and fortifications   165

2. The pillared building (Area A)   167

3. The citadel (Area B)   169

4. The water-system (Area L)   172
   a. General   172
   b. The water-system   173
      1. The shaft   173
      2. The sloping tunnel   175
      3. The entrance-structure   176
   c. The date of the water-system   177

XV. THE LATER PERIODS   179

  1. Stratum VI (Jeroboam II)   179
    a. Area A   179
      1. Building 2a   179
      2. Building 14a—The house of Makhbiram   181
    b. Area G   182
      1. Building 10037c   183
      2. Storehouse 10030c   184
      3. Silo 10034   184
    c. Area B   184

  2. Stratum V (King Pekah)   185
    a. General   185
    b. Area A   185
    c. Area B   187
      1. Stratum VB   187
      2. Stratum VA   187
    d. Area G   190

  3. Stratum IV (still Israelite)   190

  4. Stratum III (Assyrian)   191

  5. Stratum II (Persian)   194
    a. Area B   194
    b. Area A   195
    c. Area G   196
    d. Ayeleth-Hashahar   196

  6. Stratum I (Hellenistic)   196

XVI. THE HISTORICAL AND ARCHAEOLOGICAL DATA: CONFRONTATION   198

APPENDICES   201

  1. The identification of Hazor with Tell el-Qedaḥ established   201
  2. New data concerning Hazor in the MB II period   201
  3. Mari Letter A. 1270   207

INDEX   209

LIST OF PLATES

at end

I. *a.* Aerial view. Looking north. Foreground—the Tell of the Upper City. Above—the enclosure of the Lower City.

   b. Aerial view. Looking south. The bottle-shaped Tell of the Upper City (right—Area B). Foreground—southern part of Lower City (right—Area C and earthen rampart).

II. *a.* Area C. Looking west. Above—earthen rampart. Most of the buildings shown are of LB periods. The MB II strata—bottom left.

   b. Area F. Aerial view, looking west. Big altar—centre left.

III. *a.* Area D. Looking south-west. Tripods above rock-hewn cisterns. Buildings of MB II and LB periods.

   b. Area 210. Strata 4–1A (MB II–LB III).

IV. *a.* Area A. The 'Big Trench'. Looking south. Section through the MB II brick-wall.

   b. Area G. Looking south. The MB II stone glacis and moat.

V. *a.* Area A. Looking south-east. The MB II palatial building. Below left—the Early Bronze strata. Above—the pillared building of Stratum VIII (ninth century B.C.).

   b. Area F. A section of the MB II underground rock-hewn tunnel 8108.

   c. Area F. Rock-hewn cave 8207. MB II.

VI. *a.* Area C. Looking north-west. The MB II strata.

   b. Area 210. Burials in jars. Left—Stratum 3 (T1); right—Stratum 4 (T3–T4). MB IIB–C.

VII. *a.* Area K. Looking south-west. The city-gate at the commencement of excavations.

   b. Area K. Looking south-west. Eastern face of southern half of the gate. Stratum 3. MB IIC.

VIII. *a.* Area K. Looking south-west. The revetment wall of the gate approach. MB IIC (B?).

   b. Area K. Looking north-west. Section along gate's passageway. Paving (1A–B) covered by ashes and brick debris from final destruction.

IX. *a.* Area P. Looking west. The two-roomed western tower of the city-gate. MB II, with some LB additions.

   b. Area P. Looking south-west. The terraced stone foundations of the brick wall between the city-gate and the earthen rampart. MB IIB.

X. *a.* Area H. The clay liver-model. Stratum 2 (LB I).

   b. Area F. Burial 8112 (Stratum 2—LB I) inside drainage-channel of the Stratum 3 (MB IIC) 'Double Temple'.

   c. Area H. The bronze plaque. Stratum 2 (LB I).

XI. *a.* Area C. Looking south-west. A general view of the IB–A strata (LB II–III). Building 6225 (below) and 6063.

   b. Area C. Looking north-west. Room 6217 with nest of pithoi. Note upper potter's wheel at bottom left. Stratum IB (LB II).

XII. *a.* Area F. Looking north-west. Burial-cave 8144 with hundreds of LB II (IB) vessels.

   b. Mycenaean IIIA vessels from above burial (fourteenth century B.C.).

   c. Two Cypriote 'Bucchero' ware juglets from the same burial (fourteenth century B.C.).

XIII. Area C. Looking west. Section through western earthen rampart (MB IIB), and 'Stelae Temple' (IA–LB III), at bottom of rampart.

XIV. *a.* Area C. Looking north-west. The niche of the 'Stelae Temple' as found (head of statue was found at bottom). IA–LB III (thirteenth century B.C.)

   b. Area A. Looking west. Stelae and offering bowl, in front of the ruined LB I 'Long Temple' (LB III)—Stratum XIII (thirteenth century B.C.).

XV. *a.* Area C. Potter's workshop (locus 6225), with potter's wheel and clay mask. Stratum IB (fourteenth century B.C.).

   b. Area C. The clay mask shown above.

   c. Area C. A bronze silver-plated cult-standard. Stratum IB (IA?). Fourteenth–thirteenth century B.C.

   d. Area D. A clay mask similar to that from Area C. Fourteenth–thirteenth centuries B.C.

XVI. *a.* Area H. The 'Orthostats Temple'. Looking south-east. The 'Holy of Holies' (2113) in its Stratum IA (thirteenth century B.C.) phase.

   b. As above. Looking east. 'Holy of Holies' 2123 of Stratum IB. Above earth bulk, pillar and base of Stratum IA.

XVII. *a.* Area H. The 'Orthostats Temple', looking north. Bottom, porch 2128 with two bases of pillars, Stratum IA. Lion shown in following pictures was found under heap of stones at bottom left.

   b. Area H. 'Lion orthostat' as buried under heap of stones (see also above, *a*).

XVIII. *a.* Area H. The big lion orthostat. Originally of LB I period, buried in LB II or LB III.

b. Area C. The small lion orthostat, found in secondary use in the IA (LB III) phase of the 'Stelae Temple'. Originally LB I.

c. Area A. The 'lioness orthostat', found broken in debris of Stratum XIII.

XIX. *a*. Area H. Vessels in 'Holy of Holies', as found in Stratum IA. Note the incense-altar, the basin, two libation-tables, and basalt krater near four-handled pot.

b. Area H. The incense-altar with the 'four-pointed star', within the circle, the emblem of the temple's deity.

c. Area A. A clay bull's head, with circle and four-pointed star on foreground. Found in Stratum IXB.

XX. *a*. Area H. The deity statue with its bull base, found broken in front of the Orthostats Temple. Note the emblem of the deity (circle and four-pointed star) on pendant.

b. Area H. Orthostats Temple. A bronze bull (5 cm. in length) found in the 'Holy of Holies' of the temple, Stratum IA.

c. A Mycenaean IIIB clay bull figurine, found in Stratum IA of the Orthostats Temple.

d. Area H. A cylinder seal showing a deity with winged 'solar disc', found in Stratum IA of 'Holy of Holies'. (An heirloom from earlier strata?)

XXI. *a*. Area C. Three views of the deity statue of the Stelae Temple. Note the deity's emblem: inverted crescent.

b. Area H. A seated figure (a king?) found in the burnt layer of Stratum IA; 'the Holy of Holies' of the Orthostats Temple. Height of statue: 18 cm.

c. Area H. 'The Picasso figurine' from Stratum 2 (LB I). Bronze, 5 cm.

d. Area H. 'Peg' bronze figurine. Stratum IA; 11·5 cm.

XXII. *a*. Area A. Looking west. The orthostats entrance to the 'Long Temple', Stratum XV–LB I.

b. Area A. Looking west. The vaulted corridor to the water reservoir. LB.

XXIII. Area A. Aerial view, looking south at end of 1958 season. Solomonic city-gate and casemate-wall (Strata X–IX) below. MB and LB buildings at the centre and pillared building (Stratum VIII) and the Stratum VI courtyard building, above.

XXIV. *a*. Area A. Looking south-west. Oven made of upper part of upturned store jar. Stratum XII (twelfth century B.C.).

b. Area B. Cult-place of Stratum XI. Jar with bronze votives (eleventh century B.C.).

c. Area B. A bronze deity figurine and a lugged axe blade, from *b* left.

XXV. *a.* Area A. Aerial view, looking south-east. Solomonic city-gate and casemate-wall (bottom and left) and pillared building (Stratum VIII) and courtyard building (Stratum VI) above.

b. Area M. Looking south-east. Bottom—corner of case-mate-wall (Stratum X) turning west (right), and joint of solid wall (Stratum VIII) to the left. Above—Area A.

c. Detail of above.

XXVI. *a.* Area A. Looking south-west. The northern row of pillars of the pillared building (Stratum VIII) as excavated by Garstang.

b. The pillared building (Stratum VIII). Looking south-east, at the end of the 1956 season.

XXVII. *a.* Area A. Looking south-east. The two northern halls of the pillared building (Stratum VIII). Note the rect-angular depressions in the floor and compare the following picture.

b. The same as above, after the removal of the Stratum VIII floor. The building's Solomonic (Strata X–IX) plan corresponds to the form of the depressions.

XXVIII. *a.* Area B. Aerial view (looking south-west) of the citadel (top centre) of Stratum VIII, the ancillary admini-strative buildings—right and left, of Stratum VIII–V, and the partially filled casemate-wall (left).

b. Area B. A Proto-Aeolic capital of the citadel of Stratum VIII.

XXIX. Area L. The water-system as seen from the air at the end of the dig. Note the casemate-wall (Stratum X) on right; the 'four-roomed' administrative building (Strata VIII–V) top, right, and the 'entrance-structure' to the vertical shaft—top centre.

XXX. Area L. The water-system, looking west. The rock-hewn shaft and the entrance to the tunnel.

XXXI. Area L. The water-system, looking west into the tunnel, from its entrance, showing the debris as found.

XXXII. *a.* Area L. The water-system, looking west. The water at the end of the tunnel. The wooden planks support the ceiling to prevent collapse, during the excavations.

b. As above, showing the top basalt steps, at the bottom of the rock-hewn stairs in the tunnel.

XXXIII. *a.* Area A. Looking south-east. The courtyard building (2a) of Stratum VI. Note the tilted pillars resulting from an earthquake.

b. Area A. Looking east. The destruction of Stratum V. (Room 4 in building 1.)

XXXIV. *a.* Area G. Looking south-east. Building 10037c (Stratum VI), with the stone staircase leading to upper floor or roof.

   b. Area G. Looking south (from outside city). The postern gate with stone blocking of Stratum VA.

   c. The same; looking north. The brick blocking as seen from inside city.

XXXV. *Inscriptions*

   a. Area D. A sherd (2·5 cm. wide) with proto-Canaanite inscription: [']lt?

   b. Area B. A fragment of a stele with hieroglyphic inscription. Unstratified. For decipherment see p. 126, n. 1.

   c. Area B. Stratum VA. Outer face of a bowl with a Hebrew inscription. The second word is קדש = *Holy.* The same inscription is incised also on the rim.

   d. Area B. Stratum VA. A Hebrew inscription on the shoulder of a jar: לפקח סמדר = *belonging to Pekah. Semadar* (wine of tender grapes).

   e. Area A. Stratum VI. A Hebrew inscription on a shoulder of a jar: למכברם = *belonging to Makhbiram.*

   f. Area A. Stratum VI. A Hebrew inscription painted on a jar:

      ירבעם = Jeroboam

      בן אלמ = Son of Elm(atan?).

XXXVI. *a.* Area A. Stratum VI. Three sides of a carved bone handle.

   b. Area A. Stratum VI. Three views of an ivory cosmetic spoon.

LIST OF FIGURES AND PLANS

1. General map of Mesopotamia, Syria, and Palestine, with main cities mentioned in the present book.   3

2. Map of North-east Galilee.   14

3. Topographical map of Hazor with excavated areas.   16

4. Garstang's unpublished sketch of excavated areas.   20

5. Area C. MB IIC—Stratum 3. Building 6205.   30

6. Area C. LB II–III, Strata 1B–A, with mainly 1B.   34

7. Area D. MB II–LB. Cisterns 9024; 9027.   39

8. Area F. MB II. The tunnels and shafts.   43

9. Area E. LB I—Cistern 7021.   47

10. Area 210. Plans of the MB II–LB III strata.   49

11. Earthen ramparts. Section A–A. Above: looking west; below: looking east.   55

12. Area K. The earliest gate—Stratum 4 (MB IIB).   59

13. Area K. The gate of Stratum 3 (MB IIC).   61

14. Area K. The gates of Strata 1B–A (LB II–III).   62

15. Area C. The Temple of 1B (LB II).   68

16. Area C. The Temple of 1A (LB III).   70

17. Section—looking west of temples 1B–1A.   70

18. Area H. Temple of Stratum 3 (MB IIC).   76

19. Area H. Temple of Stratum 2 (LB I).   76

20. Area H. Temple of Stratum 1B (LB II).   88

21. Area H. Temple of Stratum 1A (LB III).   88

22. Area H. Temple of Stratum 1A—layout of cult-objects as found in the Holy of Holies.   92

23. Area F. Conjectural restoration of the Stratum 3 (MB IIC) 'Double Temple'.   97

24. Area F. The 'Square Temple' of Stratum 2 (LB I), with the temple of Amman for comparison.   99

25. Area F. The cult-area of Strata 1B–A (LB II–III).   102

26. Area A. Schematic plan of the Long Temple (MB II–LB I).   103

27. The Upper City. Schematic key plan.   111

28. Area A. The MB–LB underground water-reservoir.   127

29. Area B. Stratum XI—the cult-structure.   133

30. Area A. Stratum X—the Solomonic city-gate.   136

31. Area A. Stratum XB—Building 200–2 (d) and the casemate-wall.   138

32. Area A. Stratum XA—Building 200–2 (c) and the casemate-wall.   139

33. Area A. Stratum IXʙ—Building 200–2 (b) and the casemate-wall. 144

34. Area A. Stratum IXᴀ—Building 200–2 (a) and the casemate-wall. 145

35. Gezer. The Solomonic fortifications—'The Maccabean Castle'. 149

36. Gezer. Reconstruction of the Solomonic fortifications. 149

37. Megiddo. Solomon's city-gate and the 'associate' city-wall—
    325, as published in *Megiddo II*, fig. 105. 151

38. Megiddo—building 1723 under city-wall 325. 152

39. Key plan of Megiddo in Strata IVᴀ; IVʙ–Vᴀ. 153

40. Megiddo. The excavations of 1960; 66–7. The new Solomonic
    palace and the casemate-walls. Note the position of Strata Vʙ, VIᴀ. 154

41. Megiddo—city-gates, Strata VIᴀ–IVᴀ. 159

42. Megiddo—city-gates, Strata IVᴀ–III. 160

43. Megiddo—the 1967 excavations near Gallery 629. 162

44. Area A. The pillared building of Stratum VIII. 168

45. Area B. The Citadel, the filled casemate-wall and the ancillary
    buildings—Stratum VIII. 170

46. Area L. The water-system and the adjacent buildings and sec-
    tions. 174

47. Area L. Sections of the water-system. 174

48. Area A. Stratum VI. 180

49. Area G. Building 10037c of Stratum VI. 183

50. Area A. Stratum V. 186

51. Area B—Stratum Vʙ. 188

52. Area B—Stratum Vᴀ. 188

53. Area G—Stratum V. 191

54. Area B—Stratum III. 192

55. Area B—Stratum II. 193

56. Area B—Stratum I. 193

ABBREVIATIONS AND SHORT TITLES

AAA	*Annals of Archaeology and Anthropology* (Liverpool)
AASOR	*Annual of the American Schools of Oriental Research*
AfO	*Archiv für Orientforschung*
Ain Shems V	E. Grant and G. E. Wright, *Ain Shems Excavations*, Part V, Text, Haverford, 1939
Alalakh	Sir Leonard Woolley, *Alalakh, An Account of the Excavations at Tell Atchana in the Hatay, 1937–49*, Oxford, 1955
ANEP	*The Ancient Near East in Pictures* (J. B. Pritchard, ed.)
ANET	*Ancient Near Eastern Texts* (J. B. Pritchard, ed.)
AOTS	*Archaeology and Old Testament Study* (D. Winton Thomas, ed.), Oxford, 1967
ARM	*Archives royales de Mari*
BA	*The Biblical Archaeologist*
BASOR	*Bulletin of the American Schools of Oriental Research*
CAH	*The Cambridge Ancient History* (revised edition of vols. I and II)
EB	Early Bronze
Encyclopaedia of Archaeological Excavations	*Encyclopaedia of Archaeological Excavations in the Holy Land* (Hebrew), Jerusalem, 1970
Enc. Miqr.	*Encyclopaedia Miqraith* (Encyclopaedia Biblica—Hebrew), Jerusalem
Et-Tell ('Ay)	J. Marquet-Krause, *Les fouilles de 'Ay (Et-Tell)*, Paris, 1949
Hazor I	Y. Yadin, Y. Aharoni, Ruth Amiran, Trude Dothan, I. Dunayevsky, J. Perrot, *Hazor I*, Jerusalem, 1958.
Hazor II	(As above) Jerusalem, 1960
Hazor III–IV	*Hazor III–IV* (Plates), Jerusalem, 1961
HUCA	*Hebrew Union College Annual*
IEJ	Israel Exploration Journal
JBL	*Journal of Biblical Literature*
JEA	*Journal of Egyptian Archaeology*
JNES	*Journal of Near Eastern Studies*
Joshua, Judges	J. Garstang, *Joshua, Judges*, London, 1931
Lachish II	Olga Tufnell, C. H. Inge, L. Harding, *The Fosse Temple*, London, 1940
Lachish IV	Olga Tufnell, *The Bronze Age*, London, 1958
LB	Late Bronze
MB	Middle Bronze
Megiddo I	R. S. Lamon and G. M. Shipton, *Megiddo I*, Chicago, 1939
Megiddo II	G. Loud, *Megiddo II*, Chicago, 1948

OIC	*Oriental Institute Communications* (Chicago)
PEQ	*Palestine Exploration Quarterly*
QDAP	*Quarterly of the Department of Antiquities of Palestine*
RA	*Revue d'assyrologie et d'archéologie orientale*
RB	*Revue Biblique*
RSO	*Rivista degli studi orientali*
The Glueck Festschrift	*Near Eastern Archaeology in the Twentieth Century, Essays in Honor of Nelson Glueck* (J. A. Sanders, ed.), Garden City, N.Y., 1970
VT	*Vetus Testamentum*
ZAW	*Zeitschrift für die alttestamentliche Wissenschaft*
ZDPV	*Zeitschrift des deutschen Palästina-Vereins*

PART I

THE SITE AND ITS HISTORY

I

THE HISTORICAL DATA

§ 1. GENERAL

HAZOR is known to have been a very important city in ancient Palestine, not only from biblical sources, but equally from the frequent references to it in a series of external sources. In fact, it is almost unique amongst Palestinian cities inasmuch as these sources cover a period from the beginning of the second millennium B.C. down to the first century A.D. with few gaps, and their geographical range spans almost the entire Fertile Crescent. Like many of the cities of the Holy Land, its importance to biblical scholars lay for many years mainly in the role it played in the history of Ancient Israel. However, the abundance of historical data discovered in recent years turns Hazor into a focal point in the understanding of many historical events related to its neighbouring countries, and the results of the archaeological excavations now add a new means towards solving the complex problems of Near Eastern chronology in the first half of the first millennium B.C. It is, therefore, of the utmost importance to begin our survey with a detailed description of Hazor's role as it can be deduced from written sources.

§ 2. THE EGYPTIAN EXECRATION TEXTS

Hazor is first mentioned in the Egyptian Execration Texts of the so-called Posener Group.[1] The City's name is spelt *ḥḏwiȝi* (variant: *ḥḏwiȝ*) and its ruler is a certain *gti*. It is interesting to note that while *gti* is in all probability a non-Semitic name, some

---

[1] G. Posener, *Princes et Pays d'Asie et de Nubie. Textes hiératiques sur des figurines d'envoûtement du Moyen Empire*, Bruxelles, 1940, p. 73: E 15.

B

rulers in the same texts bear names clearly derived from the West Semitic onomasticon.[1]

There is a general agreement that the Posener Group is later than the so-called Sethe Group, but opinions differ widely concerning their absolute date: XIIth Dynasty[2] or XIIIth Dynasty.[3]

While the problem of the absolute date of the Posener Group is of vital importance to the interpretation of the archaeology of Hazor as revealed by the excavations (see Chapter X, §§ 2–3), it is sufficient to note at this stage that the reference to Hazor in this group (as in fact to the other cities) indicates that, unlike the situation in Palestine as reflected in the Sethe Group, we are dealing here with a settlement with a single ruler.[4]

§ 3. HAZOR AND MARI

Notwithstanding the importance of Egyptian Execration Texts, it is in the Mari archives that Hazor emerges for the first time as a major city and centre of large-scale economic and political activities, together with such great city states as Yamḫad, Qatna, and other centres of commerce in the Fertile Crescent (Fig. 1). Indeed, Hazor and its neighbour, Laish (Dan), 30 km. to the north (also mentioned in the Posener Group, E 59), are the only Palestinian cities mentioned at all in these archives, with Hazor playing the dominant role. These references, as will be discussed later (Chapter VIII, § 2), can be related only to the great Hazor of the Middle Bronze (MB) period, as revealed by the excavations. Thus, and unexpectedly, the results of the excavations can contribute in a modest way to the solution of the vexing problem of the chronologies of Hammurabi and Mari, rather than the other way round as we would have wished. But, irrespective of chronological problems, the data concerning the status and nature of Hazor is of much importance, so much so that a detailed analysis of these

---

[1] e.g. *Ῑκmṭ–ʿmw* (E 14); *tḇ3–hdd* (E 16). On this see B. Mazar, 'The Middle Bronze Age in Palestine', *IEJ* 18, 1968, p. 81.

[2] Posener (see above, p. 1 n. 1); idem, *CAH* i, 'Syria and Palestine', pp. 25 ff. W. F. Albright, 'Remarks on the Chronology of Early Bronze IV—Middle Bronze IIA in Phoenicia and Syria—Palestine', *BASOR* 184, 1966, p. 28 n. 10 (1850–1825 B.C.).

[3] W. Helck, *Die Beziehungen Ägyptens zu Vorderasien im 3. und 2. Jahrtausend vor Chr.*, Wiesbaden, 1962, p. 53, followed by M. Noth ('Thebes', *AOTS*, p. 24) and B. Mazar (see above, n. 1), p. 81; M. G. Posener, *Syria* 43, 1966, pp. 277 ff.

The newly discovered Execration Texts from Mirgissa are apparently older than the Posener group; see J. Vercoutter, 'Textes exécratoires de Mirgissa', *Comptes rendus de l'Académie des Inscriptions et Belles-Lettres*, 1963, pp. 97–102; Noth (ibid.), p. 23; Albright (see above, n. 2).

[4] Cf. also Mazar (see above, n. 1), pp. 81–2.

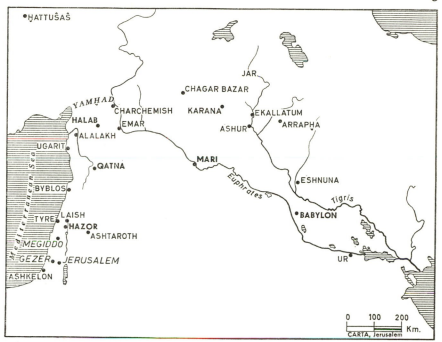

Fig. 1. General map of Mesopotamia, Syria, and Palestine, with main cities mentioned in the present book.

references would be very useful.[1] Hazor's name is spelt *Ḥa-ṣú-ra*, *Ḥa-ṣú-ra-yu^ki*, or *Ḥa-ṣú-ra-a* with a long final vowel.[2] The following are the most important references to Hazor in Mari:

1. Baḫdi-Lim—the Chamberlain of Mari's palace during the reign of Zimri-Lim, informs his master about a group of messengers who arrived at Mari, including among them men from Hazor.[3]

        1   [To] my Lord
             speak
             [Thus] (speaks) Baḫdi-Lim
             [Thy servant:]
        5   [A group of messengers[4] from Haz]or

[1] The following discussion draws heavily on the excellent treatment of this subject by A. Malamat, in two articles: (1) 'Hazor "The Head of all those Kingdoms" ', *JBL* 79, 1960, pp. 12 ff. (2) 'Hazor and its Northern Neighbours in New Mari Documents' (Hebrew), in *Eretz-Israel*, vol. 9 (The Albright Volume), 1969, pp. 102 ff. (with a short English summary). See now an English version of this article (with some additions), in *The Glueck Festschrift*, 1970, pp. 164 ff.

[2] In another source (The Babylonian Dream-Book), to be discussed later, Hazor is spelt: Ḥa-ṣú-ur. See also Appendix, § 1.

[3] J. R. Kupper, *Correspondance de Baḫdi-Lim*, ARM vi, 1954, no. 78. The translation used here is that of Malamat (*JBL*, see above, n. 1, pp. 13–14).

[4] *ṭeḥîtum* from *ṭeḫû* 'to approach'. For this term, Malamat is indebted to A. L. Oppenheim, *JNES* 13, 1954, p. 147.

[and Qatna has arriv]ed here

. . . .

. . . .

[Servants of my Lo]rd,
10 [and a man of Ha]zor
[as their] escort
(have come) to my Lord
Two messengers from Babylon
who have long since resided at Hazor
15 With one man from Hazor
as their escort are crossing
to Babylon.[1]

The importance of this document can hardly be overestimated. It shows that the King of Babylon (Hammurabi) had special ambassadors[2] residing at Hazor and for some considerable time. The close relations between Hazor and Babylon, further attested by other sources, are undoubtedly responsible for such inscribed objects found by us as clay liver models (Chapter VII, § 2,*c*), a jar bearing an Akkadian personal name inscribed in cuneiform (Chapter IV, § 2,*b*), and a fragment of the lexical series HAR-ra-*ḫubullu* (Chapter X, § 3).

2. In another letter,[3] Baḫdi-Lim reports the movement of emissaries in the opposite direction:

Further, a group of travellers in transit from Babylon, Eshnuna, Ekallatum, Karana, Qatna and Arrapḫa on their way to Yamḫad, Qatna, Hazor and . . . have arrived here. Shall I let them go or stop them?

It is interesting to note—as pointed out by Malamat—not only that Hazor is mentioned here together with such great cities and states as Yamḫad (with Ḥalab as its capital) and Qatna (present-day *el Mishrefeh*) but that the order of mention is geographically from north to south.[4]

1 The rest of the document deals in a similar manner with messengers from Babylon and their escort from Qatna, who were crossing to Babylon.

2 *mār šiprim*, i.e. ambassadors of the highest rank, as Malamat points out (*JBL*, see above, p. 3 n. 1, p. 14).

3 *ARM* vi, no. 23; Malamat, ibid., p. 15.

4 A similar geographical order occurs in a fragment of a Babylonian Dream-Book found in Babylon from the Kassite period (A. L. Oppenheim, 'The Interpretation of Dreams in the Ancient Near East', *Trans. Amer. Phil. Soc.* 46, 1956, p. 313; Malamat, ibid..

The following cities are mentioned there: Mari-Emar-Ḥalab (i.e. capital of Yamḫad)—Qatna—Hazor. Malamat (ibid., p. 16) concludes 'that for the Mesopotamian the Kingdom of Hazor was the last political centre in the West'. Yet, in the above quoted letter, there existed another name after that of Hazor, which, alas, is not preserved. A. Alt ('Beziehungen zu Ägypten in den Briefen von Mari?', *ZDPV* 70, 1954, pp. 130–4) suggested that the missing name was Egypt, and Malamat infers that it might have been an important centre

3. A very important document, which unfortunately has not hitherto been published in full, mentions the name of the King of Hazor. It is extremely important also because it is the oldest reference to Hazor in the Mari documents.[1]

The letter is from Shamshi-Adad, King of Assyria, to his son Yasmaḫ-Adad who was the King's viceroy, ruling Mari. The letter deals with envoys of the King of Hazor as well as of those of the Four Kings of Amurru. The King orders his son to see to it that the King of Qatna appoints a special escort to bring the envoys into his city.

As mentioned above, this is also the only document from Mari which mentions the name of the King (thus) of Hazor: Ibni-Adad, the Akkadian form of the West Semitic name Yabni-Hadad. It is difficult to say whether this form was current in the court of Hazor, thus further testifying to a Babylonian influence, or whether this form was given thus by the scribes at Mari. It has also been suggested[2] that the form of the name is just a hypocoristicon of the full theoric name. If this is true, it is possible that the name Yabin was a royal dynastic name of the Kings of Hazor. In this case it would seem that the ruler of Hazor, bearing the non-semitic name *Gti*, mentioned in the Execration Texts, *preceded* Ibni-Adad rather than[3] succeeded him.

4. Ibni-Adad is mentioned several times in other documents which have not yet been published.[4] According to these, the King of Hazor was in contact not only with Mari, but also with Ugarit and even with *Kaptara*.[5] In another unpublished letter,[6] in which Ibni-Adad is mentioned several times, there is also mention of Laish, the only other Palestinian city to occur in the Mari documents. Contact between Mari and Hazor is

to the south of Hazor. It is possible that the missing name may have been Laish, the only other Palestinian city mentioned in the Mari letters. Its position after Hazor could have been prompted by the fact than on the itinerary from Mesopotamia it was reached after Hazor, although it lies further to the north.

[1] Malamat, *JBL* (see above, p. 3 n. 1), p. 17; idem, *Eretz-Israel* (see above, p. 3 n. 1), pp. 101 ff. For further details see: A. Pohl, *Orientalia* 19, 1950, p. 509; J. R. Kupper, 'Les nomades en Mésopotamie au temps des rois de Mari', Paris, 1957, p. 179 n. 1; G. Dossin, 'Kengen, pays de Canaan', *RSO* 32, 1957, pp. 37 ff. (all mentioned by Malamat). For further aspects of the Mari documents see also, 'La civilisation de Mari', *XVᵉ Rencontre Assyriologique Internationale*, Paris, 1967.
[2] W. F. Albright, *The Biblical Period from Abraham to Ezra*, New York, 1963, p. 102 n. 83.
[3] As is the view of Mazar (see above, p. 2 n. 1, p. 83 n. 51).
[4] Malamat, *Eretz-Israel* (see above, p. 3 n. 1), p. 10.
[5] See also, G. Dossin, *Comptes rendus 3me recontre assyriologique internationale*, Leiden, 1951, p. 21. Professor Malamat now informs me that these references are doubtful. See Appendix, §3.
[6] Oral communication of Dossin to Malamat, Malamat, *Eretz-Israel*, ibid.

attested by another document,[1] administrative in nature. According to this document a man from Hazor (Ḫa-ṣú-ra-yu[ki]), together with seventeen other emissaries and artisans (from Babylon and Eshnuna, Carchemish and Emar, as well as from Yamḫad), received meat rations while they stayed at Zimri-Lim's court. However, the most important of these administrative documents[2] deals, *inter alia*, with a consignment of tin[3] for Hazor. This certainly has to do with the manufacturing of bronze vessels at Hazor, and it further attests the close and intricate political and economic ties between these two centres. The discovery of the Hazor of Mari times has become, therefore, one of the most interesting of our discoveries, and its nature will be discussed in Part II.

§ 4. THE EGYPTIAN SOURCES

a. *General*

Hazor is mentioned several times in the conquered-towns lists of the Pharaohs of the New Kingdom.[4] While it is sometimes difficult to assess whether Hazor was actually conquered, or was just under control of the Pharaohs, these references provide us with further data concerning Hazor. The earliest of these references goes back to Thutmosis III,[5] and Hazor is spelt, *ḥḏr* or *ḥḏ⟨w⟩[r]*. A more important mention of Hazor during the reign of this monarch occurs in the Papyrus Hermitage No. 1116A,[6] which contains a list recording the allocation of beer and corn to messengers from *Djahy*. The envoys are further designated as *mryn*. This list includes such known cities as Megiddo, Kinnereth, Achshaph, Shimron, Ta'anakh, Ashkelon, as well as a few less known or clearly identified. Hazor (ḥ-[ḏ]-r) occurs between Ashkelon (no. 9) and *Ḥ-t-m* (unidentified), but no precise geographical references can be drawn from the order in which the cities are listed.

As will be seen later, the spade revealed that Hazor attained an unprecedented prosperity during the fifteenth century.

---

[1] M. Birot, *ARM* xii, Paris, 1964, no. 747.

[2] J. Bottéro, *ARM* xii, 1957, no. 236; Malamat, *JBL* (see above, p. 3 n. 1), p. 17.

[3] *Anākum*. See Appendix, §3.

[4] Most conveniently arranged in *ANET*², 1955, pp. 242 ff.

The following numbers and references are given to J. Simons, *Handbook for the Study of Egyptian Topographical Lists Relating to Western Asia*, Leiden, 1937, unless otherwise stated.

[5] Simons, no. 32, pp. 111, 116; no. 27, p. 123.

[6] W. Golénischeff, *Les Papyrus hiératiques Nos 1115, 1116A et 1116B de l'Ermitage Impériale à St. Petersburg*, St. Petersburg, 1913. For a recent treatment of the relevant lines, see Claire Epstein, 'A New Appraisal of some Lines from a Long-Known Papyrus', *JEA* 49, 1963, pp. 49 ff.

The next mention of Hazor is in the reign of Amenophis
—*ḥdr*.[1]

As far as the town lists are concerned, the last mention of
Hazor is in the days of Sethi I[2]—*ḥd*⟨*w*⟩*r*.

The last reference to Hazor in the Egyptian texts is perhaps
also the most enlightening. Papyrus Anastasi I, which is
ascribed to the reign of Rameses II,[3] contains the following
passage, in which Hori, a royal official, challenges Amen-em-
Opet the scribe: 'Where does the *mahir* (a swift military courier)
make the journey to Hazor (*ḥ d r*)? What is its stream like?'

The above brief references to Hazor attest to its existence in
one form or another, in the fifteenth, fourteenth, and thirteenth
centuries.

b. The el-Amarna letters

By far the most important source concerning Hazor in the
Late Bronze period generally and in the first half of the fourteenth
century in particular—is no doubt the el-Amarna letters. Two
dispatches of the King of Hazor have been found so far, and in
two other letters Hazor and its king are the main subjects of
the correspondence. These texts are so well known, and the
amount of literature dealing with the el-Amarna letters so
vast[4] that it will suffice here to single out the main points of
interest relating to Hazor.

Letter no. 227

In this letter, written by the monarch of Hazor to the Pharaoh,
the writer refers to himself as the 'King of the city of Hazor'
(*šàr ᵃˡHa-su-ri*ᵏⁱ), a case unparalleled in all the letters of the
Canaanite cities in the el-Amarna archive. Furthermore, in
another letter (no. 148—to be discussed later), he is so referred

---

[1] Simons, no. 18, p. 129.

[2] Simons, nos. 66, 64—pp. 137, 141. The suggested restoration of [ḥd] ⟨w⟩r in Rameses
III lists (Simons, p. 177) has no firm basis.

[3] See J. A. Wilson, *apud ANET*, p. 477.

[4] The numbers of the letters referred to here are (unless otherwise stated) those in J. A.
Knudtzon, *Die El. Amarna-Tafeln*, Leipzig, 1915. An English translation can be found in
S. A. B. Mercer, *The Tell El-Amarna Tablets* . . ., 1939, as well as in *ANET*. On the problems
of the el-Amarna letters generally, or on those related to a particular subject (such as the
ḥabiru), see the following studies, where additional bibliography can be found: E. Täubler,
'Chazor in den Briefen von Tell el-Amarna', *Festschrift für L. Beck*, 1938, pp. 9–30;
E. F. Campbell, Jr., 'The Amarna Letters and the Amarna period', *BA* 23, 1960, pp. 2–22;
W. F. Albright, 'The Amarna Letters from Palestine', *CAH* ii, chap. 20, fasc. 51, 1966; F. F.
Bruce, 'Tell el-Amarna', *AOTS*, pp. 3–15; J. Bottéro (ed.), *Le problème des Ḥabiru*, Paris, 1954
(Cahiers de la Société Asiatique, 12); M. Greenberg, *The Ḥab/Piru*, New Haven, 1955
(American Oriental Series, 39); idem in *The Patriarchs and the Judges* (ed. B. Mazar—Hebrew
edition), Jerusalem, 1967, pp. 95–102, M. Weippert, *Die Landnahme der israelitischen Stämme*,
Göttingen, 1967, pp. ff. On the chronology of the period, see K. A. Kitchen, *Suppiluliuma and
the Amarna Pharaohs, A Study in Relative Chronology*, Liverpool, 1962.

to by the ruler of Tyre.[1] No. 227 is unfortunately rather fragmentary,[2] but it is interesting to note that the King reassures
the Pharaoh that he is safeguarding the *cities* of the Pharaoh
(*a-na-ku na-aṣ-ra-ti* [*ala*]-*âni^{ni} šarri bêli-ia*) until the latter's
arrival. This indicates no doubt that the King of Hazor's rule
embraced more than the city itself. This is further corroborated
by the letters of the rulers of Tyre and Ashtaroth (see below).

Letter no. 228

The second letter of the ruler of Hazor includes two further
precious pieces of information. We learn the name of the king
or, the 'man of the city Hazor' as he refers to himself this time
(*amêl ^{al}Ḫa-ṣu-ra*), 'Abdi Tirshi (^{m}Abd[i]-Tir-ši).[3] Furthermore,
there is an intriguing reference to some hostile acts which
befell the city and the king: 'Let my Lord the King remember
all that was done against the city of Hazor—your city—as well
as against your servant.' We do not know, of course, to what he
is referring, but it must have been something of some magnitude,
since 'Abdi-Tirši takes it for granted that the actual event
was known to the Pharaoh. It is perhaps possible that it is
related to another obscure event mentioned in the letter from
the King of Tyre 'Abi-Milki (No. 148). Near the end of the
very long letter, 'Abi-Milki abruptly says: 'The King (!) of
Hazor left his city[4] and joined[5] the *ḫabiru*.' He concluded the
letter with a general warning connected with this: 'Let the
King know that they (the *ḫabiru*) are hostile to the Supervisor.[6]
The King's land is falling into the hands of the *ḫabiru*. Let the
King ask the High Commissioner[7] who is familar with Canaan.'[8]
It is not clear why the King has left his city to join the *ḫabiru*.
If he did it deliberately, why did he have to leave the city? Or
maybe the actual incident refers to an internal coup which
forced the King temporarily to find refuge with the *ḫabiru*?
If this is so, we have here a striking similarity to what happened
to King Idrimi of Alalakh.[9]

Idrimi, after having been ousted by a revolt, took refuge at
various places, till in the end he wandered to Canaan and

---

[1] For a similar phenomenon regarding the King of Hazor in the Mari Archives, see above
§ 3.

[2] On some of these problems, see W. F. Albright, in *BASOR* 163, p. 40 n. 20.

[3] For this name, see idem, *BASOR* 139, 1955, p. 18.

[4] *Alâ-šu* (Bottéro), or 'his house'—*bîta-šu* (Greenberg). Cf. also W. F. Albright, *JEA* 23,
1937, p. 202.

[5] Or *'placed himself'* (the Canaanite word is here used: *it-ta-ṣa-*[*a*] *b*) with the *ḫabiru*.

[6] Greenberg's suggestion.   [7] *li-iš-al šarru* ^{lu}*rabiṣa-šu*.   [8] *ša i-de* ^{mât}*Ki-na-aḫ-na*.

[9] See conveniently, D. J. Wiseman, in *AOTS*, pp. 121 f.

stayed for seven years with the *ḥabiru*. He eventually regained control and returned to Alalakh. Could the previously mentioned words of 'Abdi-Tirshi about the calamities which befell him refer to the very event mentioned by 'Abi-Milki, but differently interpreted? Whatever the case, 'Abdi-Tirshi the monarch of Hazor in the first half of the fourteenth century, was otherwise, or at different phases of his reign, quite ambitious and his territorial expansion reached the sphere of suzerainty of 'Aiâb King of Ashtaroth in cis-Jordan. This we learn from the relatively recently published letter written by 'Aiâb:[1] 'The man of the city of Hazor took from me three cities.'

§ 5. THE BIBLE

The main references to Hazor in the Bible fall into two distinct groups: 1. Hazor's role in the conquest process. 2. Brief historical references apropos of the description of Solomon's building activities and the conquest of Galilee by Tiglath-Pileser III. While the second group of references creates no textual or historical problems, the former constitutes one of the most controversial subjects in the study of Ancient Israelite history, and in the basic approach of scholars to the understanding of the Books of Joshua and Judges in particular. At this stage, before the result of the recent excavations is presented, it will suffice to refer to these passages briefly and to mention only the main trends of opinion regarding their interpretation which were current before the excavations.[2]

a. *Joshua 11: 10–13*

Of the detailed description of the battle against the northern Canaanite league and Jabin King of Hazor contained in Joshua 11, the following are the main salient points relevant to the present discussion:

'And Joshua turned back at that time, and took Hazor, and smote the King thereof with the sword: for Hazor beforetime was the head of all those Kingdoms . . . and he burnt Hazor with fire . . . But as for the cities that stood on their mounds (lit. on their *tells*) Israel burned none of them save Hazor only; that did Joshua burn!'

The main interest lies in the compiler's gloss—explaining why Hazor was the main object of Joshua's attention: 'for

---

[1] F. Thureau–Dangin, *RA* 19, 1934, p. 96; Mercer, 256A.

[2] We shall return to this subject in the discussion of the LB Strata in the Lower City (Chapter IV) and Upper City (Chapter X), and particularly in the section (Chapter XI) dealing with the first Israelite settlements in Hazor as evidenced by the excavations.

Hazor beforetime was the head of all those Kingdoms'. It seems to me that the logical explanation for this is that, by the times of the compiler, Hazor was no longer an important city and the 'beforetime' refers to its status on the eve of Joshua's conquest.[1]

b. Judges 4–5

In the prose version of Deborah's war, preserved in Chapter 4, we read: 'And the Lord sold them into the hand of Jabin King of Canaan, that reigned in Hazor; the Captain of whose host was Sisera, which dwelt in Harosheth of the Gentiles . . .

'Howbeit Sisera fled away on his feet to the tent of Jael the wife of Heber the Kenite: for there was peace between Jabin the King of Hazor and the house of Heber the Kenite . . . So God subdued on that day Jabin the King of Canaan before the children of Israel. And the hand of the children of Israel prevailed more and more against Jabin King of Canaan.'[2] The crux of the problem lies in the apparent contradiction between these passages and the one from Joshua 11, and that Deborah's song (Chapter 5) contains no reference whatsoever to Jabin. Furthermore, both in the prose version and in the song, the actual battlefield is the western part of the Esdraelon Valley, far, far away from Hazor.

The main or basic approach in biblical studies to these problems may be grouped under four 'Schools of thought':

(i) This view adheres closely to the biblical texts and was held by the Jewish medieval commentators who, stressing the fact that Judges 4 refers to Jabin in the past tense, 'that *reigned* in Hazor', took it to mean that by the time of Deborah he was no longer alive. In this they were followed most recently by S. Yeivin.[3]

(ii) The view that Joshua 11 has no historical basis, and in fact sees the whole process of the conquest as a peaceful infiltration culminating in local conflicts, some of which are reflected in the biblical narratives of Judges.[4]

---

[1] Another view is that of Malamat (*JBL* above, p. 3 n. 1, p. 19) who maintains that the expression 'beforetime' refers to Hazor's greatness in the MB Age.   [2] Cf. also 1 Sam. 12: 9.

[3] S. Yeivin, 'The Israelite Settlement in Galilee and the Wars with Jabin of Hazor', *Mélanges Bibliques, Rédigés en l'honneur de André Robert*, Paris, 1957, pp. 95 ff.; idem, *Encyclopaedia Miqraith* (Hebrew), vol. iv, 1962, pp. 79 ff.

[4] For this view, which may be called the German School of A. Alt and his followers (with variants and modifications), see the exhaustive treatment, with generous bibliography, of M. Weippert: *Die Landnahme der israelitischen Stämme in der neueren wissenschaftlichen Diskussion*, Göttingen, 1967, pp. 14 ff., 40 ff. Cf. also very recently V. Fritz, 'Die sogennante Listen der besiegten Könige in Josua 12', *ZDPV* 85, 1969, pp. 136 ff. See also W. F. Albright, '† Albrecht Alt', *JBL* 75, 1956, pp. 169 ff.

(iii) The view that accepts the chronological and historical basis of Joshua 11 and Judges 5, but takes the references to Jabin in Judges 4 as a late editorial interpolation, influenced by Joshua 11. Furthermore, this view—which may be ascribed to the Albright School[1]—takes the archaeological evidence revealed at such sites as Bethel, Lachish, etc., as a conclusive proof for the historical accuracy of the Joshua narratives.

(iv) A 'compromise view' which, although it considers the nucleus of both Joshua and Judges as reflecting historical happenings, changes the order of events, and places the destruction of Hazor as described in Joshua *after* the one dealt with in Judges 4. This school of thought was originated by B. Mazar.[2] This view was adopted by Y. Aharoni, who, basing it on his survey of Upper Galilee, came to the conclusion that the two battles—which occurred after the infiltration phase —took place towards the *end* of the twelfth century; in other words, it envisaged that Jabin's Hazor was flourishing in the second half of the twelfth century.[3] A critical reaction to some of the above-mentioned views, in the light of the excavations, will be presented in Chapter IV, § 2, *c*, and in Chapter XI, § 2.

c. 1 Kings 9: 15

This passage will be discussed in detail in Chapters XII–XIII, and therefore it is sufficient to stress at this point only that the above passage—about the historical accuracy of which there has been no division of opinion—indicates quite clearly that the turning-point in Hazor's history took place in the time of Solomon, when, together with Megiddo and Gezer, the ruined city was rebuilt as one of the most important strategic bases.

d. 2 Kings 15: 29

The following short passage is the last historical reference in the Bible to Hazor, and indicates that the city fell in 732 B.C., together with most of the northern part of Israel.

As will be shown later on, this piece of information was invaluable towards the interpretation of the archaeological

[1] Apart from his known comprehensive books on biblical archaeology, cf. *inter alia*, 'Archaeology and the Date of the Hebrew Conquest of Palestine', *BASOR* 58, 1935, pp. 10 ff.; 'The Song of Deborah in the Light of Archaeology', *BASOR* 62, 1936, pp. 26 ff.; *BASOR* 68, 1937, pp. 22 ff.; 'The Israelite Conquest of Canaan in the Light of Archaeology', *BASOR* 74, 1939, pp. 11 ff. For a critical treatment of these views, see Weippert (see above, p. 10 n. 4), pp. 51 ff., and ibid. Bibliography. Cf. also most recently, A. Malamat, in *The Patriarchs and Judges* (B. Mazar (ed.)—Hebrew), 1967, p. 21 f.

[2] *HUCA* 24, 1952–3, pp. 80 ff.; *Enc. Miqr.* iii, 1958, p. 259, and most recently in *The Patriarchs and Judges* (see above), pp. 193 f. Cf also Malamat, ibid., p. 221.

[3] *The Settlement of the Tribes of Israel in Upper Galilee* (Hebrew), 1957, pp. 89 ff., idem, *Enc. Miqr.* iii, 1958 (s.v. *Jabin*), pp. 449 ff.; idem in *Antiquity and Survival* 2, 1957, p. 149.

evidence: 'In the days of Pekah King of Israel came Tiglath-Pileser [the 3rd] King of Assyria, and took Ijon, and Abel-beth-maacah, and Janoah, and Kedesh, and Hazor, and Gilead, and Galilee, all the land of Naphtali, and he carried them captive to Assyria.'

§ 6. LATE SOURCES

a. 1 Macc. 11: 67

This is the last reference to any historical event connected in one way or another with Hazor. Here we are told that Jonathan fought against Demetrius (147 B.C.) in the 'Plain of Hazor'.[1] Whether this remark indicates the existence of some settlement at Hazor at that time, or, that only its location was still known —there was no means of determining before the excavations (see Chapter XVI).

b. Josephus, Antiquity V, 199

This, the last mention of Hazor in the ancient sources, has no value for the history of the city but has been helpful in locating its site. According to Josephus, Hazor lay 'over the Lake Semechonitis',[2] i.e. the present day Lake Hûleh, in Upper Galilee.

[1] ' . . . τὸ πεδίον Ασωρ'.   [2] 'ὑπερκαιται τῆς Σεμεχωνίτιδος λίμνης'.

II

THE SITE

§ 1. IDENTIFICATION, LOCATION, AND GENERAL TOPOGRAPHY

THE first modern scholar to identify the site of Tell el-Qedah (or Tell Waggâs as it is alternatively called after the name of a village which once stood nearby) was J. L. Porter, who in 1875 wrote the following: 'We soon afterwards cross a deep glen [i.e. Wadi el-Waggâs] on whose northern bank is a scarped mound and beside it a broad terrace which was apparently the site of a town. Upon it now stands the little village of Waggâs. The ancient and long-lost Hazor might possibly have stood on this spot.'[1]

Porter's ingenious suggestion was not sheer intuition, but came as a result of thorough study. After rejecting other identifications he continues:[2] 'The site of Hazor, however, could not have been very far distant [from Kedesh]. Josephus says it "lay over the Lake Samochontis", and two passages of scripture seem to imply that it lay southward of Kedesh (Josh. 19: 35–7; 2 Kings, 15: 29). . . . Hazor, I think, must be sought for on the lower slopes of the mountains along the western or south-western border of the Hûleh.'

In a later book he not only repeats his conviction, but adds some details about the site as he saw it. It is worth quoting this rare book:[3] 'Beside where I sat was the mouth of the ravine of Hendâj.[4] Mounting my horse, I followed a broad path, like an old Highway, up its southern bank, and soon came upon the ruins of an ancient city. Not a building—not even a foundation was perfect. Large cisterns, heaps of stones, mounds of rubbish, prostrate columns, the remains of a temple and an altar with a Greek inscription[5]—such were the ruins strewn over this site. I thought at the time that these might be the ruins of Hazor, and I have since become more and more confirmed in the belief.'

[1] J. L. Porter, *Handbook for Travellers in Syria and Palestine*, London [John Murray], pp. 414–15.   [2] Ibid., p. 422.

[3] *The Giant Cities of Bashan and Syria's Holy Places* [T. Nelson and Sons], London, Edinburgh, and New York, 1881, p. 270.

[4] This time he approaches the site from the north.

[5] Nothing remains today of this inscription.

Nevertheless, the credit for bringing the site to the attention of modern scholars should go to John Garstang, who not only re-identified the place with Hazor in 1926,[1] but was also the first to conduct excavations on the site (see below Chapter III, § 1).

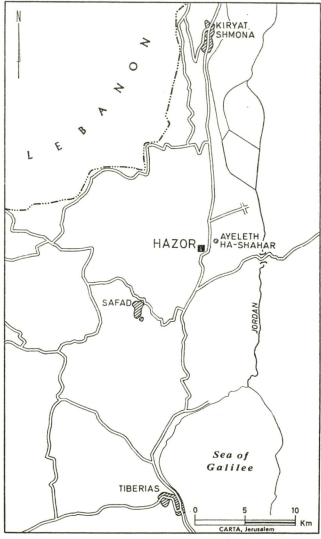

FIG. 2. Map of North-east Galilee.

Tell-el-Qedaḥ is situated at the foot of the eastern ridge of the upper Galilee mountain range at the south-west corner of the Hûleh Plain (Fig. 2). It lies 15·5 km., as the crow flies,

[1] *AAA* 14, 1928, pp. 35 ff. Garstang was unaware of the previous identification as can be gathered from his book, *Joshua, Judges,* London, 1931, p. 184 n. 1.

north of the Sea of Galilee, and about 8 km. from the southern tip of Lake Hûleh (before its partial draining).

The site is situated strategically; it is aptly described by Garstang: 'Standing in the south-west of the Huleh Basin, at the meeting point of the main road from Sidon to Beisan with that from Damascus to Meggido, it occupied the most strategic position in the land, the real key to Palestine. Its situation and character accorded fully with its importance.'[1]

The site (Fig. 3) comprises two distinct areas; the Tell proper and a vast rectangular plateau to its north and east (Pl. I*a*).[2]

§ 2. THE TELL

The Tell is a bottle-shaped mound (Pl. I*b*) with its 'neck' in the west and its 'base' in the east. It rises about 40 m. above the bed of Wadi el-Waggâs. It is 540 m. long at its base from east to west and 470 m. from north to south at its top. At its widest point it measures 260 m. at its base and 175 m. at its top. Thus the total area at its base is about 26 acres, while at its top it is 15 acres, roughly the area of Megiddo. The Tell, in its present state, slopes from west (240 m. above sea level) to east (210 m.), in four terraces; the 'neck', the bulk of the western half, the bulk of the eastern half, and a forward eastern terrace. As will be indicated, these terraces were partially caused by the extension of the city in various periods. A shallow depression, visible at the southern edge of the second terrace, will be discussed in detail in Chapter XIV, § 4.

The present-day road to the north skirts the mound on the south and on the east. To the south of the road the bed of the Wadi el-Waggâs is covered by a thick growth of shrubs and canes, as a result of the many springs which still rise along its course in close vicinity to the mound. Today, most of the water is tapped by the Meqoroth Water Corporation.

§ 3. THE PLATEAU

The vast enclosed plateau (which on excavation turned out to be the lower city of Hazor—see Chapter IV) lies to the north, and partially to the east, of the Tell, and is basically rectangular in shape. The northern and main area is 1,000 m. from north to south and 700 m. on the average from east to west, 175 acres

---

[1] *Joshua, Judges*, p. 183.

[2] As can be seen on the map, the true north lies about 45° to the east of the actual orientation of the plateau. For reasons of convenience, we shall refer hereafter to the narrow sides of the 'plateau'—south and north, and to the long sides, west and east. Thus the Tell lies to the south of the main area of the plateau. See further below Chapter III, § 2, *b*.

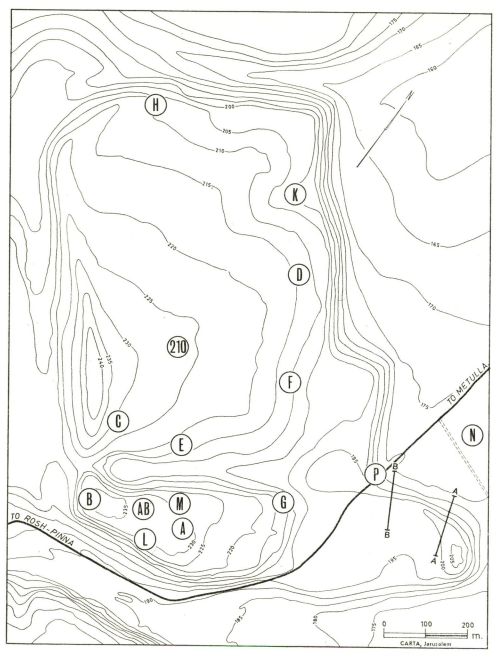

FIG. 3. Topographical map of Hazor with excavated areas.

in all. The eastern spur measures 400 m. from east to west and 250 m. from north to south, and its area is 25 acres. The total area is thus 200 acres. While the western and northern sides of this Rectangular Plateau (as it is hereafter called) are more or less straight the eastern side is stepped and widens from north to south. A study of the topography of its contours indicates that the original area sloped from south-west to north-east, about 35 m. (absolute altitudes: 235–30 m.). It is also apparent that while the northern and eastern boundaries conform to the original slopes of the natural terrace, the western side was artificially formed by separating the natural plateau to the west from the newly formed enclosure by a deep fosse and rampart (see further Chapter V). The northern side is limited by a deep wadi, while the southern end is separated from the Tell by a ravine further accentuated by a fosse and a deep oval depression in the south-western corner (Chapter V, § 2). The eastern spur, while being part of the enclosed plateau, topographically was originally separated from it by the ravine and is, in fact, the extension to the east of the ridge on whose western part the Tell was formed. Both the Tell and the spur are separated in the south from the higher terrain by the deep Wadi el-Waggâs.

III

THE EXCAVATIONS

§ 1. GARSTANG'S SOUNDINGS IN 1928

a. The published results

THE site was first excavated by Garstang in 1928, but no report was ever published. Some indications of his excavations are embodied in a short description of the site given in *Joshua, Judges*,[1] accompanied by a rough sketch. According to these notes 'extensive soundings were made upon the site'.[2] While Garstang gives no details of where he excavated within the 'enclosure', he remarks: 'During M.B.A. occupation of this area was shown to have been fairly intensive and of a permanent character (with stone-built houses); but in L.B.A. there appears to have been only a surface occupation, in tents or huts, which was brought to a close by a general conflagration.'[3] Garstang was more generous in supplying information about the nature of his excavations on the Tell proper:[4] 'This [the city—*Y.Y.*] proved to have been encircled in M.B.A. by a stone rampart,[5] repaired during L.B.A., but there were traces of much earlier fortifications in the slopes [the southern—*Y.Y.*] of the Tell . . . in E.I.A. ii the city sprang again to life, with traces of Solomonian work including stamped bricks, and a building supported by a row of square stone monoliths, possibly a stable.[6] On the west end of the Tell stood a palatial building or temple, the origin of which could not be determined; but it seems to have been in use in E.I.A. ii, and to have lasted on until Hellenistic times:[7] it was separated from the rest of the hill by a deep ditch, which produced on excavation nothing but loose earth.[8]

---

[1] pp. 381–3.

[2] p. 382.

[3] p. 383. Further observations made by Garstang concerning the nature of the enclosure, and the date of its destruction will be referred to and dealt with in Chapter IV, § 1.

[4] p. 383.

[5] Proved by our excavation to be Solomon's, see Chapter XII, § 1, *c*; § 2; Chapter XIV, § 4.

[6] Turned out to be a store-house of the ninth century B.C. See Chapter XIV, § 2.

[7] Generally correct. See Area B, Chapter IX, § 3.

[8] Most probably the depression created by the water-shaft, see Chapter XIV, § 4.

(b) *Garstang's unpublished reports in the files of the Palestine Archaeo-logical Museum*

Recently,[1] Garstang's report to the Department of Anti-quities,[2] preserved in the files of the Palestine Archaeological Museum, became available to the writer.[3] Since this report, with the accompanying sketch-plan (Fig. 4), contains very important data concerning Garstang's activities and con-clusions—sometimes more accurate than those published in *Joshua, Judges*—it is worth while quoting it in detail,[4] with some annotations. In a preamble, Garstang, *inter alia* notes concerning the Tell that the 'city was refortified apparently by King Solomon (on evidence) and continued in occupation during the whole of Iron Age ii (i.e. till 700 B.C., or just later)'. Garstang refers to the enclosed plateau as 'the camp enclosure', and his report deals first with this part of the site (cf. the sketch-plan):

1. ϵ A section was cut with some difficulty into the rampart which proved to be made of an agglomerate resembling concrete mixed with earth.[5]

2. $\delta_1 \delta_2 \delta_3$ Within the enclosure a space some 20 m. $\times$ 15 was explored disclosing:[6]

   (i) on and beneath the surface traces of occupation in the Late Bronze Age;[7]

   (ii) at a depth of about 1·30 m. walls and contents of houses of the Middle Bronze Age, or first phase of the Late Bronze Age;

   (iii) below the floor level of these houses a child burial and various pottery fragments also of Middle Bronze Age.[8]

3. δ_4 A second area[9] was explored with similar historical results, but fewer objects. Just below the surface was found a large one-handled pottery vessel of a kind dated at Beisan to the era of Amenophis III. 1600 B.C.[!—*Y.Y.*].

4. δ_5 A third area disclosed rock and fragments of Late Bronze Age pottery.

---

[1] June 1969.   [2] Dated 25 October 1928.

[3] This report was not available to us when we began our excavating in 1955. As will be shown, this turned out to be, in a way, a blessing in disguise, since had we known at the time the exact sites of Garstang's soundings, some of the most significant discoveries of our expeditions would not perhaps have been made. We would have been deterred from excava-ting areas near those which, according to the report, proved to be of no particular significance. It seems that, in one or two cases, Garstang just missed the mark.

[4] I wish to thank Dr. A. Biran, Director of the Israel Department of Antiquities, for the permission to quote from Garstang's report, and to reproduce the sketch accompanying it.

[5] This is approximately at the same area, at the bottom of which we discovered our Stelae Temple; see Chapter IV, § 2; Chapter VII, § 1.

[6] This seems to be just east to our Area C, see Chapter IV, § 2.

[7] Our Strata IA–B.   [8] See Chapter IV, § 2, *b*.

[9] Very close to our Area 210, Chapter IV, § 6.

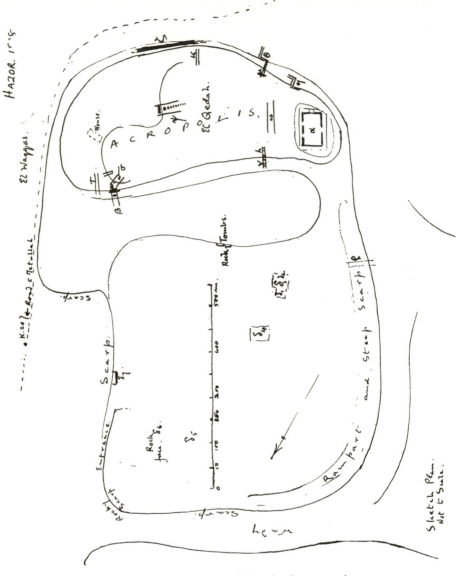

FIG. 4. Garstang's unpublished sketch of excavated areas.

5. δ₆ A fourth area was occupied by a rock with cup marks and water channel.[1]

6. δ₇ A portion of exposed rock scarp on the E. slope was examined, disclosing numerous fragments of pottery of several ages, and under the rock two intact pottery vessels (1 cooking pot and a one-handled jug) of Late Bronze Age. Various other exposed features of the site were examined and photographed.[2]

[1] The latter two areas are just north of our Area D; see Chapter IV, § 3.
[2] This area is just south to our Area K, see Chapter VI, § 1.

With this ends the description of the sounding in the enclosure, all told eight areas or sub-areas. The following are the sections dealing with the Tell:

The Tell or Acropolis

7. A continuous section β of the northern slope (towards the East) disclosed a wall of Canaanite character built upon debris of the Middle Bronze Age, and with an accumulation against it of debris of the Late Bronze Age.

Superimposed upon the Canaanite wall, and protruding from the surface, were traced the foundations of a curving angle-wall enclosing remains of a brick construction (σ). One of the bricks bore the sign familiar as a mason's mark in the age of King Solomon (10th Century B.C.). Pottery fragments found in the clearance confirmed the date, pertaining to Early Iron Age (ii). The area, developed, contained a ramp and doorway.[1]

8. A parallel trench γ[2] towards the West of the same face produced parallel results. The Canaanite wall was traced; pottery fragments of kindred date and character were found; but upon topping the Acropolis and continuing the trench (λ) into the interior a number of Israelitish houses of the period B.C. 900–700 were disclosed.[3] Pottery fragments of Early Iron Age (ii) gave the date.

A thin deposit of Early Iron Age (i), Eleventh Century B.C., was found below the floors of the houses.[4]

9. Trench ζ disclosed the Canaanite defensive wall for a length of 50 metres, and to a height in places of 2·50 m. This wall, by arrangement with the owner, was left exposed and the ground outside was terraced for ready access of visitors.[5]

Trench θ disclosed the Canaanitish defensive wall, and within it at a higher level a wall of the Early Iron Age.[6] Trench η gave results parallel to those of θ.[7]

10. *On the Surface of the Acropolis*

Trench κ heading in from ζ disclosed house-walls of the Early Iron Age, and fragments of pottery dated generally to 1000–700 B.C.[8]

[1] Presumably τ in the sketch. The whole area is exactly our Area G (Chapter IX, § 5) where the city wall was found (of the ninth century and not Canaanite), based on a MB wall. It is a pity that Garstang does not indicate more precisely the nature of the sign on the brick. The only marked brick found by us was in Area A, Stratum V (eighth century), bearing a sign similar to an *aleph* (see, *Hazor III–IV*, pl. xxvii, 3). In fact the bricks referred to by Garstang appear to belong to the ninth–eighth centuries.

[2] To the east of our Area B.

[3] Correct. The nearest to this spot is our Area AB, see Chapter IX, § 4.

[4] Most probably our Stratum XI, see Chapter XI, § 3.

[5] Indeed the wall is still visible today. It turned out, however, to be not Canaanite, but Solomonic; see in particular Chapter XII, § 1,*b*, Chapter XIV, § 4. Cf. also *Joshua, Judges*, pl. XLIX, bottom.

[6] Most probably one of the Strata VIII–V additions. See the above references.

[7] This trench must have been carried out in an area just east of the southern end of Area B; see Chapter IX, § 3.

[8] i.e. our Strata X–V.

Trench μ heading in from θ disclosed between the Canaanite enclosing wall and the higher Israelitish wall a space in which were traces of occupation during the Late Bronze Age, including a fragment of Cypriote 'milk bowl' and various other fragments of the period.

11. A broad cutting[1] up the face of a secondary acropolis[2] upon the Tell (ψ) disclosed:

(i) An enclosing wall at the foot of the slope;[3]

(ii) A hall of columns, monoliths, nine in number.

. . . The pottery fragments ranged from Early Iron Age (ii) (c. 700 B.C.) on the top to Early Iron Age (i) (c. 1000 B.C.) below.[4] The building is then apparently attributable to the Israelitish re-occupation of the Tell in the age of Solomon.

12. Upon the highest part of the Acropolis, towards the South,[5] traces of a building were visible in the surface, and this was more fully explored. It proved to be a large single building surrounding a central area about 15 m × 12. The main entrance was from the West,[6] and doorways around communicated with a series of chambers. The pottery was that of the Eighth Century B.C., with the exception that, corresponding to certain intrusive walls, there were found a lamp and other fragments of Hellenistic date.[7] At no other spot was there sign of any occupation later than the Seventh Century B.C.

13. Finally a deep trench ω disclosed an earth deposit lying between the buildings aforementioned, namely α and ψ. The highest building α was thus separated by a considerable dip from the rest of the Acropolis, and probably marks the site of a temple or public edifice.[8]

The debris of some tombs was examined on the face of the scarp opposite to and northwards of the Tell. The tomb contents were of two periods, viz. Middle Bronze Age (at the bottom) and Early Iron Age above. The tombs had been rifled and the contents were all broken, but useful forms can be restored.[9]

The report concludes by stating that all 'these preliminary Soundings lasted just over three weeks. . . . Number of workmen employed varied from 80 to 140'. We are not told how many archaeologists supervised the work of this large contingent of workers, nor could we discover any more sketches or plans related to the soundings.

[1] Our Area A; see Chapter IX, § 2.   [2] i.e. the terrace between Areas A and B.

[3] The Solomonic casemate-wall.

[4] Actually ninth-century.

[5] Must be towards the west.

[6] Erroneously referring to an inner doorway. See *Hazor I*, the plan on pl. CLXXVII.

[7] See also Chapter XV, § 6.

[8] It turned out to be a Citadel. Trench ω seems to have been made right in the depression of the water shaft, and has nothing to do with a ditch. See Chapter XIV, § 4.

[9] These tombs are described in the section dealing with our Area E (Chapter IV, § 5). No Iron Age pottery was found. In addition to the MB, many LB I and LB II vessels were recovered.

§ 2. THE JAMES A. DE ROTHSCHILD EXPEDITION (1955–8)

a. Organization and staff

Extensive excavations were carried out on the site under the directorship of the writer between the years 1955 and 1958. Altogether, four seasons of excavations took place, each lasting on the average three months (August–October). The permanent senior staff included Y. Aharoni, Ruth Amiran, J. Perrot, Trude Dothan, and (the late) I. Dunayevsky who served as the architect of the expedition. In addition M. Dothan joined the expedition of 1958 in place of J. Perrot. Claire Epstein also participated during certain seasons.[1]

The excavations were carried out on behalf of the Hebrew University, and were sponsored in addition by the Palestine Jewish Colonization Association, the Anglo-Israel Exploration Society, and the Government of Israel. The number of labourers varied from 120 (1955) to 220 (1958), and their work was supervised by a staff of about 45 archaeologists and senior students.

The staff were lodged in the guest-house of Kibbutz Ayeleth Ha-Shahar which is situated east of the site. A special working camp (which included several barracks and sheds) was erected nearby. To facilitate the removal of earth a special network of light railways was built on the Tell proper.

b. Methods, areas, and stratigraphy

1. The grids

The excavation grid was not parallel to the geographic grid, but orientated according to the bearings of the Rectangular Plateau and the Tell. This promised—in part fulfilled—a better adjustment between the grid squares and the building plans.

The area was divided into squares of 100 × 100 m. In order to cover the whole area of the site and adjacent ruins, the south-west corner square was fixed at about 1,000 m. south-west of the Tell. The squares were always numbered from west to east in each row. In the excavated areas, each square was further divided into sub-squares, each 5 × 5 m., i.e. each main square contained 400 sub-squares. The latter are marked by letters A–U from west to east and numbers 1–20 from

---

[1] For the detailed lists of the staff members (which included many students of the Hebrew University, Jerusalem, who are now archaeologists in their own right) see *Hazor I–II* (Members of the Expeditions), and *IEJ* 8, 1958, p. 1 n. 2.; ibid. 9, 1959, p. 74 n. 2.

south to north. A full reference, therefore, to a particular locus is, e.g., 110/K 14.

2. *The excavated areas*

The vastness of the area of Hazor, and the two distinctive features of the site (the Tell and the Rectangular Plateau) induced us to start from the very beginning at various areas simultaneously, each named by a letter (Fig. 3). On the Tell proper areas A and B were excavated in all the four seasons (under Y. Aharoni and Ruth Amiran respectively), Area G in the 1957 season (under Trude Dothan), and also in the same year a trial trench BA[1] (under A. Ben-Tor).

In the Rectangular Plateau the following areas were excavated: Area C in 1955 (under J. Perrot) and 1956 (under Trude Dothan), Area D in 1955 (under Claire Epstein), Area E in 1955 (under J. Perrot), Area F in 1956–7 (under J. Perrot), Area 210 in 1957 (under E. Stern), Area H in 1957 (under Claire Epstein, 1958—Trude Dothan), Area K in 1958 (under M. Dothan).

Because of the great distance between the various excavated areas, and in order to ensure a strictly objective study of the stratification of each area, it was our practice to name each stratum in each area independently, and use arabic numerals for this purpose. Only when correlation between the strata of the various areas was possible, were they replaced by Latin numerals. This method was employed particularly on the Tell, where, as will be seen, the full sequence of occupation of Hazor emerged. In the present book the original arabic numerals will be maintained for some areas (particularly in the Rectangular Plateau) but will be equated later with the absolute numbers in the summing-up.

3. *Loci and registration*

Since all the areas were organized as self-maintained units, each area was allocated a group of numbers to mark its loci, e.g. A–1–3000; B–3001–6000, etc. Walls were normally given a fresh series of numbers preceded by W. This system was also applied to tombs, which were preceded by a T. The artefacts were marked in such a way that the inscription borne by each object or sherd indicated immediately the season, area, and (indirectly) the locus. Thus $\frac{\text{H 56}}{\text{A 125/2}}$ means Hazor, season 1956, Area A, Basket 125, object no. 2 from this basket. Each area

[1] Sometimes referred to as AB.

had an independent list of baskets (marked in the field-diary according to locus, absolute altitude, contents, etc.); thus, the number of the basket was in fact the key to its exact provenance. Right from the beginning the expedition maintained a fully equipped photographic department. Developing and printing were done the same day so that prints issued to the field staff the next morning enabled them to check each detail before removing an object.

c. *Publications*

The results of each season were published in a preliminary report the following year in the *Israel Exploration Journal*.[1] The results of each season were subsequently published again in definitive volumes.[2]

§ 3. THE 1965 SOUNDINGS

In 1965 Kibbutz Ayeleth Ha-Shahar decided to erect a public building near the northern rampart of the eastern spur. Permission was granted by the Department of Antiquities on condition that a trench would be dug near the spot in order to ascertain the nature of the slope. This was carried out on 15–16 September and 31 October–1 November in the same year, with the aid of mechanical equipment. The soundings were made by I. Dunayevsky and A. Kempinsky under the supervision of the writer. These soundings provided very important data concerning the nature of the Rectangular Plateau fortifications[3] and are dealt with here in Chapter V, § 4.

§ 4. THE 1968 CAMPAIGN

After an interval of ten years from the last full season of excavations in 1958, a fifth season was conducted at Hazor from mid-July to the end of October 1968. The purpose of the renewed excavations was to clarify various problems left unsolved, and to open several new areas which were expected to shed additional light on Hazor's town planning in various periods. The excavations were carried out under the direction of the writer, on behalf of the Hebrew University and the Israel Exploration Society, and with the aid of the Israel Ministry of Labour.

[1] 1955–6, 1956, pp. 120 ff.; 1956–7, 1957, pp. 118 ff.; 1957–8, 1958, pp. 1 ff.; and 1958–9, 1959, pp. 74 ff.
[2] *Hazor I* (The 1955 Season), 1958; *Hazor II* (The 1956 Season), 1960; *Hazor III–IV* (to date the plates volume only), 1961.
[3] See *IEJ* 19, 1969, pp. 10 ff.; *BA* 32, 1969, pp. 61 ff.

Excavations were made in the following areas: Area A (under the supervision of A. Ben-Tor), to clarify the stratigraphy of the Bronze Age; Area BA (under A. Eitan), for the same purpose; Area L (Y. Shiloh), the site of the Iron Age water-system; Area M (Malka Batyevsky), the extension of Solomon's city—all in the Tell; Area N (B. Hofri), outside the site area, water installations; and Area P (A. Mazar), a gate in the Rectangular Plateau. The architects were I. Dunayevsky, G. Kertes, G. Klir, and E. Menzel.[1] The general organization and excavation methods were similar to those adopted in the previous seasons, but the Expedition staff lived in Rosh-Pinnah. The results of this season are incorporated in the following pages according to the subjects of discussion.

[1] For other members of the staff see *IEJ* 19, 1969, p. 1 n. 1.

PART II

THE LOWER CITY

IV

NATURE, STRATIGRAPHY, DATES,
AND FINDS

§ I. INTRODUCTION

a. The problem

U P till now, we have defined the large enclosed area to the
north of the Tell as the Rectangular Plateau; this was done in
order to maintain the objective description of the area prior
to excavations.

The initial purpose of our excavations at this area was to
examine the validity of Garstang's repeated assertion that the
Rectangular Plateau was a 'fortified camp', rather than a
proper city. It was not easy to accept this view, both because
of the tremendous earthen fortifications and because of
Garstang's actual archaeological finds in his soundings. His
views were based also on his interpretation of the meaning of
the name Hazor:

The name Hazor, meaning strictly an enclosure, signifies in this
context a fortified camp. . . . It [the site of Hazor] thus comprised at
one and the same time a permanent city of large size [i.e. the Tell] and
an associated camp enclosure . . . the camp enclosure was large enough
to accommodate in emergency 30,000 men with a corresponding
number of horses and chariots. . . . During the Middle Bronze Age,
about 1800 B.C., it had attained already the zenith of its prosperity and
extension . . . such had been its activity in those days *that houses had arisen
in numbers even inside the camp enclosure* [my italics—*Y.Y.*], disclosing
a city of proportions altogether without parallel in southern Syria. . . .
In the fifteenth century B.C. in which the story of Joshua begins, this
exceptionally intensive period had given way to more normal conditions, under which Hazor remained still pre-eminent . . . while the great

enclosure was apparently occupied only by temporary structures, for troops or travellers passing through, whether *tents of goat-hair or maybe huts built of papyrus reeds* [my italics—*Y.Y.*] after the fashion still much in vogue in the locality. . . .[1]

The second objective of the excavations in the 'fortified camp' was to attain a more precise date for its final abandonment. Garstang concluded that this happened about 1400 B.C.— a date in accordance with his placing of Joshua and corroborated by the finds:

. . . in L.B.A. there appears to have been only a surface occupation, in tents or huts, which was brought to a close by a general conflagration. Some 2,500 fragments of pottery from the surface deposits were examined, and while L.B.A. i was well represented, both by Cypro-Phoenician and local fabrics, no Mykenaen [*sic*] specimens were found. The latest single dateable specimen ranges down to the Tell el Amarna period (found at Beisan in that stratum); but as a whole and in round terms the complete absence of Mykenaean [*sic*] specimens, as at Jericho, suggests a date of destruction about 1400 B.C. . . .[2]

This assertion was also susceptible to doubt, to say the least. While there is no doubt that Mycenaean pottery was not detected by Garstang, his dating of the LB strata, based on the then accepted dating of the Beisan strata, had to be examined in view of the corrections proposed by Albright in 1937, which showed *inter alia* that the 'Thotmes III' level (ix) had to be reduced to the late fourteenth century, Level vii (Amenophis III) to the thirteenth century, and Level vi (Seti I) to the twelfth century, etc.[3]

b. The areas of excavation

The first area which was chosen to test Garstang's assertion was in the south-west corner of the 'camp enclosure' and was designated Area C. After startling discoveries here, which not only indicated that the area was still a properly built city in the LB period, but also produced Mycenaean pottery, we decided to verify these facts in other areas of the vast enclosure. Altogether eight areas were excavated, evenly spread throughout the enclosure (C, D, E, F, H, K, P)—and all produced the same data. Thus we may proceed, from now on, to call this area the Lower City.

[1] *Joshua, Judges*, pp. 184–5. These general conclusions are repeated in more or less the same way, in the caption to his pl. XLIX, and on p. 198, as well as on p. 383 in the summing-up of his excavations.   [2] Ibid., p. 383.
[3] See Albright in *AASOR* 17, 1938, pp. 76–9. Cf. also G. M. Fitzgerald in *AOTS*, pp. 188, 191.

§ 2. AREA C

a. General

Area C lies, as stated, in the south-west corner of the Lower City, in Square 168 (Pl. IIa),[1] and the total area of excavations covers about 1,250 sq. m. The aims of the excavations here were to ascertain the nature of the 'enclosure' and the dates of its foundation and destruction, as well as to probe into the character and method of construction of the great earthen rampart extending along the western side of the 'enclosure', which on this spot attains an enormous size (see Chapter V). The area had a further advantage, technically speaking, since it was nearest to the areas of excavations on the Tell proper. The excavation in Area C revealed for the first time the nature of the 'enclosure': the Lower City of Hazor. Immediately below the ploughed surface, remains of building were found. Nearer the rampart, the remains were found under a sterile layer of brown earth (which had been washed down from the top and slope of the earthen rampart) and were better preserved, while further to the east the remains came to light immediately under the ploughed disturbed surface. Virgin soil was reached in a considerable part of the excavated area (at c. 222·5 m. above sea-level), and altogether five main strata of occupation were found. They were designated by arabic numerals from top to bottom 1A, 1B, 2, 3, and 4; Strata 1A–B of the LB III and LB II respectively; Stratum 2 of the LB I, and Strata 3 and 4 of the MB II.

b. Strata 4–3: The MB II period

Basically, two strata (Pl. VIa) pertaining to the MB II were found. In the lowest (Stratum 4)—which lay directly on the virgin soil—building phases were noted in *some* of the structures. Although it was not possible, due to the fragmentary nature of these phases, to achieve a coherent plan of units of these sub-phases,[2] their existence indicates that Stratum 4 was of considerable duration. Stratum 3 was much better preserved, and under the floors of both Stratum 4 and Stratum 3 a considerable number of burials was found.[3] The majority consisted of typical MB II infant-burials in store-jars (accompanied by one or two juglets) while three burials were of adults, buried within an

---

[1] For the detailed reports of the excavation at Area C, see *Hazor I*, pp. 71 ff.; *Hazor II* pp. 76 ff.

[2] For a detailed discussion, see *Hazor II*, pp. 79–80.

[3] Ibid., plan on fig. 4, p. 83.

area roughly marked with field stones. In some rooms the number of infant-burials was very large and the burials touched each other. In one room,[1] each of the burials contained the remains of two infants.

A similar phenomenon was discovered in Area 210 (see below § 6).

All the pottery discovered here—both on the floors and in the burials—does not precede the MB IIB period and a considerable part of it can actually be defined as MB IIC.[2] The same data was revealed in the other areas of excavations at the Lower City (see below).

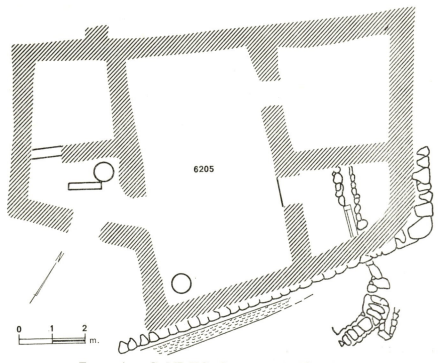

6205

0   1   2
m.

FIG. 5. Area C. MB IIC—Stratum 3. Building 6205.

The main structure of Stratum 3 (which may have been constructed in parts already in Stratum 4) is a large dwelling (6205) with four rooms flanking a big court (7×4 m.), two on each side (Fig. 5).[3] The building is, in fact, a corner-house built on an elevated area, limited on its southern part (due to the

---

[1] See there, Tombs 24, 25, 26.
[2] For a detailed discussion of the pottery with parallel material from other sites in Palestine, see *Hazor II*, pp. 86 ff.
[3] Ibid., pp. 78 ff., Building 6205.

sloping of the natural surface) by a retaining wall. Under this wall a series of drain-channels was found, the upper of which was made of one well-dressed U-shaped basalt block[1] measuring 1·85 m. It is quite probable that the water was drained from this area towards the southern moat (see below). Additional buildings of the same nature were found to the north of Building 6205, but they were in a fragmentary state. The plans of the buildings, as well as the pottery and objects found in them, indicate that we are dealing with a normal dwelling-quarter, apparently not associated with any cult structure. Stratum 3 came to its end as a result of a violent conflagration, and a thick layer of ashes separated it from the one which followed.[2]

Some structures were found at the very foot of the slope of the earthen rampart. Some of these were composed of a series of parallel walls in the form of revetment walls. These structures, too, contained MB IIB–C pottery.[3] Of special interest is a group of three jugs which were found in a niche formed by the above-mentioned walls.[4] On one of these was incised a short Akkadian inscription—the earliest of its kind yet found in Palestine. It was not possible to establish with certainty whether the locus was to be attributed to Stratum 4 or Stratum 3, since we found no direct stratigraphic connection between it and the structures of these two Strata. Nevertheless, as this locus is situated directly on the conglomerate of the earthen rampart, it can be assigned perhaps to Stratum 4. The inscription was made on the shoulder of the jug. Over it was incised—before firing—the sign of a trident,[5] which was found also on a number of other vessels discovered in Area C and Area F, all of MB II. It is possible that the sign is of a deity. On the other hand, it is strikingly similar to the one incised on a copper ingot from Hagia Triada in Crete of the MM period.[6]

The inscription[7] was read as: ᵐIš-me-ᵈAdad by Albright and ᵐIš-me-Ilamˡᵃᵐ by L. Böhl. The latter reading is preferred by Artzi and Malamat. In any case it is interesting that the first element in the name which is clear, has—as Malamat pointed out[8]—an Akkadian rather than West-Semitic form.[9]

---

[1] *Hazor I*, p. 74, and pl. XXIII, 2; *Hazor II*, pp. 78–9.

[2] *Hazor II*, pl. XXVI, 3.   [3] Ibid., p. 81, Sub-area 6174.

[4] Ibid., pl. XXVII, 2.   [5] Ibid., p. 116, pls. CXII, 9; CLXXX.

[6] Cf. Claude F. A. Schaeffer, *Enkomi-Alasia*, Paris, 1952, p. 30, fig. 5, p. 33. The relations between Mari and Crete on the one hand and the shipment of tin to Hazor on the other, should perhaps be recalled in this connection (see above, Chapter 1, § 3). Could the sign indicate a trade-mark? Could the bearer of the jug be associated with the trade with Mari?

[7] Studied by P. Artzi and A. Malamat, see *Hazor II*, p. 116.

[8] *JBL* 79, 1960, p. 18.   [9] See further Chapter I, § 3.

The general conclusion drawn from the excavation at Area C is that the 'enclosure' is in fact a built-up area which formed the Lower City of Hazor from the MB IIB period down to the end of the LB (see next paragraph). These two basic and important conclusions were borne out by the excavations in the other areas.

c. The LB periods (Strata 2, 1B, 1A) excluding the Stelae Temple

1. LB I—Stratum 2

Above a layer of ashes covering the MB II period a new city was built in Stratum 2. Except for one minor case in which walls of the previous stratum were reused, all the walls of Stratum 2 were laid afresh with no relation to those of the stratum below them.[1] The pottery associated with this stratum is LB I including a few vessels with two coloured patterns, but not of the common Bichrome Ware.[2] The most characteristic locally made vessel of this period is the bowl decorated with red concentric bands on the interior. Of the foreign ware one should mention bowls of Cypriote Monochrome Ware, similar to those found in Megiddo in LB I tombs and in Strata IX–VIII, and in Lachish Temples I–II.[3]

Considerably more material of this period was found in Areas E (below, § 5), 210 (§ 6), H (Chapter VII, § 2, *c*), and D (below, § 3), including Bichrome Ware. Furthermore, in the light of the 1968 season, there are grounds for believing that some of the basalt orthostats found in this area originated in this stratum.[4] This Stratum 2, representing the sixteenth–fifteenth centuries in Hazor, emerges as one of great prosperity and cultural standards. This is no doubt the Hazor of the Thutmosis III period.[5] In view of a considerable accumulation between Stratum 2 and Stratum 1B above it, it may be assumed perhaps that there was a gap in the history of Hazor, some time in the middle of the fifteenth century.

2. LB II—Stratum 1B

The two upper strata in Area C belong to LB II and LB III respectively. Structures of these strata were found in all the excavated area including the Stelae Temple—the prize find which will be discussed separately together with the other temples of Hazor (Chapter VII). Stratum 1B, in particular, was well preserved and in many places the walls stood, when

---

[1] See *Hazor II*, pp. 92 ff.
[2] Ibid., p. 94. For Bichrome Ware in Hazor, see below, § 4, *c*.
[3] *Hazor I*, pp. 151–2.
[4] Below Chapter VII, § 2, and particularly Chapter X, § 4.
[5] Above Chapter I, § 4.

found, to a height of 1 m. The two strata were dated by us to the fourteenth and thirteenth centuries respectively, based on the abundance of the local ware and the few Mycenaean fragments belonging to groups III A and B. The great quantities of Mycenaean vessels which were found in the other areas in the corresponding strata (D, F, H, and in the Upper City) leave no doubt that Stratum 1B was flourishing in the fourteenth century (the el Amarna period) while the last of Canaanite Hazor was destroyed when Mycenaean III B pottery was still in use, i.e. during the thirteenth century B.C.[1]

The whole area, to the east of the 'Stelae Temple' and its terraces, was occupied by a number of building complexes (Fig. 6) which were perhaps associated with the Temple, although their nature was not strictly cultic: pottery workshops, store-rooms, and proper dwellings which perhaps served the temple personnel. Two of these structures will be described here on account of the rich harvest of vessels and other objects found in them. A third, which may have belonged to Stratum 1A, will also be discussed here because its content is similar.

Building 6063

This building[2] (Pl. XI*a*) is built on the plan of a square central courtyard—6215—(5 × 5 m.) surrounded by rooms on its four sides: two rooms in the north, east, and south, and five on the west. To some of the rooms there were no entrances and they may have been used as service and store-rooms. It is very important to note that particularly in this building (but not solely) there was evidence of two phases during the existence of Stratum 1B. It is equally important to stress that these two phases are distinguished mainly by a change in *plan* of some of the rooms: blocking of openings within the house or changing its relation to adjacent buildings. While these changes may indicate perhaps a less secure phase in the life of Hazor, they are definitely a sign of a relatively long duration.

The contents of the court and rooms may contain a clue as to the function of the building. A bench of undressed stones is set along the east wall of the courtyard in which two roof-rollers (one broken) were used as building material. The court also contains a silo. The courtyard was very rich in pottery, its main

---

[1] The historical and chronological conclusions to be drawn from the above facts are dealt with below in Chapter VIII, § 3. For the Mycenaean and Cypriote Ware found in Area C, see *Hazor I*, pp. 83, 85, 91; *Hazor II*, p. 109. See now also V. Hankey, 'Mycenaean Pottery in the Middle East: Notes on finds since 1951', *The Annual of the British School at Athens* 62, 1967, p. 123.

[2] *Hazor II*, pp. 98 ff., pl. XXXII, 1; XXXIII, 1.

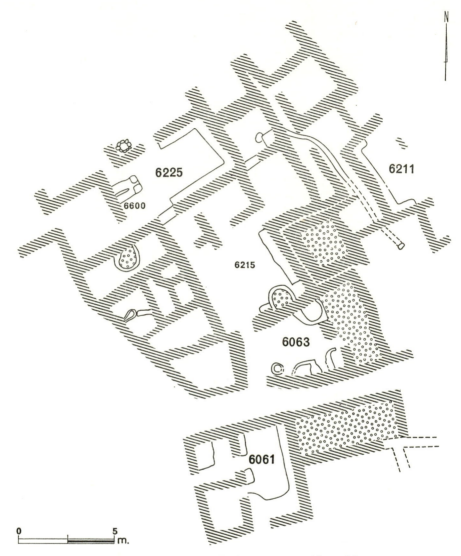

FIG. 6. Area C. LB II–III, Strata IB–A, with mainly IB.

concentration being along the bench. Among the vessels were
conspicuous the big pithoi so typical of the Hazor LB II–III
periods, but they included many storage-jars, bowls, cooking-pots,
and jugs—some with decorations. In the other rooms, too, many
pithoi were found (Pl. XIb). In the building, two upper stones
of potters' wheels were also discovered. The peculiar character
of the building, the numerous objects found in it, and the potters'
wheels, all suggest that at least part of it was used as a potters'
workshop, as indeed was the next building to be described.

Building 6225

Although only the southern part of this building was uncovered it merits special attention (Pl. XI*a*). It too seems to
have a central courtyard surrounded by rooms. On the southern
side, it is limited by Building 6063 (previously mentioned).
Indeed the two were at one stage connected by a door, which
was later blocked up.

The chief locus (6225) of this building is of particular interest,
and is distinguished by its peculiar plan, size (7 × 3·5 m.), and
by the finds made in it. It served, perhaps, as a central courtyard, a function suggested not only by its dimensions but also
because of its four openings.

Characteristic of this 'court' are the benches built along the
walls: in the eastern halves of the northern and southern walls,
as well as along its eastern wall. The most important structure
in this locus is the installation (6600) built in the form of a
double wall set at right angles against another wall. Between
the two walls is a narrow interval filled with earth. On this
installation, at a height of about 0·4 m. above floor-level, was
found a pair of potters' wheels, the upper and the lower, and
near them an intact clay mask (Pl. XV*a*). It seems that this
area served as a potters' working-place—most probably connected with the temple activities.

The wheels

The wheels are admirable in their precise execution and the
way they fit together. The upper stone is flat on top while the
lower is hemispherical. The two parts are fitted into one another
by a conical projection in the upper stone and a conical
depression in the lower.[1]

The cult mask

The mask (Pl. XV*b*) was first thrown as a bowl on the potters'
wheel. The eyes are cut out of the mask; the long eyebrows join
the upper end of the straight, slender nose; the ears are well
moulded. Two holes are perforated in the upper end and four
others in the sides, two on each side, above and below the ear.
A similar mask (Pl. XV*d*) was found in Area D (see below § 3, *b*).

The mask is small (height *c.* 14 cm.), and is beardless.[2] The
possible use of this mask, the parallel finds from other places,

[1] A similar upper-stone was found in a pottery workshop in a cave at Lachish, of about
the same age. See *Lachish IV*, pp. 291, 293; pl.49: 12. Cf. also R. Amiran's article in *Eretz-
Israel* 4, 1957, pp. 46–50.
[2] *Hazor II*, p. 115, pl. CLXXXIII.

and the mask's relation to the adjacent Stelae Temple are discussed in Chapter VII § 1, *d*.[1]

Building Complex 6211

This most important complex might as well be ascribed to Stratum IA (for reasons to be indicated), but since its contents definitely fall within the general nature of the other buildings we can equally well deal with it here. The main feature of this complex is a trapezoid room ($5 \cdot 5 \times 6 \cdot 5 \times 3 \cdot 3$ m.). Its eastern side opened on to a lane. This opened frontage was apparently so large that its roofing was supported by a pillar. Along the other walls parts of benches were found. The very rich accumulation of pottery found in this room,[2] particularly in its northern part, included many bowls, chalices, goblets, juglets, lamps, and a stand. Some of the vessels were found stacked in heaps. While stratigraphically the original building was definitely built in Stratum IB, I have strong suspicions that the actual finds belong to IA. Two complete juglets were found on the top of the wall stump. This indicates that the building was in a state of dilapidation when the pottery group was placed in it.[3] Since in both Strata IB and IA the Stelae Temple was in use, and the repertoire of the local pottery is identical, it is very difficult indeed to come to a firm decision.

The standard

The most important discovery in this locus was made near the western face of the pillar referred to above, where three bowls, one on top of the other, were found and underneath them a peculiar jar containing a bronze silver-faced standard (Pl. XV*c*).[4] It is rectangular ($12 \cdot 5 \times 7$ cm.) with a tang in its lower part. The standard is made of bronze and its face bears a representation made in both relief and incision. The surface is plated with a very thin layer of silver which is pressed tightly on to it. The subject of the representation is not clear in its details, but one can observe the face of a woman holding a snake in each hand, and wearing a pendant of a stylized snake. On the upper edge of the standard, over the image's head, is a crescent and within it the stylized snake is repeated. This object is definitely of cultic nature and most probably was associated

---

[1] See also, Y. Yadin, in *The Glueck Festschrift*, pp. 221 ff.

[2] *Hazor II*, pl. XXXV.

[3] The detailed analysis of the stratigraphy of this locus may be found in *Hazor II*, pp. 104–5.

[4] For a detailed discussion see ibid., p. 117.

with the Stelae Temple; and therefore it will be further discussed in Chapter VII, § 1. In fact, the very character of the other vessels found—many of which bore no traces of use—indicates, also, a relationship with the shrine or with potters' activity in the neighbourhood.

3. *LB III—Stratum 1A*

This stratum—the topmost occupation of the Lower City—represents some decline in comparison with the activities of the previous stratum. Furthermore, in many cases (the Stelae Temple is a good example), the inhabitants of Stratum 1A reused buildings of Stratum 1B. On the other hand, several cases were observed in which walls and floorings of this stratum were clearly erected and built *over* the destroyed remains of Stratum 1B. This stratum appears to have had a relatively short life, since in only a few cases could we detect a raising of floors or other alterations.

With all that, there seems to be no doubt that the population belonged to the same cultural and religious nature as those of 1B. This was evidenced by the pottery which was identical, and particularly by the reuse of the previous temples.

The relative poverty of this stratum should not, in my opinion, be over-exaggerated because of the somewhat meagre remains found there. One should remember that this last stratum was exposed for a long time to the elements, only to be destroyed further by the plough. This fact was particularly evident in Area C, where the remains of 1A found under the protective sterile layer of the wash from the ramparts were much more coherent in plan and execution than those found further to the east just below the ploughed surface.

Apart from the temple proper which was reconstructed in this stratum the activities of 1A were particularly obvious in its vicinity. The inhabitants of 1A introduced far-reaching changes mainly into the area between the temple and the buildings to the east of it. They improved the terraces which provided a better approach to the temple, and added new ones. In the other part of the area many floors and walls were found above the previous stratum. However, because of its fragmentary nature, it is difficult to achieve coherent plans of the buildings.

The end of Stratum 1A came about as the result of a violent fire, as indicated by ashes found in the less exposed areas excavated in Areas H and K.

§ 3. AREA D

a. General

Area D lies in the central and eastern part of the Lower City, about 600 m. north-east of Area C. Even before the beginning of the excavations there were visible many surface rocks which had been vertically scarped and dressed. The total area excavated was about 500 sq. m. The object of the dig here was to ascertain the nature of the rock scarps as well as to probe further into the nature of the Lower City and its history. The area, rich in finds, was also most difficult to excavate from a stratigraphical point of view: the rock lay at surface level, so that all periods of occupation on it had been washed away by the rains and the plough (Pl. IIIa). Furthermore, since the rocks form a sort of terrace and the levels of occupation were both on the terrace and below it, it was impossible to achieve an uninterrupted sequence of strata. The great number of cisterns which had been cut into the rock at the very beginning of its occupation, but were reused several times, and later for different functions— all added to the difficulties. Therefore, in order to maintain an objective reading of the stratification, the small area was further divided into five sub-areas (according to the terrain, etc.)— each studied individually. It is beyond the scope of the present work to describe them in detail,[1] and therefore only the most salient finds and conclusions will be dealt with.

b. The main phases of occupation

The earliest occupation is evidenced by rock-cut tombs, cisterns, and some dwellings around them. The most important of the tombs was well cut with a vaulted entrance, which led through a narrow corridor into a room, rectangular in shape. Although the ceiling of the cave was found to have collapsed, traces of the tooling on the remaining blocks of stone indicated that an aperture had been cut in the central part. Caves of this type are found over a wide area in and around Hazor. It may be assumed that the apertures were used as a means of descent into the caves by the inhabitants of the area above. The earliest contents of the tombs—like the dwellings and cisterns—are of MB IIB. Interesting too are the cisterns (Fig. 7), all bottle-shaped and some reaching the depth of over 8 m. (Pl. IIIa). Of particular interest is Cistern 9024 which gives us good stratification, important for fixing both the date of these cisterns and their function. The lowest level was composed of clayey earth

[1] See *Hazor I*, pp. 99 ff.

and sediment about 1 m. thick—indicating that the original purpose of the cistern was to store water. In this level was found quite a number of vessels—all MB IIB, such as cooking-pots, lamps, jugs, and bowls, which had fallen into the cistern during this phase. A surprising find was in a neighbouring cistern (9027), the upper and more porous parts of which were covered with plaster. Since this cistern went out of use for the storage of water in the LB I, it is the earliest example of its kind known in Palestine.[1]

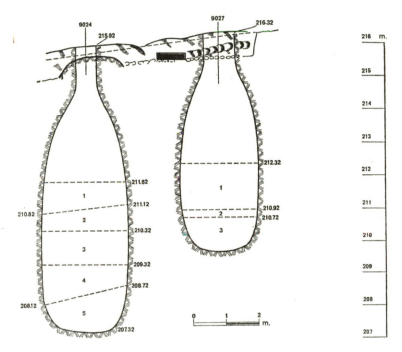

FIG. 7. Area D. MB II–LB. Cisterns 9024; 9027.

The storage capacity of the cisterns was 23 cu. m. Because of the rocky surface of the ground in the vicinity and the absence of large channels, it cannot be assumed that rain-water collected on the surface could have filled the cisterns; we must suppose that they were filled by water running off the roofs of dwellings built above or near them. Assuming the average annual rainfall to have been about 600 mm., a roof-surface of 25–30 sq. m. would have sufficed to fill most of the cisterns. In fact the

[1] Thus it precedes by several centuries the alleged introduction of plastered cisterns attributed to the Israelites in the Early Iron Period, see W. F. Albright, *The Archaeology of Palestine*, London, 1949, p. 113. See now also, Paul W. Lapp, 'The 1968 Excavations at Tell Ta 'annek', *BASOR* 195, 1969, p. 33 where it is indicated that waterproof plaster was used in LB I cistern.

remains of houses in the very vicinity of the cisterns indicate that the built-up area of a certain house was of these dimensions. A similar system of cisterns in the beginning of the MB IIB was found also in the Upper City.[1] Since, as indicated, most of these cisterns were later used as tombs, silos, etc., one has to assume that by then other solutions were found to supply the city with water.[2]

Returning to Cistern 9024, the next stratum, above the clayey and silt layer, indicated that by now—and still within the MB IIB–C periods—the cistern served as a burial-place. This stratum contained a large number of human skeletons with great quantities of burial furniture and scarabs lying near them. It was possible to ascertain that some of the dead were buried one on top of the other during a fairly short period.[3] In the stratum above the one containing the burials—i.e. local Stratum 3—a rich find of vessels of LB I was found. From the general arrangement of the vessels and their character it can be assumed that by now the cistern was used as a silo. Of particular importance for the dating of this stratum is the fragment of a typical Bichrome krater.[4] Similar ones were found in other areas of the Lower City[5] and Upper City.[6]

The next stratum was sterile, and it must be ascribed to a certain gap in the settlement here during the later part of LB I.

The top stratum contained many LB II–III fragments of pottery.[7] The outstanding find in this upper stratum is a clay mask similar to the one discussed in Area C.[8]

Thus this cistern represents all the periods of settlement of the Lower City; furthermore it demonstrates how a cistern was used for various functions in different periods.

Cistern 9027

This cistern had a slightly different story to tell (Fig. 7). The lowest stratum was 1 m. thick and contained no artefacts. The entire stratum was composed of very hard clay produced by water sediments. Since the next stratum contained already LB II–III pottery, it has to be assumed that this cistern served as a water-cistern for a long time. Above this stratum a most

---

[1] See below Chapter XIV, § 4, *a*.
[2] See below § 4, *b*; Chapter V, § 2; Chapter X, § 4.
[3] For a detailed discussion of the great quantity of pottery and scarabs discovered here, see *Hazor I*, pp. 130 ff. and pl. CXVIII.
[4] Ibid., pl. CXXIV, 8.   [5] See below § 4, *c*.
[6] Chapter X, § 4.
[7] Including a krater of a type found in Temple III at Lachish, *Hazor I*, p. 137, Krater no. 11.
[8] See above, § 2, *c*.

important burial was found belonging to LB II–III. 5·5 m. below the mouth of the cistern the skeleton of a young woman was found. Several vessels were discovered next to the skeleton, the most important of which were two intact Mycenaean pyxides. These pyxides[1] are very similar to types 94 and 95 in Furumark's type classification. They are related by Furumark to late Mycenaean IIIA: 2–IIIB,[2] i.e. late fourteenth or thirteenth centuries. Other fragments of Mycenaean pottery found in this cistern belong to Mycenaean IIIB.

Cistern 9017

The last cistern to be discussed is Cistern 9017, which was found in the lower terrace, i.e. in an area which yielded good occupational stratigraphy.

This cistern was hewn out of the rock at the same time as the other cisterns. At that period its mouth was on the rock level of the MB II stratum. Since in this area several occupation strata were found, an 'additional mouth' was added in later periods, built up with several courses of undressed stones. The upper course reached the LB strata. It may be assumed, perhaps, that the occupants of the LB II–III levels discovered the cistern after the earth had subsided at this point, cleaned it out completely, and used it for their own purposes. In this cistern *scores* of complete vessels were found—all belonging to LB II–III. Their nature (bowls, cooking-pots, etc.) indicate that in this period the cistern was used as a silo. In fact this cistern provided us with one of the richest groups of LB II–III vessels.[3] The vessels include many of locally painted ware, some resembling very much Levanto-Mycenaean IIIB type.[4] Indeed, a number of actual Mycenaean IIIB fragments as well as Cypriote 'Milk Bowls' and Base Ring II were found here.[5]

A reference should also be made to a couple of kilns discovered in Area D. One was perhaps used for making pottery while the other was most probably used for metal-working, to judge by the several pieces of copper slug found in it. For technical reasons[6] it was difficult to assign these kilns either to the MB II period or the LB II, although the first possibility seems perhaps more probable.[7]

---

[1] *Hazor I*, pl. CXXXI, 9, 10.

[2] A. Furumark, *The Mycenean Pottery, Analysis and Classification*, Stockholm, 1941, p. 43, fig. 12: 94, 95. See also V. Hankey above, p. 33 n. 1.

[3] *Hazor I*, p. 119 ff.   [4] Ibid., p. 121, *Decorated Vessels*, 4.

[5] Ibid., p. 122, *Imported Vessels*.   [6] Ibid., pp. 115 f.

[7] In this case it is interesting to refer back to the references of shipment of *tin* to Hazor in the Mari period. See above Chapter I, § 3.

And finally, mention should be made of a tiny fragment of a locally made LB II–III pot, found on the surface. The sherd (Pl. XXXV*a*) bears two letters in the proto-Canaanite script.[1] The two letters are painted in dark brown and may be read as: . . . *lt*. The inscription may be compared to the famous Lachish Ewer (Temple III) the inscription of which ends with the word '*lt* (goddess).[2]

I have discussed the finds from this area at some length in spite of the fact that the results were fully published in *Hazor I*. The reason for this is twofold. Due to the stratigraphical problems, the detailed descriptions of the results in *Hazor I* are somewhat difficult to digest by non-archaeologists. The above simplified summary may help. The other reason is the fact that this area not only corroborated the general picture of the history of occupation of the Lower City but yielded one of the richest ceramic evidences for dating both the foundation of the city and its destruction.

§ 4. AREA F

a. General

Area F (Pl. II*b*) is situated in the centre of the eastern part of the Lower City, some 200 m. south of Area D. For reasons similar to those affecting Area D, it was very difficult to excavate here. Indeed, although results from this area are of much importance for the study of the history of the Lower City, some of its finds are still enigmatic. The area was selected for excavation on account of a large rectangular dressed stone block that projected from the ground here, resembling an altar. Some 25 m. to the north of the altar the top of a wall of large undressed stones projected from the ground.[3] The excavations revealed that in a phase of MB II, as well as in LB I–III, most of the area was occupied by temples or cult-places. Since these will be discussed in a separate chapter (below Chapter VII, § 3) we shall confine ourselves here to other aspects of the area, stressing those finds which shed further light on the history of the settlement in the Lower City and produce more precise data for the dating of its establishment and final destruction.

---

[1] *Hazor I*, pl. XCIX, 20.   [2] *Lachish II*, pp. 49 ff; pl. LX 3.
[3] These ruins are marked on Garstang's first sketch (see above Chapter III, § 1) as 'masonry'. For a detailed description of the LB II remains of Area F, see *Hazor II*, pp. 127 ff.; for the earlier remains see the plates in *Hazor III–IV*, pls. LX–LXXVII.

b. The Middle Bronze strata

The earliest activities in this area (with the exception of a possible MB I tomb) are represented by a network of huge underground tunnels cut in the rock (Fig. 8). These tunnels (Pl. V*b*), reaching quite often to the height of 2 m. and the width of 1 m., slope from west to east, i.e. from inside the City towards its perimeter. A total length of 100 m. of tunnels had been excavated under very difficult conditions by the time work was stopped in this area in 1957. Except in one possible case,

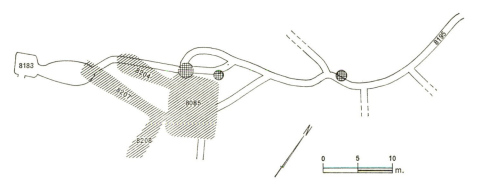

FIG. 8. Area F. MB II. The tunnels and shafts.

neither the tunnels' source nor their termination was discovered. Fragmentary as the picture is, it is clear that various tunnels originated in several directions (west, south-west, and north-west) and then converged into one tunnel extending eastwards (8195). The excavation of the latter had to be abandoned after about 30 m., on safety grounds. It is difficult to reach a firm conclusion regarding the function of these tunnels at this stage, but the following facts might point towards a solution.

At one place the source of a tunnel was apparently found: an oval-shaped artificial cave reached through a big vertical shaft (4×4×8 m.). This shaft (8183) was not completely excavated; but on its other corner (south-west) the beginning of an opening was found. It cannot be stated, however, whether this led to another cave or whether it constitutes the continuation of the tunnel. If the first possibility is proved, then we may assume that these tunnels served as communication-corridors between a series of deeply cut burial caves; furthermore, the fact that eventually all these tunnels sloped towards the perimeter of the city, might indicate that their main function was to drain the water which accumulated in the burials through the shafts.

The possibility that Area F served as a necropolis at the very beginning of MB IIB, is corroborated by another discovery. In the centre of the excavated area, another huge shaft (8085) was found, measuring $8 \times 6 \times 8$ m. From the bottom of the western side of the shaft accesses were found leading to three well-cut big caverns (Pl. V*c*), the largest of the three extending to a length of 15 m. This complex was definitely intended to serve as a tomb. When discovered, however, the caves were found to have been rifled in antiquity, or not to have been used. But for a few intact MB IIB vessels, they were completely empty. The interesting fact is that the shaft had cut through some of the tunnels, thus indicating that it was later than the original tunnels. If this theory is confirmed, it is possible that the area served as a burial-place for the nobility of the early MB IIB Hazorites—to judge by the gigantic size both of tunnels and of caves. Another possibility, although less probable, is that the whole network served as a huge drainage system of the Lower City, but at later times tombs were cut into it. In the 1968 season a further system of canalization was found outside the city.[1] One branch of these canals seemed to originate in Area F, thus forming the external outlet to this amazing complex of tunnels. Perusal of the pottery plates of *Hazor III–IV*[2] shows that the earliest activities on the site discussed above do not antedate the MB IIB. The next MB II stratum—a huge rectangular building—was built above the deliberately filled shafts. This is the latest MB II stratum on the site and must belong to phase C of this period. The intricate system of canalization of this structure was clearly connected with the tunnel-system. The building, perhaps a temple, will be discussed later on.[3]

c. The Late Bronze Strata

The area was densely settled throughout the LB periods. The main buildings were either temples or other cult installations, and they too will be discussed separately.[4] Here we shall concentrate on some of the more important finds from a chronological point of view.

LB I

All around the main building of this stratum (Stratum 2), the area was strewn with graves which yielded a rich collection of LB I pottery. Of particular interest are the Bichrome vessels—

---

[1] Area N, to be discussed below, Chapter V, § 5. [2] CCXXXIX–CCXLV.
[3] See below Chapter VII, § 3, *b*. [4] Below Chapter VII, § 3, *c* –*d*.

the largest collection of this type of pottery found so far at Hazor.[1] As noted already, the type was found in lesser quantities in all the excavated areas, both in the Lower and the Upper cities, and its profusion indicates that Hazor was densely populated in the latter part of the sixteenth century and the first half of the fifteenth century.[2] Of particular interest among the LB I finds in this area is a burial (Pl. X*b*) found inside the by now disused drainage channel of the building of Stratum 3.[3] This find not only indicated that the earlier building was by now derelict, but also furnished an interesting group of LB I pottery including an ivory stopper in the shape of Hathor's head.[4]

LB II–III

Aside from the interesting cult installations found in this period,[5] the area yielded most important data for dating the last Canaanite strata at Hazor. In Stratum IB the whole area was covered by buildings, mainly like those in Area C—of the central-court type, with many cobble-floored units.[6] The buildings, the reused earlier canalization systems, and the tombs produced a rich harvest of pottery, both locally made and imported. Tomb 8144–57[7] was particularly important. The large quantity of vessels found in it (Pl. XII*a*)—over 500 in number—has not only enriched our knowledge of the ceramic repertoire of this period, but has also given us the pottery types common throughout the existence of Stratum IB. In fact, it enabled us to fix firmly its duration from the el-Amarna period down to the end of the fourteenth century. The tomb was cut in the natural rock near the north-eastern corner of the Stratum 3 building. The circular shaft which led to it was found covered with two stone slabs. It is clear that the tomb was no longer in use in Stratum IA, since a wall (8624) built in Stratum IA was erected over the earth fill, which was nearly 2 m. thick and covered the stone slabs blocking the entrance to the shaft.

The *terminus post quem* of the period is fixed by the discovery in the tomb of a rare scarab bearing the name of Thutmosis IV

---

[1] *Hazor III–IV*, pls. CCXLII–CCXLIII, CCCXL.

[2] K. M. Kenyon's remarks (*Archaeology in the Holy Land*[3], 1970, p. 341) that there was (at Hazor) at best a much reduced population in the latter part of the sixteenth century and for much of the fifteenth century, and there may even have been a gap—seem to be contradicted by the discoveries in the areas already described, and particularly those by made in Areas H, K, and E, to be discussed later.

[3] *Hazor III–IV*, pl. LXXVII, 3 (Burial 8112).

[4] Ibid., p. CCXL.   [5] See Chapter VII, § 3, *d*.

[6] Strata IB and IA are described in detail in *Hazor II*, pp. 127–60, plan on pl. CCX, and finds in pls. CXXVIII–CLII.

[7] Ibid., pp. 140 ff.

(*Men-Kheperw-Re*). The duration and particularly the end of this stratum is effectively dated by the unusually rich Mycenaean pottery (Pl. XII*b*) found in the Tomb. This is of the IIIA: 2 type (with few A: 1). Some of the vessels belong to the very end of the IIIA: 2 type.[1] Similar Mycenaean pottery was found in another Tomb (8065),[2] as well as on the floors of the houses.

Thus Stratum IB extended throughout the fourteenth century. This conclusion was further corroborated by a large group of Cypriote vessels: 'Milk Bowls', Base-ring, and Bucchero Ware (Pl. XII*c*).[3]

Stratum IA, like in Area C, was found just below the surface, and in many phases erosion and the plough have played havoc with its remains. Nevertheless, enough was found[4] to indicate its existence in this area too. Furthermore, the numerous Mycenaean IIIB fragments (as well as isolated intact vessels) found decisively date its duration within the first two-thirds of the thirteenth century B.C.[5]

§ 5. AREA E

This small area (150 sq. m.) lies in the central part of the southern edge of the Lower City perimeter. Excavations were initiated here to probe into the nature of the rock-cutting, which looked like burial-chambers. It was particularly important to check this, since in his sketch of the site Garstang indicated that he found here 'Tombs'.[6] The general nature of the area was not entirely different from Area D,[7] with the same use of rock habitations and cisterns. On the whole this area, too, showed that the earliest habitation goes back to the beginning of the MB IIB, and the latest belongs to the thirteenth century. Of particular interest was a large bottle-shaped cistern (7021) some 9 m. deep (Fig. 9). The mouth of the cistern was found blocked by stones and fragments of basalt vessels (7020) and covered by a floor (7019) belonging to Stratum IB or IA. This cistern, unlike those of Area D, was rich in pottery, all of which belonged to Late Bronze I. Hundreds of pottery vessels were found in the lowest layer (*c*), which was composed of grey earth. The nature

---

[1] For a detailed discussion of this pottery see *Hazor II*, pp. 150–1. Because of their importance we submitted them to a special examination by Professor A. Furumark, and the above remarks are based also on his conclusions conveyed to us.

[2] Ibid., p. 153.   [3] Ibid., pp. 151 ff.
[4] Ibid., pp. 128–9, 142 ff.   [5] Ibid., pp. 157.

[6] See above Chapter III, § 1, *a–b*. Garstang's remarks in the Palestine Archaeological Museum report, that he found here a tomb with MB and Early Iron Age remains, are puzzling. The checks in the vicinity revealed no Iron Age pottery and the caves excavated by us revealed only MB and LB pottery.

[7] For a detailed report of Area E, see *Hazor I*, pp. 145–59, and the plan on pl. CLXXXIV.

of the accumulation (highest at the middle—some 2·5 m. from the bottom) indicates that the vessels were thrown or fell into the cistern. No remains of the MB II were found in it, although it is clear that it was actually made in this period. It must have been completely cleaned by the LB I peoples.

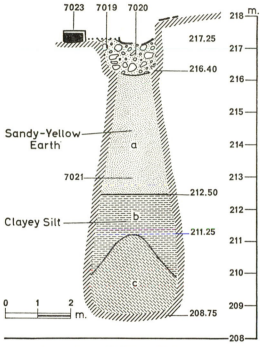

FIG. 9. Area E. LB I—Cistern 7021.

The vessels found here represent most of the LB I types known (including Bichrome Ware).[1] In addition, it included a new type in the repertoire of Palestinian pottery forms. This is a carinated bowl with quatrefoil mouth.[2] The type seems to have originated in Anatolia, where it occurs throughout the period of the Hittite Empire.[3] This find, too, indicates the extent of the LB I settlement, and points to its contacts with the northern cultures. As indicated, the last stratum belonged to LB II–III, and its remains were found both in structural remains above the rock and in two caves below.

§ 6. AREA 210

This small area (5 × 5m.) is of the utmost importance for the study of the nature and chronology of the Lower City (Pl. III*b*).

[1] Ibid., pl. CXL, 17–19, and p. 151.   [2] Ibid., pl. CXXXVI, 12–16.
[3] For discussion see *Hazor I*, p. 149.

Since the areas previously excavated in the Lower City (C, D, E, F) were either on the outskirts of the enclosure or were of a special nature (tombs, temples, etc.), it was decided to excavate a trial spot right in the centre, where no particular remains were to be seen on the surface. The intention was to clinch our main discoveries concerning the nature of the Enclosure and its dates. The area is situated at the south-west corner of Square 210 according to the excavations grid.

Since the results were of importance, and have not yet been published,[1] we shall describe them here in greater detail (Fig. 10). Altogether, as in Area C, five strata were found: 4–3–MB IIB–C; 2–LB I; 1B–LBII; 1A–LB III. The level of the latest stratum was just below the ploughed surface (225·5 m. above sea-level) while that of the lowest (Stratum 4) 223·1 m.[2]; i.e. the total thickness of debris is 2·4 m., encompassing a period of about 500 years.

Stratum 4

This is the lowest stratum here, and the houses are founded in the virgin soil, on which the floors, too, were laid. Altogether parts of four rooms (2009, 2010, 2011, 2012) were identified in these limited areas (*Hazor III–IV*, pl. CXLVII). The general orientation is roughly north to south. One of the units (2010) had a cobble floor while the floors of the others were of earth. Few sherds were found on the floors (*Hazor III–IV*, pl. CCXCVI 1. 4. 5)—all MB IIB. Of special interest was the south-western room (2011), under the floor of which three infant burials (Pl. VI*b*) were found in jars (*Hazor III–IV*, pl. CXLVIII, 1 : T₂, T₃, and T₄), similar to those found in Area C. There was a slight difference between the two areas; while in Area C most of the juglets were found within the burial jars, in Area 210 most of them were found nearby; otherwise they were the same, and so was the pottery (*Hazor III–IV*, pl. CCXCVI)—all of MB IIB.

Stratum 3

This stratum belongs, too, to the MB II period. The general plan of the rooms (now numbered 2005–8) is the same as in the previous one, but the floor was raised some 0·4 m. Furthermore, while some of the previous walls were reused, others were built afresh. In one of the corners of room 2008 (*Hazor III–IV*, pl.

[1] For plates see *Hazor III–IV*, pls. CXLVI–CXLIX. For the pottery see pls. CCXCVI–CCXCIX. The following references will be to these plates. The description of the results are partially based on the report of the Area Supervisor, E. Stern, submitted for the Text Volume of *Hazor III–IV*.
[2] Erroneously marked in Fig. 10.

CXLVIII, 3), a raised paved platform was found with a nest of vessels consisting of cooking-pots and baking-trays (*Hazor III–IV*, pl. CCXCVI). This, together with the layer of ashes, indicates that the platform served as a 'cooking corner'. Under

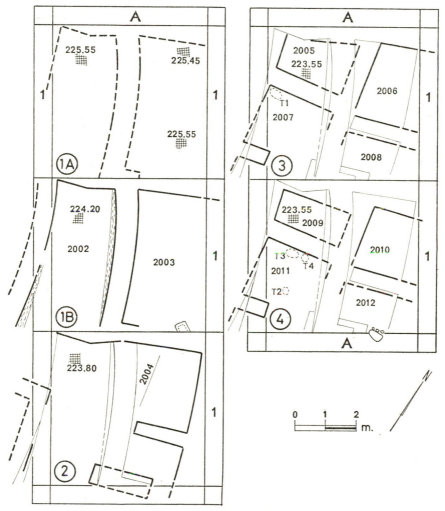

FIG. 10. Area 210. Plans of the MB II–LB III strata.

the floor of one of the rooms (2007) an infant-burial (T1) was found in a jar (*Hazor III–IV*, pl. CXLVII). This room is above the one from Stratum 4 (2011), under whose floor also infant-burials were found.

Stratum 2

In this stratum there occurred a complete change and devia-tion from the previous ones. Instead of the four rooms observed in Strata 4–3, most of the area now is occupied by a court, surrounded on all its sides by walls and openings which obviously led to other rooms. The earth floor of this court was laid above the stumps of previous walls. In the south-east corner of the court, on a paved enclosure (2004), a few vessels were found (*Hazor III–IV*, pl. CCXCVII), all of the typical LB I period at Hazor.

Stratum 1B

A completely new layout is apparent in this stratum. Instead of the previous court, two rooms (2002, 2003) were discovered, orientated roughly north to south. But for the northern wall, which is based on a Stratum 2 wall, all the walls of Stratum 1B were newly erected ones. The western of the two rooms (2002) is long (5 m.) and rectangular and its southern limit is beyond the excavated area. It seems that the room served as a store; this is further corroborated by eight pithoi (pl. CXLIX, 4) found in it. The bases of the pithoi were stuck deep in the floor of the room. They are of the typical Hazorian type found in abundancy both in Stratum 1B and 1A.[1] The type is unique in Palestine, but very close parallels were found in Ugarit in the LB strata.[2]

Stratum 1A

No fresh buildings were found in this stratum. The proximity to the surface must have eliminated the structures. All that remains is a floor on which was found a group of sherds (pls. CXLVI; CXLIX, 4).

Thus, this small trial trench at the heart of the Lower City revealed the same strata of occupation as in the other areas—from MB IIB down to LB III.

§ 7. OTHER AREAS IN BRIEF (H, K)

Three more areas were excavated in the Lower City, but they will be better discussed in separate chapters. In Area H, in the northern part of the city, a series of temples were found, and therefore they will be dealt with in detail in Chapter VII (§ 2). In Areas K and P, on the eastern edge of the city, the remains of the city-gates were discovered and will be discussed in Chapter VI. Nevertheless, it should be emphasized here, in concluding this chapter, that in all these three areas the general picture depicted here was confirmed, and in fact, enriched by abundant stratigraphical and ceramic data.

---

[1] Cf. pl. CCXCVIII.   [2] *Hazor I*, p. 155.

V

THE EARTHEN RAMPART AND FOSSE

§ I. GENERAL

HAVING established that the 'enclosure' was indeed a great flourishing city, it is possible now to examine some aspects of its fortifications. The most conspicuous elements of the site are, of course, the stupendous earthen ramparts, particularly large on the western side of the perimeter. Their nature is very clearly seen on the ground, but aerial photographs and photogrammetric maps further emphasize their layout.[1]

Similar ramparts are known from Carchemish,[2] Qatna,[3] Tell Mardikh,[4] Tell Dan,[5] and other places,[6] but their exact anatomy is not sufficiently known.

A glance at the aerial photographs (Pl. I*a*) reveals a very important clue to the understanding of the main purpose of these ramparts and the relation between them and the other element which is very characteristic of these types of cities, namely the fosse. One can observe that the rampart on the western side has no constant measurements. It is very wide (90 m.) and high (15 m.) at the southern end and it tapers off in size towards the north. In the same photographs (and maps) one can see quite clearly to the west of the rampart, and parallel to it, a deep gulley which is obviously a man-made moat or fosse. Its artificial and military nature were indeed recognized even by the local Arab settlers, who called it *El-Ḥandaqiyeh* (= fosse). This moat, too, tapers off towards the north where it merges with a natural *wadi*. Thus it is clear that the earthen rampart on the western side was created mainly with the earth scooped out of the moat. Where the moat had to be dug deeper, the rampart was wider and higher. The topography of the natural plateau[8]—which is well protected in the north and east

---

[1] See *Hazor I*, Frontispiece and pls. I–II; *Hazor III–IV*, pl. I.

[2] C. L. Woolley, *Carchemish II*, London, 1921, p. 43.

[3] Du Mesnil du Buisson, *Le site archéologique de Mishrife-Qatna*, Paris, 1935, pp. 40–2; pls. I–II.

[4] *Missione archeologica in Siria-Campagna di scavi 1964*, Roma, 1965, fig. 2; pls. III–IV.

[5] Cf. *IEJ* 19, 1969, pp. 121–3, 240.

[6] Cf. Y. Yadin, 'Hyksos Fortifications and the Battering-Ram', *BASOR* 137, 1955, pp. 23 ff.

[7] As recorded by Garstang (*AAA* 14, p. 35).   [8] See Chapter II, § 3.

by the sloping terraces—left the western (or, more precisely, the south-western) side of the Lower City unprotected by any natural obstacles. For this purpose the moat was cut here. The moat is 40 m. wide at the base and 80 m. at the top, and at present (unexcavated yet) is 15 m. deep.

It became evident from the start of the excavations that the constructional nature of the rampart will have to be examined— no easy task.

During the 1955–8 seasons this was done, with moderate success in Areas C and H, and only in the trial trenches of 1965 we succeeded in achieving a clearer view of this problem. So, firstly, we shall recount the result reached in C and H.

§ 2. AREA C[1]

At the start of the excavations, a 5-m. trench[2] (6062) was dug at right angles to the rampart in order to find out how it was built (Pl. IIa). Because of its great thickness—and the unexpected discovery of the Stelae Temple at the foot of the rampart[3] —we have not succeeded in reaching the core of the rampart, but it was possible to observe some of its characteristics. The trench showed that it was composed chiefly of a mass of small stones and beaten earth. No structures were found at this point, on top of the rampart, but several were discovered on its inner slopes. The entire lower part of the rampart had been strengthened, at least as early as Stratum 3 (end of MB II), by a number of parallel supporting walls built up to a wall which revetted the foot of the rampart.[4] Furthermore, the slopes of the rampart were sheathed with several layers of small rubble stones, perhaps for the purpose of protecting the buildings inside the city, and more especially those at the foot of the rampart, from floods and landslides.[5] The sheathing was thicker on the lower parts. On the upper parts there was usually only a very thin layer of stones. It is possible of course that this can be explained away by assuming that the accumulations at the bottom were the result of stones falling from structures lying higher up the slopes. The narrow nature of the trench prevented us from reaching more firm conclusions.

One further point should perhaps be mentioned again: the remains of buildings of the top strata inside the city were

---

[1] See *Hazor I*, pp. 74 f.   [2] Ibid., plan on pl. CLXXIX.
[3] See below Chapter VII, § 1.
[4] *Hazor II*, p. 81, Sub-area 6174. See also ibid., pl. XXVII, 1–2, and plan on pl. CCVIII.
[5] *Hazor I*, pl. XXVI, 5–6.

covered in the vicinity of the rampart with a sterile layer of earth—thicker near the slopes of the rampart and thinner at some distance from it.[1] We conclude from this that the rampart was originally higher at this point, but that the uppermost layers (with a wall?) were washed down by the rains and formed the sterile earth layer.

A word should be said here concerning the huge round depression which is situated at the south-western corner (Pl. I*b*), between Area B at the western tip of the Tell and Area C. The depression is actually at the extreme west end of the ravine and moat separating the Upper and Lower Cities.[2] Its diameter at the top is about 90 m. and its depth is 20 m. This depression seems to be man-made, but, since it has not yet been excavated, only a tentative suggestion can be offered as to its function. As is known from the results of the excavations in 1968 of the water-system,[3] the water-level of the surrounding springs is at about 190 m. above sea-level, just 10 m. below the present lowest point of the depression. It is possible, therefore, that this round depression was dug in order to reach the water-level and served as a prime water-reservoir for the whole of the Lower City.[4] Whatever the case, the topographical position of the depression afforded an additional defence by narrowing down the actual width of the gap between the rampart and the Tell to a few metres.

§ 3. AREA H

Area H lies in the extreme north end of the Lower City. Here was found a series of temples which will be dealt with separately.[5] The proximity of the temples to the perimeter of the city and the excavations of the areas surrounding the temples provided us with important data concerning the ramparts in this area too.

The main data were obtained as a result of a trial-trench made just east of the temples, and of several soundings on the northern (outer) slope of the city's plateau, in a direct line with the trial trench. It became evident that here too, as on the western side, there existed an earthen rampart, but—because of the existence of a deep *wadi* to the north—of a lesser height. Here we had also a clear stratigraphical proof that the earthen rampart was

---

[1] A similar phenomenon was noticed by Woolley at Carchemish.

[2] See *Hazor I*, p. 2.   [3] See below Chapter XIV, § 4.

[4] The suggestion offered in *Hazor I*, p. 2, that one has to assume the existence of a horizontal tunnel connecting the depression with the springs to the south of the Tell now seems to me rather far-fetched.

[5] Below, Chapter VII, § 2.

erected in Stratum 4. The temple of Stratum 3 is built *partially* on a specially levelled area at the lower part of the rampart. The maximal height of the rampart here was 8·5 m. above the virgin soil of the city. Its top is about 6 m. wide. The soundings on the northern slope showed that the beaten earth construction extended to a distance of at least 30 m. on the slope. Further to the north, towards the *wadi* we encountered a terrace, which might have been created by a revetment wall at the bottom of the slope. These facts indicate clearly that the plateau was protected by a combination of a rampart and a glacis: above the top of the natural slope of the terrace the rampart was erected, and its outer face further extended northwards and outwards towards the bottom of the slope, in a shape of a glacis built in the same manner. The inner slope of the rampart is slightly more sheer than the one on the outside (1 : 1·5) and its total length is 9 m.

The rampart was made of layers of yellowish chalky material, covered in its upper face with a layer of small basalt field-stones. At the bottom of the inner slope of the rampart—and lying upon the levels of Strata 3 and 2—there was found a considerable amount of brick debris. This indicates, perhaps, that on top of the rampart there was originally a brick wall. The latter assumption is further strengthened by the fact that the latest temple was covered by a thick sterile layer—composed of brick material—extremely difficult to excavate.

§ 4. THE 1965 SECTIONS[1]

The two sections affected in the northern slope of the 'Eastern Spur' contributed immensely to the understanding of the anatomy of the earthen ramparts.[2]

a. Section A–A (Fig. 11)

This section is located roughly along the middle part of the rampart (near the point where it turns southwards, due to the topography). The trench was deepened with the aid of mechanical equipment, to a depth of 5·5 m. A further 2 m. were excavated by hand. It became immediately apparent that we excavated here, too, a rampart, like that in Areas H and C. But because we were able to cut the section so deep we were able for the first time also to look at its 'inside'.

---

[1] See above, Chapter III, § 3.
[2] The present description is based on the account prepared by the late I. Dunayevsky and A. Kempinsky.

The trench revealed in the centre of the rampart a brick-built core, 8 m. wide at the top and between 11 and 16 m. wide at the base. This core consisted of a 'structural casemate', 3 m. wide and 5 m. deep, filled with basalt and other stone pebbles and beaten earth. The northern outer face of the brick core was nearly vertical and it was covered here and there with plaster. The bottom was not reached and the measurements of the base are conjectural. The core is built of sun-baked bricks measuring

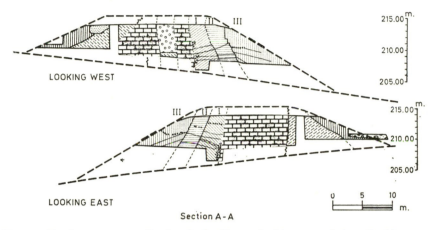

FIG. 11. Earthen ramparts. Section A–A. Above: looking west; below: looking east.

0·4×0·3×0·15 m. While the horizontal space between the courses is rather thin, the vertical ones are very thick and often reach 10 cm. The colour of the bricks varies from very dark to very light. In the lower portion of the eastern face of the section we could discern a fairly big portion built of grey bricks containing many sherds, the material for which was obviously taken from previous debris. The rampart itself was thrown up against the core in three vertical 'blocks', each composed of various layers (sandwich-like) of different types of earth, varying in thickness from 0·6 m. to 1·5 m. The two blocks (I–II) nearer the core were dumped against it inclining inwards (that is in a direction opposite to the natural slope). The throwing of the two 'blocks' was done simultaneously and thus the same materials are found in the various layers of the 'blocks' (marked in fig. 11 in thin lines), and in the same order. When the throwing of a certain layer was completed, its outer face was plastered. Thus we can discern in the section, lines of the plasters slightly slanting from top to bottom. The outer 'block' (III)—also consisting of layers—was thrown along the direction of the slope, and thus the present surface of the outer slope of the rampart was achieved. The outer face is covered by a beaten chalky layer some 15 cm. thick. Another detail of interest is that at the lower part of the northern face of the core—between it and the thrown blocks—one can see in the section a thin sheath of field-stones which were thrown here in the process of the dumping. At the inner (southern) side of the core we could discern only two 'blocks' of layers thrown against the core, and forming an inner slope of 35–45°. Its exact method of throwing was not so clear in the section.

b. Section B–B

This section, about 140 m. west of A–A, was cut near (the later excavated) Area P in which a city-gate was found.[1] This trench was but 2·5 m. deep, and revealed that here the rampart was apparently devoid of the brick-built core. It consisted mainly of a beaten-earth core strengthened within by the addition of several layers. Its nearness to the gate and its adjacent structures may explain the change in the method of its construction.

§ 5. CONCLUSIONS

The discoveries in Areas C and H (as well as those in P and K), and particularly in sections A–A and B–B, prove that the method of constructing the ramparts in the MB II was well developed and sophisticated, and adapted effectively to the topography and tactical requirements. Wherever the terrain dictated a considerable slope, the rampart had been strengthened with a built core against which the earth was dumped. Thus, a solid, stable rampart was achieved, extending downwards in the shape of a glacis, almost impossible to batter or pierce. A similar phenomenon was recently discovered at Tell Dan, where the core is built of stones. This core was 10 m. high and 6·5 m. thick.[2]

The fact that the rampart was composed of layers dumped in 'blocks' and in different directions should induce a fresh examination of other sites to see whether the numerous 'blocks' of layers in the glacis/ramparts (such as at Jericho[3] or Shechem[4] for example) are indicative of the existence of different glacis of different periods—or whether they are to be explained as a technical innovation peculiar to a single period. In any event it is clear that the building of the glacis and ramparts in this

[1] See below, Chapter VI, § 2,   [2] A. Biran, *IEJ* 19, 1969, p. 240.
[3] K. Kenyon, *Digging up Jericho*, N.Y., 1957, fig. 4.
[4] See the Section (fig. 22) in G. Ernest Wright, *Shechem*, N.Y., 1965.

period was a completely new phenomenon—both technically and in basic conception, introduced by the builders of the gigantic 'Lower Cities' of the MB IIB, with the clear purpose of defending their new cities and mounds against any possible penetration and destruction by battering rams,[1] or similar means. The new data negate, I believe, the opinion voiced, without sufficient basis, that the glacis and ramparts were mere local developments stemming from earlier periods.[2]

[1] Cf. Yadin, above, p. 51 n. 6.
[2] Peter J. Parr, *ZDPV* 84, 1968, pp. 18 ff. Parr's article is, otherwise, very useful and important for the dating of the various earthen ramparts, particularly in Syria. See Appendix, § 2.

VI

THE GATES

A MOST interesting subject for the study of the fortifications of the Lower City are, of course, the city-gates. This is particularly so in view of the fact that the nature of the gates of the 'fortified camps' is not well enough known from other sites.

Two gate sites of the Lower City were excavated, Area K[1] and Area P,[2] and since neither is yet published—except for preliminary reports—we shall discuss them here in greater detail.[3]

§ 1. AREA K

Area K is located on the north-eastern edge of the Lower City, not far from the northernmost corner. From aerial photographs and from a careful exploration of the whole area, we felt convinced that one of the city-gates must have been located in the north-eastern part of the city—a deduction made long ago by Garstang.[4] The excavation's starting point was what looked like the jamb of the gate (Pl. VII*a*), the huge ashlar stones of which were found protruding from the ground.[5] In order to facilitate the follow-up of the many phases of the gate's history, we decided to excavate only half of the gate-house, south of its axis, and leave its northern half unexcavated for future checking. Since it is very difficult to ascribe the gates stratigraphically on their own, a certain area of the city proper south of the gate was excavated too. In addition, we probed in various areas in the vicinity along the walls and revetments connected with the gate. Altogether we found here five gates and occupational strata—corresponding to those of the other sites in the Lower City—which we shall designate[6] 1A, 1B, 2, 3, and 4.

[1] See above Chapter III, § 2, *b*, 2.   [2] See above Chapter III, § 4.
[3] For preliminary reports see *IEJ* 9, 1959, pp. 84 ff.; ibid. 19, 1969, pp. 8 ff. See also, *Encyclopaedia of Archaeological Excavations in the Holy Land* (Hebrew), Jerusalem, 1970 s.v. Hazor. For the plates of the gates in Area K, see *Hazor III–IV*, pls. CXXX–CXLV.
Since there was a difference in opinion between the late I. Dunayevsky and myself, concerning the interpretation of the data related to the topmost stratum (1A), the captions to the pictures in *Hazor III–IV*, often contain the phrase: 'for stratification, see text.' The text of *Hazor III–IV* has not been published to date, and therefore the following discussion should be taken also as a shorter version of the accompanying text to the plates. The nature of the division of opinions will be explained below.
[4] *AAA* 14, fig. 3.   [5] *Hazor III–IV*, pl. CXXX, 1.
[6] As in the captions to the plates of *Hazor III–IV*.

Stratum 4

Of the gate of this stratum, belonging to the beginning of the Lower City and built over virgin soil, very little was unearthed, since it lay partially under the succeeding gates. However, enough was found to indicate its general plan (Fig. 12). A simple gate-passage was flanked on either side by a solid tower, measuring about 8 m. square and built of bricks on stone

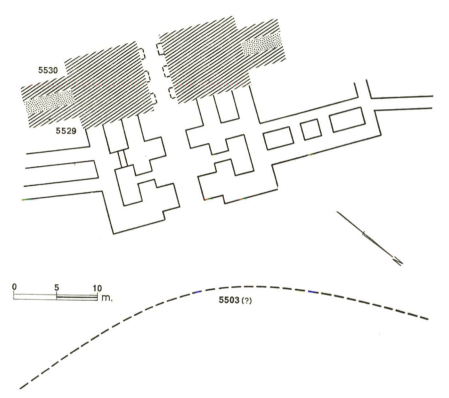

FIG. 12. Area K. The earliest gate (hatched lines)—Stratum 4 (MB IIB).

foundations.[1] Some of the stones, which are roughly trimmed field-stones, measure 60 cm. in height. It may be perhaps surmised that this gate—which seems to be similar to the southern gate at Gezer—had a number of pilasters in the passage itself. The gate was located some 22 m. away from the slope (about 13 m. away from the later gates) and was approached by a gentle ascent built of beaten earth, laid in alternate layers of basalt flakes and clay, crushed yellowish

[1] See *Hazor III–IV*, pl. CXXXVII, 1, in which one can see the stone foundations of the eastern face (5538) of the excavated tower—the southern of the two. On pl. CXXXVIII, 1, is shown the foundation of the southern face of the same tower.

chalk rock, and brown brick mud. While there seems to be no doubt that this gate was contemporary with the earthen rampart, it was connected with the latter by a special wall which bridged the natural depression in the topography between the site of the gate and the upper 'shoulders' of the ramparts to the north and south of it. This bridging wall was composed of two parallel walls (5530–29) each of just over 1·5 m. in thickness, with the space between them 1·7 m. in width. The total width of the wall was 5 m. The space between the walls—at least up to the level of the gate floor—was filled with beaten earth,[1] similar in construction to the core of the rampart discussed in Section AA[2] and in the sub-structure of a fort in Area B in the Upper City.[3] Other methods of bridging a gate with the rampart were found in Area P, to be discussed below.

Stratum 3

The gate of this stratum—the latest phase of the MB II—entirely differs, both in plan, construction, and location from the previous one, and is patterned according to the 'classical' gate-plan of this period (Fig. 13), found both in Palestine and elsewhere (Alalakh, Qatna, etc.). In the gate-passage (7·5 m. wide), three pairs of pilasters narrowed the width of the passage to 3 m. On either side of the passage stood a large tower(16 × 6·5 m.), the southern (Pl. VII*b*) of which (the only one excavated in its entirety) was divided into two interconnected chambers. The sole entrance to the chambers was in the passage, through an entrance to the eastern (outer) of the two rooms. The total length and width of the gate-house (exterior measurements) were 20 and 16 m. respectively.[4]

East of the gate, at a distance of about 10 m., a huge revetment-wall (5503) was found[5] (Pl. VIII*a*) built of large basalt boulders. This wall supported the causeways leading to the gate from the north and the south, along the slope. In front of the gate, there was a large artificial platform which enabled the chariots to enter the gate after a turn of 90°. The revetment-wall has been preserved to a height of more than 5 m. and to a length of 50 m., and is one of the finest examples of MB II fortifications. No direct stratigraphy was found between the

[1] See *Hazor III–IV*, pl. CXXXIX, 2, for the eastern (outer) wall of the 'double wall' (5529) and its junction with the Stratum 4 gate-tower (showing both the stone foundations and the bricks above them), and the same plate, 3–4, for the western (inner) wall.
[2] Above Chapter V, § 4.   [3] See below Chapter X, § 3.
[4] See *Hazor III–IV*, pls. CXXXIII, 1; CXXXIV; CXXXVII, 2, 3; CXXXVIII, 2.
[5] Ibid., pl. CXXXII.

revetment-wall and the two earlier gates, but I am inclined to ascribe it to Stratum 3 (the revetment was used, of course, by the subsequent gates too) for the following two reasons: (*a*) it is built too far away from the gate of Stratum 4; (*b*) a sounding[1] which we made under the base of the revetment, revealed a considerable amount of MB II, sherds, indicating the existence

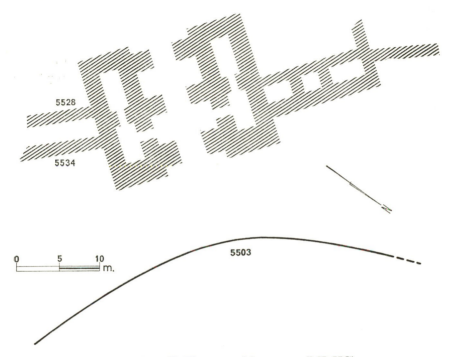

FIG. 13. Area K. The gate of Stratum 3 (MB IIC).

of an occupational period before the erection of the wall. The third element in the gate-complex is of no less importance. The gate-house was connected with the 'shoulders' of the rampart-fortifications by a huge and true casemate-wall, the earliest of its type found in Palestine.[2] Each of the two walls (5534–5528) is 1·5 m. in thickness and the space between them is 2·25 m. Well-built stone foundations, still preserved up to over 2 m., were found in the sections.[3]

[1] *Hazor III–IV*, pl. CXXXII, 2 (sounding 5003).

[2] Recently, and of the same period, a casemate-wall was found also at Taanach; see Paul W. Lapp, 'The 1968 Excavations at Tell Ta'anek', *BASOR* 195, 1969, pp. 21–2.

[3] The western (inner) wall (5528) can be seen on *Hazor III–IV*, pl. CXXXIX, 1, and the eastern (5534) wall and its junction to the gate-tower, on pl. CXL, 4. On pls. CXLIV and CXLV can be seen the section in the casemates of the wall to the north of the gate.

Stratum 2

The gate of this phase—LB I—is identical in plan with that of Stratum 3, but is built with huge and well-dressed ashlar blocks,[1] another testimony to the high cultural and technical achievements of Hazor in this period.

The destroyed casemate-wall of the previous stratum was restored too, and courses of stones added in this stratum are discernible.[2]

Stratum 1B

In this stratum the gate is identical with that of the previous one, with minor repairs and additions (Fig. 14). Amongst the

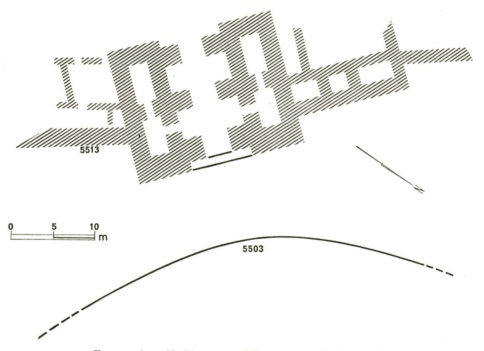

FIG. 14. Area K. The gates of Strata 1B–1A (LB II–III).

latter are the two huge basalt slabs forming the outer threshold of the gate,[3] and the raising of the floor of the passage, which is now built of cobblestone.[4] Another important change took place in the bridging wall: the casemate-wall gave place to a new wall (5513) built of bricks and 3 m. thick. Its lower and outer face is protected by a low revetment wall built of rubble.[5]

[1] See *Hazor III–IV*, pls. CXXXIII–CXXXIV.
[2] Ibid., pls. CXXXIX, 1; CXL, 4.
[3] Ibid., pl. CXXXIII, 2.   [4] Ibid., pl. CXXXVI.   [5] Ibid., pl. CXL, 2.

Stratum IA

This gate is in fact the previous one with minor repairs and additions, mainly visible in the cobble paving.[1] The floor was found to be covered with a thick layer of ash and rubble (Pl. VIII*b*), comprising brickwork of the gate and towers[2]—obviously the result of the final destruction of the city-gate by a violent conflagration—as was the case in the temple of Stratum IA in Area H.[3] Near the gate a small cult-installation was found, which included some stelae,[4] similar to those of the Stelae Temple of Area C[5] and the cult-installation near the temple in Area A.[6]

§ 2. AREA P

It was recognized from the outset[7] that another gate of the Lower City may have existed in the corner between the east and north sides of the 'eastern spur'. The modern highway to the North now passes at this point. When the road was built in the 1920s large structures, some remnants of which can still be seen today in the ditch along the roadside, were destroyed. As the Israel Ministry of Labour was planning to widen this

---

[1] Ibid., pl. CXXXVI, 1 (on right of paving).   [2] Ibid., pl. CXXXVIII, 3.

[3] See below Chapter VII, § 2, *e*. This interpretation of the evidence is mine; the late I. Dunayevsky, on the other hand, ascribed the layer of ashes to IB, and claimed that the city-gate went out of use in this period. These different approaches depend very much on the interpretation of the evidence of the structures discovered within the city, adjacent to the southern face of the city-gate.

The LBII–III periods were represented here by three clear phases of a large room (or court) which contained several installations (Room 5013, in *Hazor III–IV*, pls. CXLI, 2 and CXLII, 1). Dunayevsky, in his suggested plans, attributed all the three layers to IB and designated them IB/C, IB/B and IB/A. He was led to this conclusion by the fact that above these remains there appeared to be poor remains of yet another stratum.

A clear remnant to be attributed to this stratum (which he wanted to designate IA) was one stone face of a foundation of a hut, or similar construction, found *outside* the city wall, indicating quite probably that it was erected when the city's fortifications were already destroyed.

My points against it are the following:

(*a*) Nowhere was Stratum IB represented by *three* phases, and

(*b*) the installation looked more like those of the Early Iron I huts found in the upper city (see below, Chapter XI, § 1). I found a further corroboration in the fact that only Area K of all the excavated areas produced sherds of this period (Cf. *Hazor III–IV*, pl. CCXCV, 38).

This attested, to my mind, that some semi-nomadic Israelites settled for a while in the area of the destroyed gate. In the meantime, in the 1968 campaign, the same phenomenon was attested also in the gate of Area P (see below). A further point of contention concerned a certain wall (5514 on *Hazor III–IV*, pl. CXLIII, 2), which appeared to be partially built on the brick wall. A brief trial sounding in 1961 (in which both of us took part) failed to prove this point, and it seems that further excavations might be necessary in order to decide whether the other wall was indeed to be attributed to IA or to a later construction.

[4] *Hazor III–IV*, pl. CXLII, 2. Here it is ascribed to phase A of IB, which indeed could be IA.

[5] See below Chapter VII, § 1, *c*.

[6] See below Chapter VII, §4 and Chapter X, § 5.   [7] *Hazor I*, p. 3.

road, we had been asked by the Department of Antiquities to 'clear' the area by excavating it thoroughly. The excavations here[1] were particularly difficult from the technical point of view, due to the proximity of the road and the existence of a recently planted commemorative forest which we did not want to uproot. Nevertheless, we managed to uncover fragments of the gates there, grasp their basic plans and discover an important fact: the nature of the constructional connection between the gates—built in the natural depression—and the 'shoulders' of the earthen ramparts.

The excavation indicated that the western gate-towers were built west of the new road, while most of the area of the gate-passage and the eastern towers were destroyed completely when the road was first built. Here too, as in Area K, we discovered remains of five successive gates from the beginning of the MB IIB and up to the end of the LB: two MB II phases (4–3) and LBI (2) and two LB II–III phases (1B–1A).

No plan of the Stratum 4 gate can be offered, since its remains lie deep under the later remains, but enough is seen in the section to indicate its existence; furthermore, it is probable that it resembles in plan the gate of Stratum 4 in Area K. As in the latter case its remains do not tally in their position with the 3–1 gates and it seems to be on a smaller scale. The plans of the subsequent gates are generally identical with those in Area K, i.e. a gate-structure with six pilasters and two large gate-towers, one on either side; the towers comprised two chambers each (Pl. IXa). The gates proper were of brick on stone foundations. The upper surface of the foundations were levelled and paved with pebbles to serve as a base for the brick wall. It seems that here too, the gate of LB I was better built. Of the gate of 1B a well-preserved threshold made of basalt slabs was found near the inner pair of pilasters. Nearby the socket of one of the doors was found, suggesting that in gates of this type doors were erected at both the inner and outer pilasters.[2] Clear remains were found of the gate of 1A, in which a new threshold was built, near and above the 1B, but made of crude whitestone boulders. More changes were made in the inner part of the gate in the form of a semicircular bastion. In the top layers of the later gates a considerable quantity of broken basalt orthostats

[1] The present description is in many places nearly verbatim the one which we published in our preliminary communique *IEJ* 19, 1969, pp. 8 ff. The material is still under study and it is not yet possible to submit a more comprehensive report.

[2] A fact known also from other sites; see most recently Tell Mardikh, *Missione archeologica in Siria, Campagna di scavi 1966*, Roma, 1967, fig. 1.

was found in debris indicating that they were used as building material.[1]

By the gate, to its west, remains of a large LB II–III structure were found. We did not succeed in establishing their nature, but Mycenaean and local pottery found on its lowest floors indicate the date. Near the building a libation-table and other basalt stones were found, which may hint that a temple may have existed here.

It is interesting to note that, in this area too, as in K, some quantity of Stratum XII Iron I pottery was found on the surface, indicating that some huts of the semi-nomadic settlers of the Upper City extended their occupation even beyond the perimeter of the Upper City.

The most important results of this dig occurred east of the road, where we found the joint between the gate and the eastern rampart meeting at right angles (i.e. the meeting point of the eastern rampart of the Lower City and the northern rampart of the 'eastern spur'). The difficulty in constructing the joint was twofold: (a) because the gate was perforce lower than the rampart, and (b) because of the technical difference in the construction of the gate and the rampart. The excavations proved that the joint here was achieved through a number of stone-built terraces (Pl. IXb) gradually rising from the gate up to the top of the rampart. These terraces served as the foundations of a thick and impressive brick wall. It became clear that the joint was built in two periods: the first in MB IIB and the second in LB, although it is still impossible to define its dates more precisely. The total width of the terraces in the later stage was 15 m.

§3. THE CITY'S DRAINAGE-SYSTEM

In concluding the discussion of the Lower City's gates, another aspect, indirectly connected with the gates, should be discussed: the City's drainage-system.[2] While digging for the foundations of the Hazor Museum a few years ago, on the site of the Expedition Camp (General Square 176), a well-built channel of huge boulders was discovered covered by rough stone slabs. The channel was some 2 m. below the present surface with a general north–south direction. The large quantity of MB II pottery found around the channel indicated that it had been constructed, broadly speaking, together with the Lower

---

[1] The date of the orthostats in Hazor will be discussed in Chapters VII and X, § 4.
[2] See also *IEJ* 19, 1969, p. 8.

City. In order to elucidate the nature of this channel, several soundings (Area N) were conducted in the vicinity, during the 1968 season. While these soundings are, by their nature, not comprehensive, the following facts became clear: the direction of the channel's slope was to the north, i.e. towards Hazor's fields. Near the south-eastern corner of the Expedition Camp, a second channel was found to join the former, emanating apparently from Area F. The main channel continued southwards, but it too then curved westwards, in the general direction of the gates in Area P. The main channel continued north a little beyond the Expedition Camp until it abruptly stopped. It is interesting to note that under the foundation of the gates in Area P a section of a channel was found, apparently connected with the one mentioned above.

These discoveries may lead to some important conclusions related to the City's planning in the Middle Bronze (and continued in use also in the LB period). It is obvious that this network of channels served as a drainage of the Lower City. It adds further meaning to the underground network in Area F, and it demonstrates that several arteries drained the City's rain-water (and perhaps sewage as well), using the lower areas of the gates as an outlet for the channels. There remains the question why the channels were continued so far away from the City's ramparts. There can perhaps be two explanations: that outside the fortified city there existed some unfortified suburbs or hamlets, and the object of extending the channel was to prevent these structures from being flooded. The second alternative is that these channels were used too as part of a well-developed irrigation system. In both cases, it may be assumed that this amazing network was built under the influence of similar irrigation and drainage systems common in Mesopotamia.

VII

THE TEMPLES

A NUMBER of temples of various periods were found in the lower and upper cities, and they will be discussed in this chapter. Some of them (the Stelae Temple from Area C and the cult-area around the altar of Area F), were already published in detail in the final publication of Hazor, and, therefore, they will be treated here more briefly though with some new observations. Others, like the Orthostats Temple and the other temples from Area H were known to readers mainly through short preliminary reports and the plates of *Hazor III–IV*; therefore they will be discussed in greater detail here, and this may serve, temporarily, as an accompanying text to the plate-volume. A third group of temples—belonging to MB II and LB I and discovered in Area F in 1956–7—will be presented here for the first time, since it was only recently, while preparing the material for publication, that I became aware that these structures were actually temples. And finally, we shall deal here with a temple found in Area A in 1968.

§ I. THE STELAE TEMPLE—AREA C[1]

a. *Location and stratification*

As mentioned above,[2] while digging a trench in Area C to ascertain the nature of the earthen rampart (Pl. XIII) we found at the foot of the rampart a small temple or shrine of the utmost interest because of its unique furniture. The first object to be discovered was a basalt statue of a headless man and by it a bowl lying upside down.[3] At first it seemed as if the statue was not *in situ*, but after the excavation had been extended to its north, we saw that it was in fact *in situ* and formed part of a row of stelae (Pl. XIV*a*)[4] situated near the western wall of a small shrine, about 6 m. from north to south and 4·5 m. from west to east (exterior measurements). The building, with its narrow

---

[1] See *Hazor I*, pp. 83 ff., for detailed discussion. Cf. also *Hazor II*, p. 97.
[2] Chapter IV, § 2.   [3] *Hazor I*, pl. XXVII, 1.
[4] Ibid., pl. XXVIII.

(1 m.) entrance in the middle of the eastern wall, had at least two main phases[1] belonging to the LB II–III.

The lower building (Figs. 15, 17) was erected directly on the conglomerate of the rampart. The conglomerate had been excavated and cut into only within the temple area, and thus a floor was formed lying somewhat at a slope from west to east.

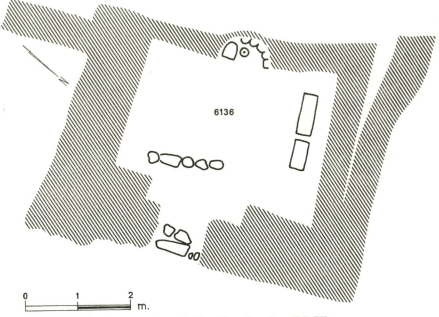

6136

0   1   2 m.

FIG. 15. Area C. The Temple of IB (LB II).

On the other hand, the conglomerate of the rampart north and south of the building had not been levelled, and it dropped here by a steep gradient from 232·2 m. to 228·8 m. A similar phenomenon was observed in the construction of the temples in Area H to be discussed later. In the centre of the western wall, opposite the entrance, a semicircular niche had been cut near the floor, its diameter 1 metre. In the centre of the niche a 'waster' jug was found *in situ*. Along the lower part of the walls, benches were built of unhewn stones with large smooth-surfaced stones set into their outer face. The whole arrangement was not unlike the benches found in the other buildings of Stratum IB.[2] The width of the bench was about 40 cm. and the height varied from 45 to 30 cm. Two well-dressed stones were found near the

[1] In *Hazor I*, p. 84, we concluded that the earlier phase originated in Stratum IB. While this may still be so, I now believe, for reasons which will be submitted below, that perhaps it was first erected in the LB I period, or, at least, that there was a shrine here at this period.
[2] See above, Chapter IV, § 2, *c*.

northern wall; they served, perhaps, as offertory tables. The building therefore had a rectangular plan with the entrance at one wide side (east) and a niche in the opposite side, similar in fact to the 'holy of holies' of the temples of Area H. It may be assumed that most of the temple-furniture discovered in the Upper Temple originated with this temple, and that it was dug out and reused after the Lower Temple had been destroyed. This is further corroborated by the fact that the northern and southern walls were reused in the Upper Temple. These walls were found standing to a height of 1·6 m. We were satisfied[1] that this building should be ascribed to IB on account of its stratification, and the LB II period on account of the intact pottery found there. Yet one has to remember that this building was built directly on the conglomerate of the rampart, and it is possible that it was first erected in some previous period, or incorporated an older building into its walls.

In addition to the ornamented pottery, one should mention among the finds from this temple a pair of bronze cymbals resting inside a bronze bowl found in the north-west corner of the building. Similar cymbals—of the LB II period—have been found elsewhere in Palestine.[2]

(b) The Upper Temple

The Upper Temple (Figs. 16–17), as has been mentioned, reused the northern and southern walls, as well as part of the eastern wall. The changes affected mainly the western side of the temple, which was more vulnerable to destruction due to floods and collapses emanating from the slope of the rampart. The main change was in the nature of the niche: the floor of the niche was higher than the floor of the building, and thus formed a sort of raised platform. In this platform we managed to discern three phases, obviously secondary repairs due to collapses, etc. In all these phases the niche had the same kind of platform, as was attested by the levels of the finds made in them. The best proof that the niche was indeed a raised platform, is the following:

(i) While the statue (see below) was found placed in situ in a level of 230·87 m., its head was found lying at a lower level—230·1 m.

(ii) The heap of pottery of the upper phase was extended from the level of the stelae to the lower level—230 m., and some of the fragments from the different levels could be pieced

---

[1] Hazor I, pp. 84–5; Hazor II, p. 97.   [2] Hazor I, p. 85,

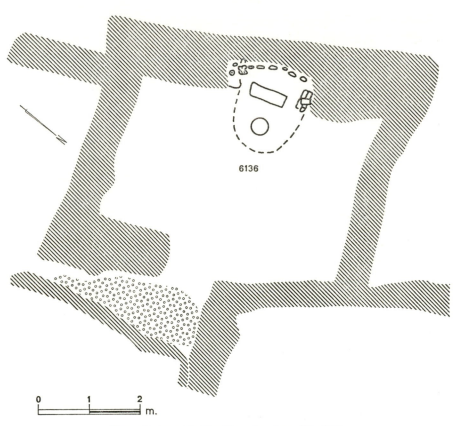

Fig. 16. Area C. The Temple of 1A (LB III).

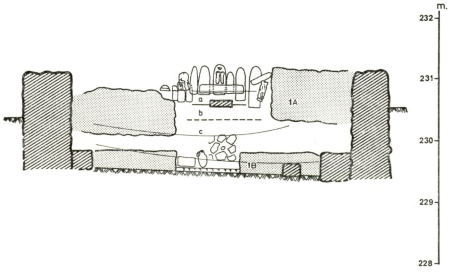

Fig. 17. Section—looking west of temples 1B–1A.

together to form complete vessels. The array of cult-furniture (statue, stelae, offertory tables) of this temple are best described as found in the upper (and last) phase of its existence.

c. The stelae and sculpture[1]

When found, a row of ten stelae (Pl. XIV*a*) stood inside the niche, next to the rear wall, all of them made of basalt. Their fronts, which faced the entrance, were flat, while their backs were convex. The tops were rounded. None of them, except the one in the centre, bore a relief. Some of them stood behind the statue (see below) to its right and left, serving, as it were, to support it.[2] One of them, to the extreme right of the viewer was found lying on a lion orthostat from the preceding phase (see below). The stelae were not of the same height: from 65 cm. for the tallest to 22 cm. for the shortest. Nevertheless—but for the small stelae which 'supported' the statue—their tops protruded above the platform, to a more or less equal height. This was achieved through the difference in depth in which the stelae were stuck in the earth of the platform. These stelae, as stated, originated in an earlier phase, but were reused. In layer c(1A) of the same stratum a recumbent stele was found. A further large group of stelae was found outside the temple; their position and nature merit description since they shed further light on their function. South of the building were found 17 stelae of various sizes, most of them only roughly worked. Of these, 11 were found atop the slope of the rampart, level with and near the southern wall of the temple, while the other 6 were found at the bottom of the slope near the eastern end of the same wall. The lowest of the stelae was found at a level of 228·8 m. It is very difficult, in these conditions, to ascribe the stelae with certainty to one or the other phase. The fact that they were discovered in, or on, a layer of masonry debris which appears to belong to the destruction of the Lower Temple indicates perhaps that these stelae were thrown in the area during this destruction only to be partially salvaged at a later stage. Another possibility is that this group of stelae—many of them in an unfinished state of working—belonged initially to a heap of stored stelae, lying outside the temple.

The stele with the relief was found in the centre of the row. The relief occupies the upper two-thirds of the surface—the part visible above the ground. It represents two hands stretched upward, and above them a symbol of a deity, composed of a

[1] For plan and layout see *Hazor I*, pl. CLXXXI.
[2] For this and the following finds, see ibid., pls. XXVIII–XXXI, CLXII.

crescent within which there is a disc. Two small tassel-like circles
are depicted below the crescent.

The statue (Pl. XXIa)—of which the decapitated head was
found lying on the floor below—was situated in the south corner
of the niche (to the left of the viewer). It is made of basalt, its
height is 40 cm., and it represents a beardless man with bare
head and feet sitting on a square stool. In his right hand he
holds a bowl, while the left fist rests on his left knee. He wears
a long tunic falling slightly below the knee, with a train sewn on
parallel to the hem. The upper part of the tunic has a curved
neckline, from which an inverted crescent hangs down upon his
chest. The head is short and round. Although the finish of the
surface is very good, not all parts of the face are equally accentuated and some have not been executed in detail: the ears
are shown without the cavity, the eyes without the pupil. This
can hardly be accidental or attributed to the hardness of the
material.[1]

In the centre of the niche a roughly finished basalt slab was
found, which presumably served as a table on which some of the
offering-vessels found scattered in the vicinity had been lying.
Amongst them were a mace-head, a rough representation of
a human-being made of basalt, part of a pottery wheel (?), and
a phallus-like piece of stone. Before commenting on the nature
of the deity of this temple and the significance of the stelae, we
should like to mention some of the objects found in the niche
but in a lower level than the offertory table and the stelae. The
most important of these is a small orthostat of a lion (Pl. XVIIIb)
found beneath the extreme right (northern) stele. The orthostat was found with its narrow face (the head of the lion)
facing the entrance, but the left side of the orthostat, bearing
the relief of the lion's body, was found turned to the north wall
of the niche and would not have been visible. This obviously
shows that even in the last but one phase it was already not *in
situ* but placed or buried there as a relic of a previous building.
This is evident in any case, since the lion is clearly an entrance-
jamb orthostat. The crouching position with hind legs drawn
up beneath the body; the curving of the tail upwards between
the leg and the body; the termination of the mane in the shape
of a horn—all these details show clearly that this orthostat is of
the same period as the large orthostat found in the Temple of
Area H.[2]

---

[1] See below, § 2, *e*, concerning a statue found in Temple H, whose details are perfectly
worked out.   [2] See below, § 2, *e*.

In the light of the discoveries of the 1968 season, we have every reason to believe that these orthostats belonged to the LB I period at the latest. Thus the small orthostat was originally definitely placed—together with another (which has not been found)—at the entrance of a building of the LB I period. Its small size (44 × 33 cm.) indicates that it came from a relatively small building, say similar to the lower temple in this area. However, since no orthostats of this size were actually found here, it is possible that the LB I period temple was somewhere in the vicinity, and was not necessarily identical with the lower temple itself.

d. The nature of the Temple

The most important questions concerning the Stelae Temple are, of course, the identity of its deity and the meaning of the stelae. There seems to be no doubt that the deity was a moon-god. This is attested by the inverted crescent pendant on the breast of the male statue,[1] which represents the moon-god Sin in Near-Eastern representations,[2] and by the top emblem on the stele bearing the relief: the full moon within the crescent. There remains the problem of the interpretation of the two upraised hands on the same stele, depicted below the above emblem. In the initial publication[3] I suggested seeing in them a gesture of supplication and submission to the symbol of the deity which appears above the hands. Although I noted then the similarity between this representation and those depicted on the much later Punic stelae, I did not at the time draw a closer affinity. Recently, in a detailed paper,[4] I suggested seeing in these hands a symbol of the goddess—the consort of the moon-god.[5] In this case the central stele bears the symbols of the two deities. This explains also, I believe, the discovery of two other cult-objects in the vicinity of the temple, discussed in a previous chapter:[6] the standard and the mask.

It will be recalled that the standard (Pl. XV*c*) bears a crescent with the depiction of a stylized snake. Below this,

[1] Which, I believe, is of the deity itself. This assumption was challenged by K. Galling ('Erwägungen zum Stelenheiligtum von Hazor', *ZDPV* 75, 1959, p. 5), mainly on the ground that the Hazor figure is the only case in which a deity's statue bears a symbol. However, subsequent to Galling's article, we found another statue bearing a symbol, of which there can be no doubt that it represents a deity (see below, § 2, *e*—Area H).

[2] *Hazor I*, p. 88.　　　　　　　　　　　　　　　　　　　　[3] Ibid., p. 89.

[4] 'Symbols of the Deities in Zinjirli, Carthage and Hazor', *The Glueck Festschrift* (ed. James A. Sanders), Garden City, N.Y., 1970, pp. 199 ff. See now also S. Moscati, *Le Stele Puniche di Nora*, Roma, 1970, pls. I–XIV.

[5] In the above article I submitted the evidence for my belief that the hands in Carthage represent *TNT*, the consort of Ba'al Ḥammon who is represented by the crescent and the disc.

[6] Chapter IV, § 2, *c*.

a woman's figure is depicted holding snakes in her uplifted hands.[1] The snake, too, is closely connected with the moon-god and his consort, and the mask must also be connected with this temple. It is interesting to note that, in the Punic cult too, masks are quite common. The fact that the Hazor mask (Pl. XV*b*) was very small, had neither nostrils nor pierced mouth, should perhaps lead one to suggest that it was not actually worn by human beings, or put on the face of the dead, but rather attached to the face of the sculpture. This may be the plastic expression of the goddess's title, *The face of Baal*, so common in the Punic inscriptions; it may perhaps explain the crudity of the depiction of the statue's face, which was meant to be covered anyway.

As for the nature of the stelae themselves, and *ergo* the nature of the temple, one should remember that the temple of Area C was not the only place where stelae of this nature were found. We have already mentioned[2] the small cult-installation in Area K, in the vicinity of the gate of the LB II–III period, which contained several stelae lying in disorder; we should also refer now to a very similar installation found in the proximity of the temple's temenos in Area A,[3] where, too, an offering-bowl was found intact. All this tends to support Albright's suggestion[4] that these stelae should be interpreted as memorials for the dead. However, this does not imply, in my opinion, that the whole temple or shrine should be interpreted as a funerary shrine in the strictest sense of the word. It is quite natural for the various temples to be used *also* for the erection of *maṣṣeboth* to commemorate the dead,[5] but this does not mean, necessarily, that this was their main function.[6]

Whatever the case, it is interesting to note that the Stelae Temple was dedicated to certain deities other than the lord of the temple to be described now.

[1] In my article (see above, p. 73 n. 4), the evidence is collected to support this assertion in connection with the Hazor standard.

[2] Chapter VI (the vicinity of the gates in Area K).

[3] See § 4.

[4] W. F. Albright, 'The High Place in Ancient Palestine', *Vetus Testamentum*, Supplement IV, 1957, pp. 242 ff. On this, see also the remarks by Galling (*supra*, p. 73 n. 4, p. 7) and, J. Gray, 'Hazor', *VT*, 16, 1966, pp. 35 f.

[5] In this connection I should mention also several similar stelae (one bearing a disc symbol) which were found in the debris of the Temple of Area H (see *Hazor III–IV*, pl. CCCXXXIII, 2–8).

[6] For the other sites in Palestine and outside in which stelae were found, see *Hazor I*, p. 90.

§ 2. THE ORTHOSTATS TEMPLE—AREA H

a. General—Location and stratification

Area H lies at the extreme end of the Lower City's perimeter, just inside the northern earthen rampart. The temples were found accidentally, when some of the top stones of the courses were seen protruding above ground. This particular part of the enclosure was not ploughed and, therefore, the remains of the latest stratum seemed unharmed, as was the case in some of the other areas. Altogether four temples were found; the older two (Strata 3-MB II and 2-LB I) were of identical plan, as were the topmost two (1B-LB II and 1A-LB III). The Stratum 1A structure was built of basalt orthostats, which clearly originated from, and were built in, an earlier phase. Their nature and date will be discussed with the Stratum 1A temple. The total area excavated was approximately 1,000 sq. m., and it included considerable parts of the areas outside the temples proper, where some of the outside court's cult-installations were found. Although the oldest temple belonged to Stratum 3, and was obviously later (at least technically) than the earthen rampart, few remains (pottery, fragments of construction) were discovered below this stratum, indicating the existence of Stratum 4 activities in this area. These were reached in only a few places and in trial soundings and therefore it is impossible to say whether any temple existed there prior to Stratum 3; the odds are against such a possibility, for reasons put forward in the following discussion of Stratum 3. The treatment of the temples should be taken as a temporary substitute for the text volume of *Hazor III–IV*.[1]

b. The MB II Temple—Stratum 3

All of the remains of this temple lie beneath the later buildings, and in many cases the contours of its walls were either detected with the help of soundings, at right angles to their courses, or were not found at all. It is, therefore, quite natural that the picture of the plan of this temple is incomplete and in some cases conjectural. There was, however, enough evidence to trace its main features and stratification. The temple (Fig. 18) comprised a large main room (2175) and a porch, consisting

---

[1] The plates referred to in the following discussion are in *Hazor III–IV*, pls. CI–CXXIX (excavation views), CCLIX–CCLXXXV (pottery and objects), and CCCXIX–CCCXXII (cylinder seals). References to numbers of walls and loci are given in order to facilitate the study of the plates. The following description is partially based on the text draft prepared by T. Dothan, I. Dunayevsky, and the present writer for the final publication.

of an entrance-hall (2163) flanked by two rooms (or towers) on the west (2183), and one on the east (2130).

The actual entrance to the porch was through basalt ashlar steps leading to a platform (2148). The whole of the southern area,

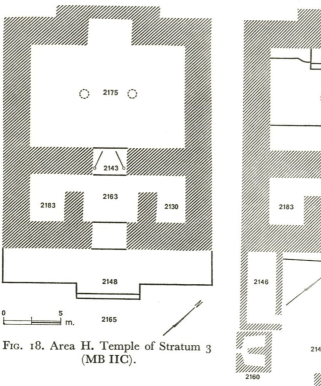

FIG. 18. Area H. Temple of Stratum 3 (MB IIC).

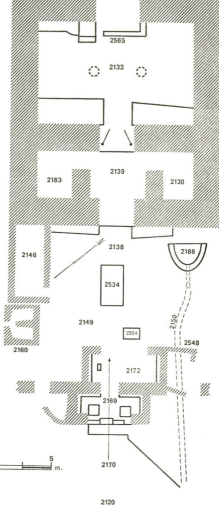

FIG. 19. Area H. Temple of Stratum 2 (LB I).

in front of the temple entrance, was occupied by a large open court (2165) paved with a fine pebble floor. The following description of the temple will deal with each of these elements separately.

The thickness of the outer walls of the temple, and most probably the wall between the main hall and the porch, was 2·3 m. thick. The measurements given below will normally be the inner measurements, unless otherwise indicated.

The main room (2175) is of the *Breitraum* type measuring 13·5 m. from west to east and 8·9 m. from north to south. These measures indicate that the roof must have rested upon pillars, since the span is too big for a roof without support. On the analogy of the later buildings, one would expect two columns placed across its width. The two 0·5 × 0·5 m. basalt capitals, or base-like stones found lying on the floor of this temple (although not *in situ*), may have belonged to the conjectural pillars of this temple. The two basalt stones are flat on one side and bear a conical protrusion on their other side.[1] There were sufficient data to conclude that the room had a niche in its northern side, which protruded also at the outside for about 1 m.[2] The following measurements of the niche are partially conjectural, since some of its walls are covered by the later buildings: 4 m. in width and 2·3 m. in depth. The border between the niche and the room was built of fairly big stones with smaller stones in the fill behind. It may be conjectured that its floor was raised in relation to the floor of the room. The top of the wall-foundations —built of rough boulders—was horizontal (about 30 cm. above the floor level), indicating that the walls themselves were built of brick. The foundations of the walls were very deep— about 1·5 m. below the floor level. This was dictated by the nature of the fill below the floors which will be discussed later on. The floor of the temple is of smooth beaten clay.[3] The passage between the main hall and the porch is 3 m. in width. The southern part of the passage-threshold (2143) was found with the two door-post sockets *in situ*.[4] The sockets lie about 30 cm. inside the entrance and are made of basalt slabs with depressions of 10 cm. in diameter. Their position indicates that the entrance was closed by a two-wing door, opening inwards towards the main hall of the temple. The main central room of the porch measures 4·9 × 4·3 m, and is separated from the flanking rooms by walls 1·5 m. thick. It is possible that the rooms served as towers, in which a staircase led to the roof or second storey, if ever there was one. These rooms (2183—western, 2130—eastern) are identical in dimensions: 2·7 m. from west to east and 4·25 m. from north to south. The outer threshold of the porch has not been found, since it was covered by later walls

[1] See pl. CIV, 3–4. [2] See pl. CVII, 1. [3] pl. CIV, 2. [4] pl. CVI, 1–3.

and, therefore, it is impossible to indicate whether or not the
porch had doors. The positions of the corners of the jambs
indicate that across the entrance to the temple, south of the porch,
and presumably along its whole facade, there was a raised platform (2148), some 3·2 m. wide.[1] In the middle of its southern side
two steps were found, each composed of two well-dressed basalt
slabs, measuring 1 metre each.[2] The top step is not in line with
the lower one, and ends slightly to the east of it. It seems that the
two steps are part of a wider system, which—based on the limits
of the cobble floor nearby—may have been some 5 m. in width,
and protruded 1·2 m. south of the platform. The outer measurements of the entire temple are, excluding the southern platform,
20·5 m. from north to south and nearly 18 m. from west to east.

South of the temple there existed a large open court, or
square (2165), with a very fine floor made of small pebbles.[3]

The extension of the pavement to the south was traced in
a trial-trench up to a distance of 30 m. (Pavement 2173), where
it ends abruptly in a straight line. Here we found traces of
bricks which may indicate the existence of a brick wall marking
the southern limit of the court. The eastern and western borders
of this great court were beyond the limits of the excavated area.
A number of trial soundings made under the floor of the temple,
and in the vicinity of the earthen rampart,[4] indicate that the
building was erected on specially prepared ground near the
foot of the rampart. Since the natural level in this area sloped
slightly towards the rampart, a sort of 'pocket' existed here—
deeper near the rampart. In order to level the ground, a slice of
the lower part of the rampart was cut out and levelled, and the
'pocket' was filled with horizontal layers of dark and yellowish
well-beaten chalk. In some places, remains of stones laid out in
line were traced,[5] possibly parts of revetment-terraces within
the fill. Both the pottery found under the fill (Stratum 4) and
that found in the temple itself and its vicinity were of MB II, and
the temple proper can be ascribed to Stratum 3 (MB IIC) on
stratigraphical grounds as well.

The plan of the temple resembles the temples of Megiddo
VIII and Shechem only in the two towers flanking the entrance,
but unlike them it is of the wide-house type.[6] The Hazor temple,

---

[1] pl. CVII, 4–6.   [2] Ibid.
[3] pl. CVIII, 2; pl. CXIV (Paved Square 2151). The latter is another locus number of the
same floor (on the eastern edge).   [4] See above, Chapter V, § 3.   [5] pl. CV, 1.
[6] For the latest treatment of the Megiddo and Shechem Temples, see G. Ernest Wright,
'The Significance of Ai in the Third Millennium B.C.', *Archäologie und Altes Testament* (Galling
Festschrift), Tübingen, 1970, p. 314, and further bibliography there.

on the other hand, is strikingly similar to the Stratum VII temple at Alalakh, to which it is also akin chronologically.[1]

c. The LB I Temple—Stratum 2

The plan of the temple of this stratum (Fig. 19) is identical with that of the previous one, although the building is a completely new construction. The main changes were made outside the temple, in the area of the previous large open court.

In various places, one can discern certain changes and additional structures which were made during the lifetime of this temple. The long existence of the temple is further attested by the raising of the floor, which was more of a natural accumulation of dirt than a result of destruction of some sort. The main hall (now numbered 2133), had a floor made of large cobble-stones further covered with a layer of plaster. This floor was laid directly on that of the floor of Stratum 3, and we had the impression that the latter was 'cleaned' before the new floor was laid out.

As mentioned above, an accumulation of beaten earth was noted in several places on this floor and belonging to this stratum. Furthermore, in various spots, additional installations were erected after the main floor had been laid, and they possibly belong to a later phase. South of the northern niche (which was of similar measurements to the previous one), and parallel to it, a partition-wall (2565) was built upon the floor. This wall[2] closed the niche also from the east, but in the west left a narrow opening which provided entrance into the niche. West of this narrow entrance a small rectangular platform was found (1·2 × 1·5 m.), to which a bench-like structure was attached at its southern end. On this an upturned basalt bowl was found.[3] Near the southern wall of the hall, and flanking the passage from the porch, further wide bench-like structures were found. Their actual width can only be estimated, since their southern limit (i.e. the actual northern face of the wall between the porch and the main hall) is buried under the walls of Stratum 1B. But it seems to have been about 1·5 m. It may be noted that the stones of the benches—as well as the cobble-floor, where it was not covered with additional plaster—were highly polished as a result of much use. A similar bench, somewhat narrower, was found near the western wall of this hall.

[1] See Sir Leonard Woolley, *Alalakh. An Account of the Excavations at Tell Atchana in the Hatay, 1937–1949*, Oxford, 1955, pp. 59 ff. and fig. 35 and pl. XIV.
[2] pl. CIX, 5.
[3] Ibid., 4.

The final destruction of the temple is represented by a thick layer (0·7 m.) of brick debris.[1] The passage between the main hall of the temple and the porch is identical in dimension with the previous one. There is now, however, a new threshold which covered the door-sockets of Stratum 3.

The eastern socket was found *in situ*; it is in the shape of a basalt bowl and shows signs of wear.[2] The central room (2139) of the porch, like the main hall, was covered with a rough cobble-floor, as well as lime plaster. In the western part of the room we found some sort of installation, most probably a stand for a krater or pot. In the eastern room (2130) a layer of 15 cm. of ashes containing organic matter was found.

As indicated, radical changes took place outside the temple in the south. Now too, a large square or court faced the entrance to the south. It was covered by a new cobble-floor made of the same coarse stones as in the building itself. Soundings showed that it, too, extended to the south at least for 30 m. from the temple. The floor is built in such a way that its northern half slants southwards, while its southern part slants northwards. Thus a sort of shallow trough was created in the centre— further accentuated by a guiding low wall—which drained the water to the south-east. On this low wall we found the bronze plaque to be discussed later on.

The main feature of the new organization of the area is the division of the open court into two main areas, separated from each other by a well-built gate-house or propylaeum and a wall; thus were created what may be called an inner court (be- tween the temple and the gate-house—2138, 2149) and outer court (2170–2120) south of it. The propylaeum consists of two elements: the entrance porch (2169) and an inner room (2172).[3]

The former is a broad room (5·2 × 1·6 m.) of which the south entrance is 3·6 m., with a threshold made of three well-dressed basalt slabs. The slabs are not equal in size and do not span the whole of the threshold; it is possible that they were taken from their original position in the steps leading to the Stratum 3 temple described above. Along the northern and eastern wall there were low, narrow benches, and it is probable that a similar bench existed along the western wall too. Just inside the entrance, near the entrance jambs, two raised platforms (1 m. square) of

---

[1] pl. CIX, 2. Similar debris was uncovered on the floors of the LB I Temple in Area A, see below, § 4.

[2] pl. CX, 1–2.

[3] pls. CXI–CXII.

rubble stones were found; one on the right and one on the left. They obviously have no constructional function, and they seemed to be cultic in nature: either bases for incense stands or offering tables. An entrance—1·5 m. wide—led from the porch to a wide room (2172)—6×2·5 m., built slightly eastward of the axis of the porch (the latter's axis is on exactly the same line as the temple porch). A bench was found along the western wall. Inside the room there were a few installations—mainly small circular or rectangular courses of rubble stone, serving as support for vessels. In the middle of the inner court (2138) on the axis of the propylaeum and porch entrances, there existed a large rectangular platform (2534) measuring 3·5×2 m., built upon the floor. When found it was still 30 cm. high. It looks like a *bammah* or an altar. Two metres to the south-east of it, a similar but smaller structure (2554) was found (1·5×1 m.).

Immediately south of the large structure, the pebbles of the cobble-floor were so laid as to form a well-marked circle,[1] 1 m. in diameter. It seems that its function was to mark the position of a certain cult-object. The whole area was littered with animal bones and ashes, and was obviously the main area of the sacrifices. This may explain the discovery of two other important finds in the area. In the eastern part of the court, about 5 m. east of the *bammah*, an interesting drainage-channel (2150) was found just beneath the court-floor.[2] The northern 1·5 m. of this channel were built of three disused incense-stands, while its continuation to the south was built of field-stones covered by undressed slabs. The channel was traced in the south to the rooms flanking the propylaeum on the east. Its course further to the south is unknown since the area has not been excavated. It may be assumed that eventually it joined the main drainage system of the Lower City. The origin of the drainage was most probably a semicircular installation (2188) in which two basalt bases of pillars were incorporated in secondary use, situated to the right of the temple-entrance. The channel seems to have drained the blood and water of the sacrifices.

In the south-eastern part of the court, just north of a wall (2548) extending east of the inner room (2172) of the pro-pylaeum, a great heap of discarded vessels was found,[3] amongst them broken incense-stands similar to those found in the drainage-channel,[4] as well as an inscribed clay model of a

[1] pl. CXII, 3.   [2] pls. CXIV; CCLXVIII, 1–3.
[3] pl. CXIII, 1.   [4] pl. CCLXVIII, 4.

liver (see below). This place was obviously the *favissa* of the temple.

To complete the inventory of the installations connected with the temple, one should mention the discovery of a brick-built potter's kiln (2160), 5 m. to the west of the *bammah*. This kiln definitely served the temple, as evidenced by the 20 miniature votive bowls found in it.[1] Only the northern chamber ($1 \cdot 5 \times 1$ m.) of the kiln was found, with its funnel to the west. North of it and adjacent to the western façade of the temple, a long room (2146) was found, with brick walls; it may have served as the potter's storage-room.

The most important objects—outside the incense stands and the pottery—connected with this temple are two figurines, a bronze plaque and the clay liver model. One of the figurines[2] (5 cm. in length), made of bronze, is of particular interest. It depicts in a schematic manner the naked body of a woman. Only half of her features are accentuated: one eye, half the nose and mouth, one breast, and half of the vulva. This Picassoesque figurine seems to represent 'life and death' or the 'born and unborn'. The other figurine—made of thin silver leaf—belongs to the well-known, tall-crown type of goddesses, with eyes, nose, breasts, and vulva schematically represented by protruding circles.[3] The bronze plaque (Pl. X*c*)[4] is of particular beauty in its execution. It is made of a thin bronze sheet, $9 \cdot 5$ cm. in length. The rivets on its back indicate that it was fastened to a wooden panel, and its position may indicate that it was once part of a whole procession. The figure is hammered and some of its details are further delineated by incisions. It depicts a Canaanite dignitary looking to the right with his right hand raised in a hailing gesture. He is wearing a long robe, with wrappings in its lower parts, similar to the depictions of Canaanite dignitaries in Egyptian wall-paintings of the fifteenth century.[5] On the upper part of the body he wears a 'poncho'-like garment terminating in fringed bands. The clay liver model[6] for divinations (Pl. X*a*), bearing Akkadian cuneiform inscriptions, is unique in Palestine. Our two fragments bear the following inscriptions,[7] pressed on the face of the models (upon and beside the protruding ridges) and on their backs:

[1] pls. CXIII, 2; CCXLXI; CCLXIX.   [2] pl. CCCXXXIX, 3.
[3] See O. Negbi's doctoral dissertation, *The Canaanite Metal Figurines in Palestine and Syria* (Hebrew, unpublished), Jerusalem, 1963, vol. ii, p. 129.
[4] pl. CCCXXXIX, 1.   [5] e.g. *ANEP*, figs. 46–7.   [6] pl. CCCXV, 1.
[7] For a full discussion of these models see B. Landsberger and H. Tadmor, 'Fragments of Clay Liver Models from Hazor', *IEJ* 14, 1964, pp. 201 ff. In *Hazor III–IV* we suggested that the two fragments belong to one model. Landsberger and Tadmor, however, tend to conclude

Fragment A

One king will bend down another
An enemy will attack my country
. . . .
Forgiveness (will be granted) by the god to the men
A servant will rebel against his lord

Fragment B

Ištar (?) will eat the land
Nergal will . . . .
The gods of the city will come back

The dating of the liver model was not an easy task. After long deliberations—and taking into account both the linguistic and orthographic peculiarities, Landsberger and Tadmor reached the conclusion that the Hazor specimens were copied about the time of Ammi-Ṣaduqa and Samsu-ditana (the second half of the sixteenth century) or slightly thereafter,[1] a date well within the chronological limits of Stratum 2. Its LB I period is well attested by the numerous LB I pottery found in the temple and its surroundings,[2] including early types of 'Milk Bowls',[3] 'Base-Rings',[4] and Bichrome Ware.[5] The temple of Stratum 2 generally and the organization of its courts in particular represent one of the most detailed temple complexes found to date in Canaanite Palestine.

d. The LB II Temple—Stratum 1B

The temple of Stratum 1B is a completely new building, built on the ruins of the temple of Stratum 2. In its northern part, it follows, more or less, the plan of the previous temples, with changes in the thickness of the walls, their exact position, etc. The innovation in the plan consists mainly in the addition of a third element in front of the building—an entrance hall. Thus the building consists of the following elements: entrance hall (2128), middle hall (2129), and rear hall (2123), which was actually the biggest in size and the most important; it was virtually its *Holy of Holies* (or *debir*) to use biblical terminology.

This hall (Pl. XVI*b*) occupies roughly the area of the previous temples' main hall. It is a wide and spacious room (13·3 × 8 m.)

---

that they belonged to two models. They designated them: Fragment A (the large, nearly complete fragment) and Fragment B (the smaller, broken one). Nonetheless, I believe that these two fragments belong to one model, based on their identical texture and finish. (Cf. fig. 4 in Landsberger and Tadmor's article for a possible reconstruction.)

[1] pp. 214–16.   [2] pls. CCLXI–CCLXX.   [3] pl. CCLXIX, 36–8.
[4] Ibid., 39.   [5] Ibid., 32–5.

with thick walls (2·1 m.). In the centre of the northern (rear) wall there is a niche (2116) 3·75 m. in width and 2·1 m. in depth. The depth equals the thickness of the rear wall, and the niche, therefore, protrudes outward with its rear wall to a distance of 1·5 m. The outer corners of the niche were built with step-like contours. The western and eastern walls of this room are built with insets in their outer face, one on each side, 4·8 m. in length. Inside the niche, in the right and left corners, there are two depressions, about 30 cm. deep—one on each side. They must have served as sockets for wooden poles, for screening the niche. Near the rear wall of the niche, and parallel to it, there is a bench-like ledge, 40 cm. wide and 1·1 m. high. At the centre of the room, roughly opposite the corners of the niche, two basalt pillar-bases were found. The eastern one is round, conical, and well-dressed (0·8 m. in diameter and 30 cm. high), while the western one is but a square slab (40 × 40 cm.).[1] This indicates that the builders just used whatever materials they found around from previous buildings. Between the two pillars a deep pit (2157),[2] 0·7 m. in diameter was cut to a depth of about 3·6 m. The upper part of the pit is built of courses of field-stones. The lowest course was found to stand on remains of the earliest temples. In the pit only a few finds were made, including fragments of a pottery goblet, the other fragments of which were found on the floor of the room.[3] The most important object was a basalt statue of a headless man (the head, broken in antiquity, was not found by us) similar in general lines to the statue of the Stelae Temple,[4] but without any emblems. It seems that this statue was put in the pit after it was broken by the occupants of Temple 1B. It may even have been an heirloom from the previous temple, which because of its holiness was stored there. The nature of the pit is not disclosed by other data, and it may be assumed that it served as an outlet for the libations performed in this part of the temple.[5]

The entrance to the Holy of Holies was situated in the middle of its southern wall, opposite the niche and roughly of similar dimensions. The entry from the Middle Room is effected down two steps, due to the difference of the room-levels: the Holy of Holies is about 30 cm. lower than the floor of the Middle Room. The Middle Room (2129), which measured 5·8 × 5 m.—and the thickness of its walls equals that of the Inner Room—is divided into three spaces: a wide central room, flanked on the west by

[1] pls. CII, CIX, 1, 3.   [2] pl. CIV, 3.   [3] pl. CCLXXIII, 9-10.
[4] pl. CCCXXX.   [5] See Temple 1A, below.

two narrow corridors (2108, 2112) and on the east by a single room (2107). The former served no doubt as a staircase leading to the second floor or roof.[1] Although 2129 was found bereft of vessels and furniture,[2] it may be assumed that this portion of the temple contained its holy vessels and votives, which were not in use in the Holy of Holies. As stated, the new architectural element added in IB was the additional porch (2128). The passage from the porch to the Middle Hall was effected through a wide entrance in the middle of the latter's south wall, and of the same dimensions as the entrance to the Holy of Holies. At the western end of the threshold, the door-socket was found *in situ*. It is made in the shape of a small basalt bowl.[3]

The porch itself is a wide room (9·8 × 4·8 m.) narrower than the front of the temple, leaving 2·2 m. insets in the west and east. Although its walls, too, are narrower than the temple's walls (they are 1·2 m. thick), they are bonded to the main building structure. Two pillars found in Stratum IA in front of the passage between the porch and the Middle Hall (see below) may have originally belonged to this stratum. The area south of the temple was completely reorganized, and all the structures found here were built afresh in this stratum. The layout of the new area, nevertheless, reforms the two elements observed in the previous stratum, with different boundaries: an inner court, south of the entrance to the porch, and a larger square or court, further to the south. The inner court (2119) measures about 14 m. from west to east, and 8 m. from north to south. It is bound in the south by a wall (2529). The entrance to this inner court was through a passage in the east. This passage was between the south-eastern corner of the porch, and an eastern wall (2540) which was built at right angles to the southern wall of the court. At the western end of the court, the boundary wall turns northwards and then westwards, and thus creates another entrance to the court. In the middle of the court, slightly west of the entrance to the porch, a cult-installation was found. It is composed of a basalt obelisk and a flat basalt slab at its foot.[4] The installation, in its present state, most probably belongs to Stratum IA. To the east of the obelisk a torso of a deity statue was found, which will be discussed together with the other

[1] The thickness of the building (2.1) indicates that there was a second storey, in contrast with the entrance hall which had only one storey, to judge by its narrower walls (see below).

[2] As in fact was the Holy of Holies. It is quite probable that most of its furniture was re-used in IA (see below).

[3] pl. CXVI, 5.

[4] pls. CXVII, 6; CXXVIII, 3.

cult-objects found in the temple of Stratum IA. Another cult-installation was found west of the porch, in the western entrance. This is a well-preserved libation-altar,[1] the position of which may indicate that it was associated with some ritual connected with entering or leaving the temple-precinct. It is composed of two elements: a high platform built of slabs and field-stones, and north of it, lying on a lower platform, a libation-table made of a basalt slab with a square depression in its corner. It is identical with those found in IA, and is another proof that the many vessels found in the later temple were actually taken from IB. The outer court or square which lay further to the south was detected up to a point 15 m. south of the inner court. Here we found a wall fragment (2546) running from west to east; it most probably constituted its southern boundary. A considerable part of the outer court's central area was occupied ᵧy a large pit (7·5 m. from south to north and at least 10 m. from west to east), which served as a *favissa* of some sort (2516). The depth of the pit, which cut through Strata 2–3, reached 1 m. It is most probably of IB, although the possibility of its being used in IA cannot be ruled out. Many disused cult and other vessels were found here, including two broken basalt libation-tables, zoo-morphic vessels, and incense-stands. It is possible that some of the pottery fragments found here actually belong to Stratum 2.

The south-western corner of the porch-wall was found destroyed by a pit, in which a big lion orthostat was found, deliberately buried. Its nature and stratigraphy will be dealt with later on, together with the problem of the orthostats. These had once adorned the rooms of this temple, but when discovered they were revealed in their final state in Stratum IA and, therefore, they will be discussed in the next stratum. The pottery found in this stratum is typical of LB and one should single out a fragment of a Mycenaean bowl found on the floor of the Holy of Holies,[2] as well as a broken cylinder-seal.[3]

The basic plan of the temple—that is, three main elements following each other with the doorways on a single axis leading to each chamber in succession—is unique so far amongst Palestinian temples, and it is similar in concept to the Solomonic Temple.[4] The discoveries in Stratum IA—particularly the two

[1] pl. CXXIX, 1–2.   [2] pl. CCLXXVI, 35.   [3] pl. CCCXIX, 1.

[4] The claim (Y. Aharoni, *AOTS*, p. 395) that the plan of the chapel in Arad 'is the essential plan of the Jerusalem temple' seems to me to be unwarranted. The 'Holy of Holies' is represented there only by a niche, and the temple has no built-up porch. The further statement (ibid.) that the Arad chapel's orientation towards the west is unique amongst Canaanite temples found in Palestine should also be corrected. The 'Stelae Temple' is also orientated

columns in the porch, further emphasize this similarity. The closest in plan is the one from Alalakh level IV.[1] It too is built of three elements arranged in the same manner, with a niche in the Holy of Holies. The only difference seems to be that the portico is of the same width as the building itself.[2]

e. The LB III Temple—Stratum IA

The temple of Stratum IA—the latest in Area H—is virtually the same building as the Stratum IB temple, reconstructed with several changes, additions, and raising of floors after the latest destruction (Fig. 21). It was found just below the modern surface, with a thick layer of brick-wash from the rampart, covering in many places the fallen white plaster of the ceiling. The latter layer actually sealed off the remains of the temple as they had been left, after the temple was destroyed and set on fire. This course of events saved for us a unique assembly of cult-vessels and furniture, practically in their original place (Pl. XIXa). Before proceeding to describe these finds, and one of the most conspicuous architectural elements of temples—the ortho-stats—here is a brief description of the changes noted by us, which took place in the new temple. In the Holy of Holies (now numbered 2113) there is a new floor (Pl. XVIa), about 50 cm. above the one of Stratum IB, with a new set of two pillars built slightly to the north, and wider apart than the pillars of IB. Of the eastern pillar, a monolith I m. high was found still standing.[3] Of the western pillar, the base was found made of a slab (65 × 55 cm.). It may be assumed that both pillars were actually made of wood, with the eastern pillar's lower part resting on the stone monolith. In front of the niche (2116), a partition-wall (2514) was erected, presumably with a passage in its centre.[4] Remains of benches were found near the walls, with nests of vessels on them. No other changes are noticeable in the Holy of Holies. The threshold (2114) of the passage from the Middle Hall (now 2115), was somehow narrowed, and on each of its sides the door-socket was found in situ,[5] with one door-pivot shoe (made of

towards the west and we now know also that the newly discovered 'long temple' on the Upper City (see below, § 4) is west orientated.

[1] *Alalakh* (see above, p. 79 n. 1) pp. 71 ff.; The plan of the temple of this level is erroneously ascribed by G. E. Wright (see above, p. 78 n. 6, fig. 4, 3) to Level VII. Some of Wright's remarks (ibid., p. 313) concerning the Hazor temples should be corrected in the light of the present discussion.

[2] This detail is unclear, since very little of the porch was actually found intact.

[3] pls. CII; CIII; CXXI, 2.   [4] pl. CXXV, 4.

[5] pl. CXXVI, 1.

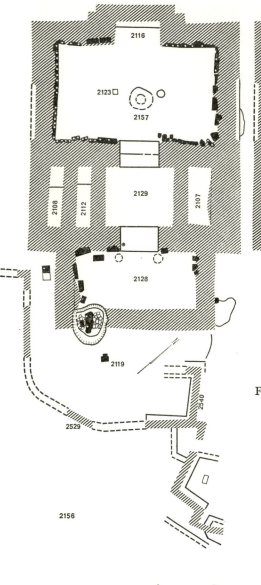

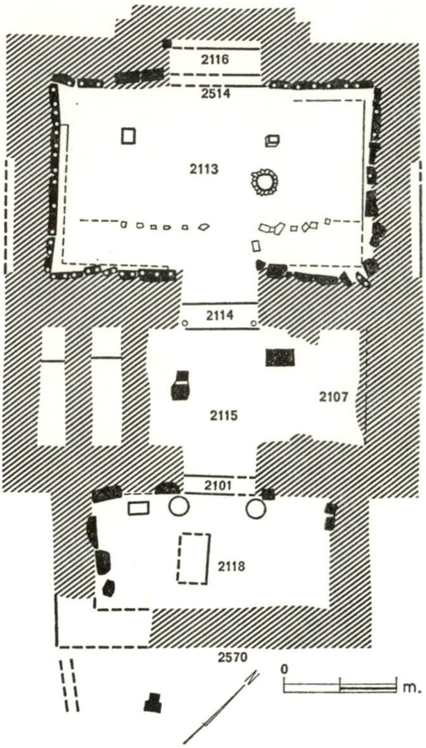

FIG. 21. Area H. Temple of Stratum 1A
(LB III).

FIG. 20. Area H. Temple of Stratum 1B
(LB II).

basalt) still stuck in one of the sockets, and another lying nearby
in a layer of ashes.[1]

A more important change took place in the Middle Hall. The
wall of the eastern room (2107) had not been reconstructed, and

[1] pl. CXXVI, 1–3.

thus Hall 2115 became larger with only the staircase-room on its west still in use. Above the stump of the eastern wall a table was erected, made of a fine basalt slab (1 × 0·5 m.). The threshold (2101) of the passage from the porch (2118) was narrowed too. No door-sockets were found there, but it is possible that the depressions in its ends served for such a purpose. Just in front of this threshold, inside the porch, two well-dressed, slightly conical pillar-bases were found (Pl. XVIIa) *in situ*.[1] The pillars in this position had no structural function, and they must have had cultic significance, placed as they were just in front of the entrance to the main building. The similarity to 'Jachin and Boaz', of the Solomonic Temple is striking indeed. The porch's limits remain the same, although it is possible that it was of poorer construction.

On the southern wall of IB, remains were preserved which, although according to Dunayevsky they represent the foundations of a thinner wall of Stratum IA, seem to me to be part of the threshold of IA. Nearby, two door-sockets made of basalt were found.[2] The changes in the outer and inner courts are more radical. Although the obelisk is still in use here the structures of IB seem to be covered with remains of the IA floor. Fragments of walls just under the present surface indicate that this court too, was bounded by a wall on the west, and most probably on the other sides as well. The most interesting architectural features of the temple are the basalt orthostats found in the Holy of Holies and in the porch. These orthostats are basalt slabs well-dressed on all sides except the back which was left rough. The height of the orthostats is between 50 and 60 cm., and their length ranges from 40 cm. to 2 m. Each orthostat has a well-drilled hole at either end of its top—5 cm. in diameter and in depth.

The orthostats were built on a protrusion in the lower parts of the walls, and their tops are flush with the top of the stone foundations of the building. Their lower parts are 1·2 m. above the floor of IB and about 0·7 m. above the floor of IA. It is quite clear that they were placed here in secondary use: they were too high above the floor—and could, therefore, not serve as a dado.[3]

---

[1] pls. CXV, 2; CXVI, 2, 5; CXXVIII, 1–2.

[2] pl. CXV, 2, in the lower part of the picture.

[3] For a detailed technical suggestion of the function of the orthostats and the top holes, see R. Naumann, *Architektur Kleinasiens*, Tübingen, 1955, p. 107 f. The orthostats were built as a dado for normal brick walls, and served as a foundation also for the beam frames which held together the massive brick wall. The holes served as sockets for pegs in the lower parts of the horizontal beams.

There is also a clear feeling that the orthostats in the porch were not originally made for this part of the building: they do not fit the measurements of the walls, and in one case,[1] a libation-table in a secondary use replaces an orthostat in the wall, and lastly—the Middle Hall has no orthostats at all. In our pre-liminary reports,[2] we suggested that the orthostats were origin-ally made for the building of the 1B temple. At the time, this assumption was strengthened by the similarity between these orthostats and those found in the Upper City in all areas, which we then ascribed to Stratum XIV (= 1B). However, in the light of the 1968 season[3] we know now that this was a mistake. The orthostats in Area A belonged to the LB I period at the latest.[4] In the light of this discovery we have to revise our attitude to the orthostats of the temples in Area H. It seems to me that they were originally made for the temple of Stratum 2.[5] The builders of 1B uprooted the stones and reused them in the new building. This may also explain why the Middle Hall was found with no orthostats. In the Stratum 2 temple this part had been the porch, and it was surely adorned with orthostats. When a new porch was added in front, in 1B, the orthostats

---

[1] pls. CXXVII, 4; CCCXXXIII, 1.

[2] *IEJ* 9, 1959, p. 83; and also in the *Encyclopaedia of Archaeological Excavations in the Holy Land* (Hebrew). Jerusalem, 1970, s.v. Hazor.

[3] See also, *IEJ* 19, 1969, pp. 2 ff.

[4] See below § 4 and Chapter IX, §§ 2 and 4.

[5] If indeed not for the even earlier structure. The possibility of ascribing the orthostats to the MB IIC period should not be ruled out, although it must be stated that nowhere in Hazor, so far, was any orthostat found in Stratum 3. On the other hand, it is clear that the Stratum 3 builders were very skilled in working well-dressed basalt slabs, as demonstrated by the discovery of the basalt steps in Stratum 3, described above.

The Hazor orthostats are very similar indeed to those found in the Level 1A temple at Alalakh (*Alalakh*, fig. 34 and pp. 84–5), and those of Stratum VII, which are without holes. This apparently indicates a date in the LB II–III period. But it is quite possible that the Alalakh orthostats of Level 1A, too, are not in their original position, which may have been Stratum IV, together with the lion orthostats (see below). A more precise indication about the earliest appearance of this type of orthostat in Anatolia and Syria might be derived from the newly discovered Palace in Tilmen Hüyük, 12 km. south-east of Zinjirli. According to a preliminary photograph published by B. Alkim, the excavator of Tilmen Hüyük (*Orientalia*, 33, 1964, pl. LII, fig. 2. and cf. also *AfO*, 21, 1966, Abb. 48 on p. 166), the orthostats of Tilmen Hüyük are very similar indeed to those of Hazor both in their size, and in their having two holes. The 'striking resemblance to the Royal Palace of Tell Atchana [Alalakh] from the VIIth Level' (*Alkim*, ibid., p. 503) does definitely not apply to this type of orthostat. The Tilmen Hüyük palace of orthostats belongs to Stratum II, most probably to its lowest phase. The destruction of this stratum is attributed to Hattušiliš I (see, W. Orthmann, *AfO* 21, 1966, pp. 165–6, and there further bibliography)—i.e. the end of the seventeenth or beginning of the sixteenth centuries (Lower Chronology). Even if this type of orthostat originated in the North, and reached Palestine slightly later than the above evidence, it would still allow us to date our orthostats in the LB I. On the other hand, one has to await more detailed reports of the Tilmen Hüyük excavations before one can come to a final conclusion regarding Tilmen Hüyük's date. For additional photographs of Tilmen Hüyük (albeit not directly related to our subject), see U. Bahadir Alkim, *Anatolia I* (Archaeologia Mundi), Geneva, 1968, pls. 145–51, p. 218.

were removed to the new element, and thus the builders remained with no orthostats for the newly formed Middle Hall.
This problem is intimately connected with another outstanding
discovery which was made in the porch.[1] The western part of
the front wall of the porch (wall 2570) was found destroyed by
a deep pit (1·8 m.), which penetrated through the cobbled
floors of Strata 2–3. In the pit, covered by a pile of stones,
a deliberately buried lion orthostat was found (Pl. XVII*b*). The
orthostat (Pl. XVIII*a*) is 1·9 m. long and 0·9 m. high, and has
two holes on its top narrow side, identical with those of the
other orthostats. One long side has a relief of a crouching lion,
as well as its head in the round, while the front narrow side
bears the head and the forelegs of the animal. This is clearly
a door-jamb orthostat and it is exactly like the smaller one found
in Area C (Pl. XVIII*b*) and similar in size to the one found in
Area A (Pl. XVIII*c*). Similar, though much cruder, orthostats
were found by Woolley in Alalakh in a secondary use in the
level IB temple. Woolley[2] recognized that these lions belonged
originally to an earlier temple (in fact a fragment of a lion was
found under the IA temple)[3]—but he wandered between temple
II and III. In the light of the present discussion, it may be
surmised that they were originally in the temple of level IV.[4]

It is clear now that the Hazor lion orthostats must be dated—
together with the unornamented orthostats which were of
exactly the same make—to the LB I at the latest.

The main problems regarding the lion orthostat are when and
why the lion was thrown and buried in the pit: it could have
been done, stratigraphically-speaking, either after the destruction of IB or of IA, since the walls of both levels were missing
here. One alternative is that it was buried by the people of IA,
when, in reconstructing the temple they had no use for it, but
buried it out of veneration. The second alternative is that this
was done by fugitives who returned to the spot after the temple's
destruction;[5] the possibility that it was the work of conquerors
seems less likely. The lion orthostat must have originally been
in the right hand (eastern) jamb of the entrance.[6]

[1] pls. CXVIII–CXX. [2] *Alalakh*, p. 86. [3] Ibid., p. 82.

[4] The following remarks of Woolley's are worth quoting (ibid): 'It is of course, possible,
that they [the lions] were taken over by the Level II architect from the temple of Level III
(the Idri-mi Statue found in the same conditions as the lions, is of Level IV date). . . .'

[5] The circumstances of the buried lion in the pit are strangely similar to the 'burial' of
Idrimi's broken statue, in a pit in the temple of Level I at Alalakh (*Alalakh*, p. 89).

[6] The western lion has, as yet, not been found. There is a strange reference in Garstang's
first paper on Hazor (*AAA* 14, p. 42) concerning a local 'story of a block of stone with a lion
carved upon it . . .' Could this refer to the other missing lion found by the Arabs?

The cult-objects

The Holy of Holies, as mentioned, was found with its cult-objects littered on the floor (Pl. XIX*a*; Fig. 22), amongst ashes and clear signs of their deliberate destruction. A short description of the most important objects found will produce a clear picture of the holy furniture of a Canaanite temple in the thirteenth century,[1] as well as revealing the identity of the temple's deity.

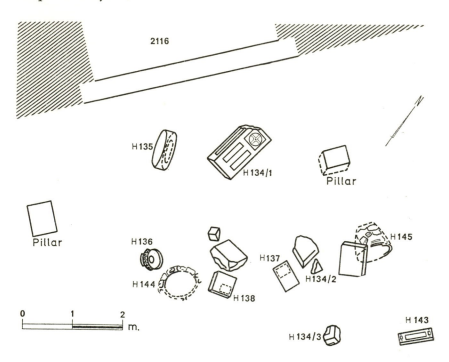

2116

H 135

H 134/1

Pillar

Pillar

H 136

H 144

H 137

H 138

H 134/2

H 145

0   1   2   m.

H 134/3

H 143

FIG. 22. Area H. Temple of Stratum IA—layout of cult-objects as found in the Holy of Holies.

An incense-altar.[2] Right in front of the niche we found, lying on its side, a basalt incense-altar—H 134/1 (Pl. XIX*b*). It is a 50×50 cm. square shaft—1·7 m. high. On the top flat side remains of burning were still visible. Two fragments—134/2–3—of this altar were found lying some 3·4 m. away near the entrance. On the upper part of one side there is a relief of a disc in a square frame with a four-rayed emblem in the centre. Below this are chiselled two elongated depressions giving the front of the altar the appearance of a relief with three columns. At

[1] And in a way of the previous periods, since many of these objects were, in fact, heirlooms from the previous temples.

[2] For the following descriptions see pls. CXXI–CXXIV; CCCXXIV–CCCXXXII.

the back, the surface is similarly dressed except that the dented square frame has no relief. The other two sides of the altar each have a long upright depression forming the impression of two columns. The emblem is similar to the one appearing on the breast of a deity statue to be discussed below. The altar is similar in many details to the one depicted in relief on one of the Alača Hüyük gate orthostats.[1]

The basin. Near the altar, to the west, a large round basalt slab —H 135—was found with a circular depression, 50 cm. in diameter in its centre. This basin-like object was found lying on its narrow side, thus giving the impression that it fell off a wooden stand when the latter was burnt.

The libation tables. About 2·5 m. south of the altar two basalt libation-tables were found, about 1·5 m. apart. One—H 137— had a deep rectangular depression on one half of its surface, a shallow rectangular depression on the other half. The other table—H 138—had a deep rectangular depression in one of its corners, and a shallow depression in another corner. One of the libation-tables was found upside down.

The 'liquids' kraters.[2] On the outer side of each of the libation-tables, stood a huge earthenware krater, one—H 144—with four handles, the other—H 145—without handles but with a vat at its bottom. The latter krater is fashioned with bands similar to the large pithoi of Hazor.

The 'carinated basalt' krater. Near the western krater (with the handles) stood a beautifully dressed carinated krater—H 136— with a Mycenaean-style spiral carved on its upper part.[3] Amongst these objects a number of dippers and bowls were lying on the floor.

The whole group of vessels belongs to the ensemble of the libation-ritual which took place, with the sacrifice of the incense, in the Holy of Holies.

An offertory table. In the south-east corner of the room a rectangular basalt offertory-table—H 143—was found, with four round and two elongated depressions around a central rectangular depression.[4] It was found standing on one of its narrow sides amongst charred wood. Originally it obviously stood on some kind of a wooden frame.

The other objects. In various places of the Holy of Holies many cult and votive objects were found strewn on the floor. A group

[1] *ANEP*, fig. 616.   [2] pl. CCLXXX, 11–12.
[3] pl. CXXII, 4; CCLXXXIV, 1.
[4] pl. CXXII, 2; CCLXXXIV, 7; CCCXXXII, 1.

of nineteen cylinder seals was found in the western part of the room amidst a great quantity of beads and shells.[1] All but one of the seals were made of brittle faïence and belong to the common so-called popular Mitannian type—typical of the fourteenth–thirteenth century and found in quantities also in other temples of Palestine.[2] The subjects depicted on them are usually connected with sacrificial scenes or with stylized sacrificial animals. The one haematite seal[3] (Pl. XX*d*) depicts a deity sitting on a chair under a winged 'sun-disc' (similar to the emblem depicted on the altar), and in front a king offering gifts, with a line of gift-bearers behind him. Above the latter there are two cherubs facing each other. This seal is rather worn and belongs to an earlier type,[4] perhaps an heirloom from the older temples. Similar in style and also of haematite, was a broken seal found in IB.[5] The same depiction of the king is shown here facing a deity (preceded by a goddess or priestess) brandishing a mace and a sickle sword. Between the deities, the same winged 'solar-disc' is depicted, while the rest of the area is filled with weapons and a humped bull. There is no doubt that these scenes are related directly to the temple's deity to be discussed below. Four bronze figurines were found too: one was of the 'peg' type (Pl. XXI*c*) which could have been a foundation deposit;[6] two were in the form of a snake and a female respectively; the fourth, perhaps the most important, is a bull made of wrought bronze (Pl. XX*b*),[7] similar in character to the bull depicted with a deity on its back, to be discussed below.

A male statue. West of the entrance to the Holy of Holies, but inside it, was a small basalt statue of a man sitting on a chair with a tall back (Pl. XXI*b*).[8] The head, broken off, was found close by together with a number of bowls amidst a thick layer of ashes. The figure has no emblems on its chest, and is identical with another statue found in Area F.[9] It seems to represent a lay figure, probably a king.

The last object from the Holy of Holies to be mentioned is a slightly broken faïence scarab, bearing the name of Amenhotep III (Neb-ma'at-Re). This gives a definite *post quem* date to

---

[1] pls. CCCXIX–CCCXXII, CCCXXXVII–CCCXXXVIII.
[2] e.g. *Lachish II*, pl. XXXIII, 43; 46; 49; 51. See also B. Parker's notes (ibid., pp. 71–4), for further discussion. [3] pl. CCCXIX, 2.
[4] Cf. ibid., pls. XXXIII, 52; p. 74; See also, H. Frankfort, *Cylinder Seals*, London, 1939, pl. XLII (Syrian 'Second Group'). [5] pl. CCCXIX, 1.
[6] See Richard S. Ellis, *Foundation Deposits in Ancient Mesopotamia*, New Haven, 1968, pp. 46 ff. [7] pl. CCCXLI.
[8] pls. CXXIII, 2; CCCXXVI–CCCXXVII. [9] *Hazor II*, pl. CXCVII.

that temple and, like others of its kind in Palestinian temples,[1] is not uncommon in a thirteenth-century context.

The Temple's deity

As already mentioned, a torso of a statue was found lying on the floor near the obelisk in front of the temple-entrance (Pl. XX*a*). Its base was found in the heap of stones above the lion orthostat. This statue is of extreme importance for the identification of the deity of the temple and for the interpretation of the other statues found at Hazor.

In *Hazor III–IV*,[2] we presented the two fragments with all their details and a suggested relationship between them. The most interesting point about this statue is that on the breast of the stick- or sword-holding figure, is depicted a pendant comprising the same circle and rays emblem found on the incense altar, indicating clearly that this is the emblem of the deity.

However, the fact that the figure stands on top of a bull is of further importance. On the one hand it demonstrates that this statue depicts a deity, and not a priest or king, and the fact that the seated figure of the Stelae Temple bears an emblem on its breast does not necessarily mean that it cannot be a statue of a deity.[3] On the other hand, it narrows down the possibilities of identification of the Orthostat Temple's deity. The emblem and the bull together indicate that it must be Hadad the storm-god, whatever his actual name was in Hazor. The relation between the deity and circle-and-rays emblem and the bull is further accentuated by the subject of some of the cylinder seals and the bronze bull-figurine mentioned above.[4]

Thus far, two contemporary temples, dedicated to two different deities—Moon-god and Weather/Sun-god—have been discussed. Before one can come to a conclusion concerning the patterns of the Hazor temple plans further temples found in the Lower City and Upper City should be discussed.

§ 3. THE TEMPLES OF AREA F

a. General

The cultic nature of Area F, at least in its latest phase of occupation, was apparent from the very beginning, by the

---

[1] e.g., *Lachish II*, pl. XXXII, 36–9 ('structure III').
[2] pls. CCCXXIV–CCCXV.   [3] See the discussion above, § 1, *b*.
[4] The tiny Mycenaean IIIB figurine of a horned animal found intact on the floor of the 1A Middle Hall (pls. CCLXXXII, 14; CCCXIV, 12) is perhaps, too, related to this subject.

existence of a huge stone altar, still protruding above the surface. However, because of the complicated nature of the area's stratigraphy[1] and the heavily robbed early structures, it was very difficult to ascertain the exact nature of these earlier buildings. Only recently, while working on the material of this area for the final publication, did I become aware of the possibility that not only in the LB II–III, but that in MB II– LB I the area had already been occupied by cultic structures. To be more precise, it was the latest discovery at Amman of a hitherto unknown temple-plan that led me to comprehend the nature of a fragmentary structure of Stratum 2. Once it became clear that this was indeed a temple, the nature of the huge structure of Stratum 3 was studied afresh, with the possibility in mind of its being a temple. The following treatment is, therefore, in the nature of a preliminary report.

b. The Double Temple of the MB II period[2]

Immediately above the filled shafts of the caves, remains of a huge building were discovered covering most of the excavated area. This was the building referred to as the 'palace' in the captions of *Hazor III–IV*.[3]

The building measures 46×23 m. (external measurements), and has very thick external walls, varying from 2·5 to 3 m. Its foundations are built of large coarse field-stones slightly trimmed for adjustment. Huge stones measuring up to 1·5 m. were used in the building's corners.[4] The northern wall is particularly wide (5·5 m.) as a result of an inner platform attached to it. Under this wall, a well-built drainage channel was found in which a LB I tomb had been discovered;[5] other drainage channels traversed the building from west to east and south to north, all eventually joining with the earlier tunnels.[6]

The fragmentary remains do not permit an exact reconstruction of all the elements of this complex and large building, but enough was there for the late I. Dunayevsky, the Expedition's architect, to elucidate the following points:

The building is rectangular (Fig. 23) and its front is on its western long side (for exact orientation, see § 5 below). Here was its entrance—8177—(about 3·3 m.) reached through a vestibule,

---

[1] For the stratification of Area F, see above, Chapter IV, § 4.

[2] For illustrations see *Hazor III–IV*, pls. LXIX–LXXVII.

[3] In the *Encyclopaedia of Archaeological Excavations* and in the preliminary report (*IEJ* 8, 1958), it is referred to more objectively as 'the large structure'.

[4] pl. LXIX, 4.   [5] pl. LXIX, 1.   [6] pl. LXX, 2.

which occupied 20 m. of the centre of its façade.[1] The entrance led to two rooms (8188, 8192), one behind the other, flanked by two identical units (8130, 8184): a central court surrounded on three sides by rooms, small and large (see plan). The size of this structure indicates obviously that it is a public building. The exact symmetry of the two wings, in the light of analogy,

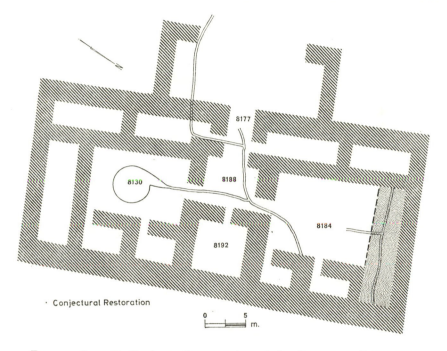

FIG. 23. Area F. Conjectural restoration of the Stratum 3 (MB IIC) 'Double Temple'.

demonstrates clearly that it was a double temple, i.e. a temple dedicated to two gods. It is difficult to indicate which of the rooms served as the *cellae*. One possibility is that the inner room, beyond the entrance-hall (8192), served as a *cella* for both deities. More probable, however, is the possibility that each wing had its own *cella*. Some of the channels emanate from the direction of the vestibule, indicating the probable existence of an open square in front of the temple, where originally the big altar (or a similar one) once stood. A striking analogy to our building is the Sin-Shamash 'double temple' at Asshur.[2] In

---

[1] Only one wall of this vestibule remains. Its position does not exclude the possibility that the vestibule consisted of two flanking towers.

[2] A. Haller and W. Andrae, 'Die Heiligtümer des Gottes Assur und der Sin-Šamaš-Tempel in Assur' (67. *Wissenschaftliche Veröffentlichung der Deutschen Orient-Gesellschaft*), Berlin, 1955, see there chapter vi (written by Haller), pp. 82 ff., concerning the Double Temple.

Hazor too, the corners of the building are orientated according to the points of the compass (the latter feature, however, is common with the other temples to be discussed in § 5 below). The Asshur building is not identical in the details of its plan, but its main feature,[1] of one temple divided into two symmetrical wings, is the same.[2] Not least important is the fact that the building was first erected, according to Haller, in the times of Shamshi-Adad I.[3] It is impossible to say to which deities the Hazor Double Temple was dedicated, but its existence in this period is another indication of the contacts between Hazor and Mesopotamia.[4] On the other hand, if the 'Double Temple' were divided into its two main elements, each would form a square temple with a central court, not too unlike the temple to be discussed in the following section.

c. The Square Temple of the LB I period

Below Stratum IB and above the 'Double Temple' just described, remains of a thick-walled building were found, which baffled us from the start. This building (Fig. 24) is situated in the centre of the northern part of the Double Temple and the remains of its thick walls were found in the area of the earlier central square of the northern wing. The main locus (8074)[5] was particularly conspicuous because of its thick white lime floor.[6] This locus is square (4×4 m., approximately) and it is surrounded by the following walls:[7] 8563 to the north, 8577 to the east, 8572 to the south. Except for the south-west corner there are no entrance-passages into this square. The somewhat baffling elements were the short walls built at right angles to the outer faces of the above-mentioned walls, and bonded well into them. The clue to the interpretation of this enigmatic structure came with the accidental discovery of a square temple at Amman, when the city's airport was enlarged. The detailed plans were made available in 1966, by J. B. Hennessy.[8] A glance at the Amman

---

[1] Unique, according to Haller (p. 84). See also A. Moortgat, *The Art of Ancient Mesopotamia*, London and New York, 1969, p. 106.

[2] The later development of the Asshur temple (fig. 26 on p. 88) is even more similar in details.

[3] Ibid., p. 86. However, see also Moortgat (see above, n. 1), p. 105.

[4] See above, Chapter I, § 3.

[5] See pls. LXXIII, 2; LXXIV–LXXV.

[6] Marked in the captions to the above plates, as the 'White Floor', see particularly pl. LXX, 1, in which the section of the floor is very visible.

[7] It is hoped that the present description will facilitate the understanding of the captions to the above plates, which are somewhat baffling, since they were written when the building's plan was not clear to us.

[8] J. B. Hennessy, *PEQ* 108, 1966, pp. 155 ff. This temple was discussed also by the architect, G. R. H. Wright, *ZAW* 79, 1966, pp. 352 ff. For a further discussion, see

temple plan, shows our building to be of the same type and it should be reconstructed accordingly. The Amman building is a perfect square about 15 × 15 m. (external measurements) with a central square court (6·5 × 6·5 m.) surrounded by six equal rooms, so arranged that two opposing sides have two rooms each, and the other two opposing sides one each. In the centre of the court, there is a flat-topped round podium. The entrance to the building is through a corner room, and the centre court

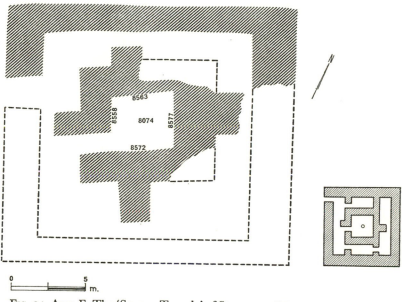

FIG. 24. Area F. The 'Square Temple' of Stratum 2 (LB I), with the temple of Amman for comparison.

has only one entrance, near one of its corners. The similarity between the Amman temple, and a building discovered by G. Welter[1] at Tananir, on the slopes of Mount Gerizim—first proposed by G. R. H. Wright[2]—was further strengthened by Campbell and G. E. Wright,[3] following the recent excavations carried out in Tananir.[4] It should be noticed, however, that the Tananir building has a different layout in the surrounding rooms (four square corner rooms and three or four long rooms, one on each side), and a much larger centre court (9 × 9 m.).

G. Ernest Wright (see above, p. 78 n. 6) and particularly E. F. Campbell, Jr. and G. Ernest Wright, 'Tribal League Shrines in Amman and Shechem', BA, 32, 1969, pp. 104 ff.

[1] Archäologischer Anzeiger, 3/4, 1932, pp. 313 ff.
[2] See above, p. 98 n. 8.
[3] Ibid.
[4] Robert G. Boling, 'Bronze Age Buildings at the Shechem High Place: ASOR Excavations at Tananir', BA 32, 1969, pp. 82 ff.

The external dimensions of this building are 18 × 18 m. In the light of the above discoveries it is now possible to reconstruct the Hazor building in a similar manner, and to regard it as a temple of the same square plan with a central cult-area. The exact arrangement of the rooms cannot be fixed with certainty, although it seems that it is closer in plan to the Amman building. The suggested plan indicates that the outer measurements of the building are about 18 × 18 m., similar to the measurements of Tananir. The date of the original phase of the Amman building seems to be in the LB I, as is indicated by the few Mycenaean II sherds found there—this date tallying with that of the Hazor building. The Tananir Temple is apparently from the end of the MB II period and thus contemporary with our 'double temple', the elements of which, as mentioned above, indicate a square temple already in existence at this time. The apparent similarity between the square temples in Palestine and the Gimil-Sin temple at Eshnuna in Mesopotamia from about 2000 B.C., was rightly observed.[1] Campbell and Wright[2] suggested that the isolated temples at Amman and Gerizim be taken for cult-centres for 'people who worshipped at them (but) did not live close by', i.e. people belonging to 'a group or tribes in covenant with one another'. This is a very attractive suggestion and it is definitely applicable to the Tananir and Amman temples. The Hazor temple, however, is within the limits of a flourishing LB I city, and therefore more in step with the Eshnuna temple, which is also within the city's boundaries. Thus it may be assumed that a 'square temple' as such is not a sufficient criterion to class it as an isolated tribal cult-place. It is conceivable though that even at Hazor the temple is a survival from an earlier tradition brought over by nomadic people.

d. The Open High-Place of the LB II–III

The layout of the buildings of Strata IB–A[3] is completely different from those of the previous stratum; nevertheless, the area conserved its cultic nature very clearly. The centre of attention in the present discussion is, of course, the large altar discovered in the south-western area of the excavations.[4] The altar is made of a large ashlar block (2·4 m. long, 0·85 wide,

[1] By G. R. H. Wright (see above, p. 98 n. 8) and rediscussed by Campbell and G. E. Wright (ibid.).

[2] In their *BA* article (see above, p. 98 n. 8), p. 9.

[3] See above, Chapter IV, § 4, and *Hazor II*, p. 128, for the reasons for assuming that the general character of the area was the same in both strata, with, of course, minor changes, such as raised floors, etc.

[4] *Hazor II*, pls. XXXIX–XL, and the plan on pl. CCX.

and 1·2 m. high) which weighs nearly 5 tons and has two depressions in its upper surface. One depression is rectangular (10 cm. deep) with three small hollows shaped like cup-marks. The second, also rectangular, is deeper (35 cm.) and forms a sort of basin. The two depressions were separated by a slender partition with a narrow passage to allow the flow of liquids. The stone seems to have originally belonged to the previous buildings.

The people of Stratum 1 utilized the top of Wall 8569 of the 'Double Temple' of Stratum 3, now in ruins, and converted it by the addition of stones into a platform for the altar. The altar is similar in its concept to the libation-tables found in Area H, and is not dissimilar to some altars found in Alalakh.[1] The assumption that the Hazor altar was actually used for slaughtering the animals is supported by the large quantity of cattle-bones found by it. It is situated at the far end of an open square to its west, in which a channel (8005) was found, possibly to drain the blood and the water used for washing the sacrifices.

On the northern part of the square we found a sort of elevated rectangular platform (8019),[2] with cooking-pots, baking-tray, and a bull's skull lying on it. To its immediate south a niche (8011) was found, and in it[3] a beautiful two-piece alabaster incense(?)-goblet. This 'high place' seems to be intimately connected with the offerings and sacrifices conducted in the area. The cultic aspect of the whole area is further attested by the enormous nests of vessels, which included incense-stands, 'cups and saucers', kernoi, and 'rattles'. A similar high place, but of the Israelite period, was found in the Upper City in Area B.[4]

East and north of the cult-area, several buildings were found, two of them (8039, 8068) of the typical central-court with rooms around it (Fig. 25). Although they may well have served as dwelling-places, it is likely that they were occupied by the 'cult-area' staff, both for dwelling and for storage. In one room (8037) a basalt table was found amidst many pithoi and other vessels,[5] while in others huge quantities of pots,[6] including unusually large kraters and cooking-pots were discovered.[7] Notable also is the unusually large amount of Mycenaean pottery found in the rooms,[8] not to mention that discovered in the tombs.

[1] *Alalakh*, pl. XIII, b.
[2] *Hazor II*, pl. XL, 1.
[3] pls. XL, 3–4; CL, 1; CXCVI, 2.
[4] See below, Chapter IX, § 3.
[5] pl. XLIV.
[6] pl. XLV, 2.
[7] pls. XLVIII, 6; CXLI, 23; CXLII, 2.
[8] pl. CXLVIII.

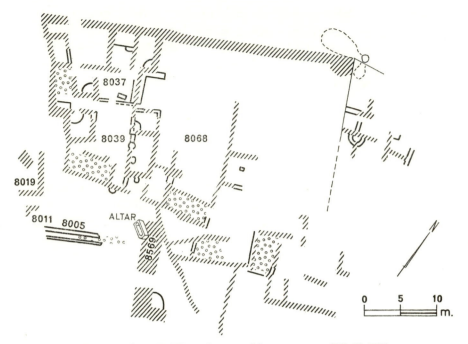

FIG. 25. Area F. The cult-area of Strata IB–IA (LB II–III).

§4. THE LONG TEMPLE—AREA A—UPPER CITY

The last temples to be discussed are those found on the Tell in Area A.[1] Here was found a long rectangular building (Fig. 26) orientated east–west (like the temple in Area C) with its entrance in the east and a raised inner platform in the west (but see below).

The recent season of excavations (1968) showed conclusively not only that the building (already partially uncovered before) was a temple, but that it was first erected in the MB II, then reused in the LB I. In the latter period an impressive orthostat entrance (pl. XXIIIa) was added,[2] with a four-slab basalt threshold, all identical in style with the orthostats of Area H. The building measures (exterior measurements) 16·2 m. from east to west and 11·6 m. from north to south.[3] Its thick walls (2·35 m. on the average) were built of bricks on stone foundations. The platform measures some 4·8 m. from north to south and approximately 1·5 m. from west to east. It is built of bricks

[1] For a detailed discussion of the complicated stratigraphy in the vicinity of this building, see below, Chapters IX, § 2; X, §§ 3–4. See also the preliminary report in *IEJ* 19, pp. 2 ff.

[2] *Hazor III–IV*, pl. X, where Stratum XIV (in the caption to the top picture) should now read Stratum XV.

[3] The measurements in the *IEJ* 19, p. 2. (15·5 × 10·5 m.) should be corrected accordingly.

covered with a thick layer of plaster. The walls too were covered by plaster painted in various colours.[1] No traces of columns were found to support the wide span of the ceiling. Although there are clear stratigraphical data for the conclusion that the building in its present plan belonged to the MB II, the finds on the floor and the platform are all of its latest phase, the LB I. These finds consist mainly of large quantities of votive bowls strewn on the platform (amidst animal-bones) and on the floor. Further quantities of the same type of vessels were found in several heaps (*favissae*) outside the building. There are no clear indications of the nature of the temple's deity. The only unusual type of pottery found uniquely in this building (in some quantity) is a conical clay phallus-like vessel with a hole at the top and a flat base.[2] A large basalt stele (see below) may have been connected with this temple.

FIG. 26. Area A. Schematic plan of the Long Temple (MB II–LB I).

The plan of the temple is quite similar to the Megiddo VIII temple, and to a lesser extent to the temple of Shechem, although it lacks the two towers flanking its entrance. This may be ascribed to the fact that the Hazor temple was adjacent to what seems to be the king's palace, and within its protected precinct. It is thus a sort of 'royal-temple'.

The remains of the LB I temple were found covered by a thick layer of brick debris,[3] indicating that the temple had never been reconstructed. Nevertheless the sanctity of the area and its immediate surroundings was maintained also in the LB II–III periods. Several cultic installations (some perhaps actual shrines) were found all around the perimeter of the ruined temple. Particularly noticeable were many heaps and pits containing sacrificial remains (bones and votive vessels). The

---

[1] The few fragments were not sufficient for ascertaining the nature of the paintings.

[2] *Hazor III–IV*, pls. CLIX, 26–36; CCCIX, 7–11, where they were erroneously ascribed to the LB II period.

[3] *Hazor III–IV*, pl. XI, 3–5.

most important find of this nature was a cult-area, just in front of the (by-now) covered entrance, consisting of one big and several small stelae (Pl. XIV*b*).[1] Two phases can be discerned in this installation: one in which a tall basalt stele with rounded top had been installed (head downwards), most probably of Stratum XIV (= 1B), and the other in which several small stelae (similar to those of Area C) were added, with an offering-bowl still found intact, probably of Stratum XIII (= 1A). This phenomenon, i.e. the abandoned temple with cult-installations of later periods around it is strikingly similar to the situation in Alalakh in the vicinity of Yarim-Lim's temple. It is worth quoting, in this respect, Woolley's description.[2] '. . . it would seem that to Yarim-Lim's shrine there attached a stigma that prevented its re-use. The site of that shrine was left desolated and its ruins were riddled with the rubbish pits of levels VI and V.'

§ 5. GENERAL CONCLUSIONS

The discovery of several temples in one city, some of which are contemporary, as in the case of Hazor, enables one to reach a few general conclusions which might apply to other sites too. The first and most significant is the fact that the various temples (with one exception) differ from one another in plan; this applies also to temples known to exist at the same time: Stratum 3 temple in Area H; the Double Temple in Area F; and the Long Temple in Area A—MB II; Stratum 2 temple in Area H; the 'Square Temple' in Area F; the Long Temple in Area A–LB I; Strata 1B–A in Area H; the open cult-area in Area F, the Stelae Temple in Area C. So also to another important factor; the temples' orientation. Until now we used mainly the excavations' conventional north[3] to indicate the general orientation of the temples, but now it is vital to refer to the 'true north'. It is apparent that all the temples, irrespective of their 'entrance to holy of holies' direction, are so built that the *corners* of the buildings are orientated according to the points of the compass. This is definitely a Mesopotamian or 'northern' trait.[4] Yet various

---

[1] *Hazor III–IV*, pl. IX.   [2] *Alalakh*, p. 65.   [3] See above, Chapter III, § 2, *b*.
[4] On the Mesopotamian temples see, conveniently, H. Frankfort, *The Art and Architecture of the Ancient Orient*, 1954, p. 5 and figs. 2–6, 10, 19–20, 23, 25, 42. See also, A. Parrot, *Les Temples d'Ishtarat et de Ninni-Zaza*, Paris, 1967, pls. II–III. The subject of the orientation of the Mesopotamian temples is discussed in great detail by a former student of mine, Mrs. Rivkah Merhav, in an unpublished M.A. thesis. The orientation of the temple's corners according to the points of the compass is noticeable in other temples in Syria and Anatolia. It is interesting to note that *all* the temples at Alalakh are thus orientated. The following references to Alalakh's temples are to Sir Leonard Woolley, *Alalakh*, Oxford, 1955: Level XV—fig. 19;

temples differ from each other in their 'entrance to holy of holies' axis. The temples of Area H are from 'south' to 'north'. The temples of Area F are from 'west to east', and those of Areas A and C are from 'east' to 'west'. These two facts, i.e. difference in plans and orientation, indicate that, unlike fortifications, dwellings, and of course pottery, one cannot use the plans of temples and their orientation as a clear-cut criterion for dating. It is demonstrated by the Hazor finds that different deities had different plans and orientation. These too may vary according to ethnic and other similar factors. Thus I believe one may explain too the fact that, of the Canaanite temples found hitherto in Palestine, very few resemble each other, although some of them are contemporary.[1]

XIV—fig. 21; XII—fig. 22; VII—fig. 35; V—fig. 29; IV—fig. 30; III—fig. 32; II—fig. 33; I—fig. 34.

In surveying the Palestinian temples, one should point out that most of them are 'walls orientated': The LB 'Fosse Temples' at Lachish; the LB Megiddo temples (Strata VIII [IX?]–VII); the LB (Strata IX–VII) temples at Beth-Shean; the MB II temple at Nahariyah and the EB large temple (The Palace) at the 'Ay. In view of these facts, two cases stand out as exceptions: Temples 5192 and 5269 at Megiddo (EB III–'Stratum XV') and the temple of Shechem. In Megiddo, which are 'corners orientated', this deliberate change of orientation may explain why (in Megiddo) the two temples were built in an angle to Temple 4040. In Shechem the 'corners orientation' is particularly conspicuous in the MB II 'Courtyard Temple, and to a lesser degree in the 'Fortified Temple' of the LB (MB IIC?) period. Do these facts indicate a northern (Mesopotamian) and a southern (Egyptian) influence?

[1] It is futile indeed to look or true similarities in plans and orientation between some of the temples of Lachish, Beth-Shean, and Hazor in the LB periods, or between those of Nahariyah, Hazor, Megiddo, and Shechem in the MB II. Those cases in which true identity is evidenced merit careful study, since, I believe, a number of important conclusions may be reached concerning religious and ethnical affinities.

VIII

THE LOWER CITY—GENERAL CONCLUSIONS

§ 1. NATURE, SIZE, AND POPULATION

BEFORE leaving the Lower City, and having surveyed most of its important facets as revealed by the excavations, let us take stock of what can be learned about it, and its implications on historical problems.

The first fact is that this huge 'enclosure' was not a 'fortified camp' or 'parking-lot' for chariots, but a full-blooded city with fortifications and public and private buildings. This type of city, like Qatna, Carchemish, Tell Mardikh, and a few others, was apparently evolved and established by large groups of people, most probably with a strong tradition of tribal affinities, who, although wishing to settle together in one big urban unit, found the existing *Tells* too small to accommodate them. Bereft in many cases of natural fortifications (as was the case in the Tell), huge new defensive obstacles had to be created, such as earthen ramparts and moats, as well as glacis, to protect slopes not steep enough or too soft.

The elaborate technique employed in massing the earth and holding it together demonstrates a combination of high engineering skill, an ant-like dedication by multitudes and, above all, the existence of strong rulers. The combination of the active employment of battering-rams as attested by the Mari documents —and highly organized 'earth engineers'—is perhaps one of the most interesting technical phenomena of the first half of the second millennium.

The Lower City of Hazor has a total area (with its eastern spur) of 200 acres, ten to twenty times larger than the largest of Tells. Assuming a coefficient of 250 people per acre,[1] the Lower City of Hazor could accommodate a population of 50,000 people. Even if we assume that the coefficient be reduced to half, the number would still reach 25,000–30,000 people. Hazor is unique in respect of its size in the Palestine of the second

---

[1] See Garstang, *Joshua, Judges*, p. 167.

millennium, and is equal in size to the few large cities of its kind in the Fertile-Crescent area. Its description in the Bible as the 'head of all those kingdoms' is evidently historically correct, and explains also its important role in the Mari documents, together with Qatna which was similar in size and nature.

§ 2. DATE OF FOUNDATION AND NEAR EASTERN CHRONOLOGIES

The above-mentioned facts make the problem of the exact date of the foundation of Hazor a matter of paramount importance for Near Eastern chronology, as has already been stressed.[1] It is quite clear that the Hazor mentioned in the Mari archives can only be the big Hazor with its Lower City. The excavations showed that nowhere in the Lower City were any remains of MB IIA found. Moreover, the large quantities of sherds extricated from within the core and layers of the earthen ramparts contained considerable amounts of MB IIB pottery. This indicates that the ramparts and the Lower City were established at the very beginning of the MB IIB at best, and most probably slightly later. A. Biran has now reached a similar conclusion concerning the date of the Dan fortifications.[2]

Now, how does this affect the hotly discussed question of the 'high', 'middle', and 'low' chronologies? In trying to assess this problem we shall remember that the earliest reference to Hazor in Mari is from the times of Shamshi-Adad I. The main dates assigned to Hammurabi (who for a short time was contemporary with Shamsi-Adad I, in the latter's last years) are as follows:[3] The 'ultra high' chronology (Landsberger): c. 1900. The 'high chronology' (mainly Goetze): 1848–1806. The 'middle chronology' (mainly Smith and now also the *CAH*): 1792–1750. The 'low chronology' (mainly Albright): 1728–1686. The 'very low' chronology (Böhl-Weidner): 1704–1662. If we follow the normally accepted date for the beginning of the MB IIB—1750 B.C.— obviously the 'ultra high', 'high', and 'middle' chronologies must be abandoned. If we raise the date of the beginning of the MB IIB to 1800 B.C.,[4] the 'middle' chronology can be

---

[1] See above, Chapter I, § 3.

[2] *Qadmoniot* 4, 1971, p. 3. See also Appendix, § 2.

[3] I follow here the detailed bibliography by Edward F. Campbell, Jr., 'The Ancient Near East: Chronological Bibliography and Charts', in *The Bible and the Ancient Near East* (*The Albright Festschrift*) N.Y., 1961, pp. 214 ff. For a further detailed discussion of this problem, see H. Tadmor, 'The Chronology of the Ancient Near East in the Second Millennium B.C.', in *The Patriarchs and Judges* (Hebrew), Tel-Aviv, 1967, pp. 40 ff. See further M. B. Rowton, in *Chronology, CAH* Revised Edition vol. 1, chapter vi, Fasc. 4, Cambridge, 1969, pp. 23 ff. Cf. also A. Malamat in *Eretz-Israel*, 9 (The Albright Volume), pp. 106–7.

[4] B. Mazar, 'The Middle Bronze Age in Palestine', *IEJ* 18, 1968, p. 84.

maintained, but with great difficulty because of the new evidence concerning Hazor and Shamshi-Adad I. Furthermore a certain time must be allowed for such a city to be built and get established. Kenyon's tentative date of 1850[1] would of course allow the 'middle' chronology to apply, but the archaeological evidence for such a high date for the beginning of the MB IIB has still to be submitted.

In summing up it seems that the results from Hazor compel us to follow either the 'middle' chronology, but raise the beginning of the MB IIB to the nineteenth century B.C., or maintain the date *c.* 1750 B.C. for the beginning of the MB IIB and follow the 'low chronology'. Of the two alternatives the latter appeals to me more. One thing is definitely clear, one can no longer follow the 'middle chronology' and the 1750 B.C. date at one and the same time.

§ 3. DATE OF THE DESTRUCTION AND THE BIBLE

The final date of the destruction of the Lower City[2] and its final abandonment seem to be clearly—as the result of the excavations—the last phase of the Late Bronze period.

The latest stratum, IA, which still contains Mycenaean IIIB pottery, must have been destroyed during the thirteenth century B.C. and not later than *c.* 1230, if we follow Furumark's dates for this type of pottery. The fact that City IA, which shows signs of decline, was rebuilt shortly after the destruction of IB is important for fixing more exact dates. If we assume that IB was destroyed by Sethi I (or at any rate while Mycenaean IIIA:B was still in use) in *c.* 1303–1290, then it seems most probable that IA was destroyed during the second third of the thirteenth century. It is not possible to be more precise. In any case, the thirteenth-century date, which cannot be doubted, poses a very serious challenge both to those who negate any historical value in Joshua 11, and to those who would like to fix Deborah's battle before the destruction described in Joshua.[3] Those who maintain the latter view are forced to date Deborah in the thirteenth century,[4] and this encounters very grave difficulties from the historical and literary points of view.

---

[1] *Archaeology in the Holy Land*[3], N.Y., 1970, p. 170. In the *CAH* ii, chap. iii (revised), 1966, pp. 13, 24 ff. Kenyon dates the beginning of this period in the early eighteenth century B.C.

[2] As well as that of the Upper City, as we shall later see.

[3] For the various opinions, see above, Chapter I, § 5.

[4] See now B. Mazar in *The Patriarchs and Judges* (Hebrew), Tel Aviv, 1967, p. 198; (but cf. Malamat, ibid., p. 221); M. B. Rowton, *CAH* (see above p. 107 n. 3) 68: 'Hence [based on the results of the excavations at Hazor] Baraq is to be dated to the second half of the thirteenth century.'

The problem would better be discussed in the light of the archaeological evidence discovered in the Upper City concerning the first Israelite Settlement in Hazor.[1] With all the problems still outstanding, we can sum up this part of the survey with the encouraging note that the excavations have cleared away many apparent obstacles created by earlier wrong data, and have opened up new avenues to a fresh examination of these vital and important problems from archaeological, historical, and biblical aspects.

[1] See Chapter XI.

PART III

THE UPPER CITY

IX

THE AREAS OF EXCAVATIONS
AND THE STRATIGRAPHICAL EVIDENCE

§ I. GENERAL

RESULTS of the excavations at the Lower City—including the brief report by Garstang—demonstrated from the start that the remains of the Israelite periods, as well as of the Early Bronze, if any, should be looked for in the Tell proper (Pl. I*a*, Fig. 27). Moreover, Garstang's published remarks were more detailed regarding the Tell, and some of the structures partially uncovered by him were still visible on the surface. With this in mind, two major areas were selected by us for excavation: Area A in the centre of the Tell, where pillars uncovered by Garstang were still standing, and Area B at the extreme western end of the Tell, where, again, remains were visible of what Garstang called a 'Palatial Building'. Both these areas were systematically excavated throughout the four campaigns from 1955 to 1958 and Area A was further excavated in 1968. A further major area, G, was excavated at the eastern end of the Tell in 1957. The small trial-trench, BA, which lies between Areas A and B, was dug in 1958 and again in 1968. In 1968 two further areas were excavated on the upper city: Area L, in the centre of the southern part of the Tell (the water-system) and Area M, near the edge of the northern part (Solomonic fortifications).

At the start, each of the major areas maintained its independent local counting of strata (arabic numerals) to ensure objectivity, but later on it became possible to replace this by one general system (roman numerals) indicating in each area the same General Stratum. Because of the ability (for reasons to be discussed below) to synchronize the stratification of all areas

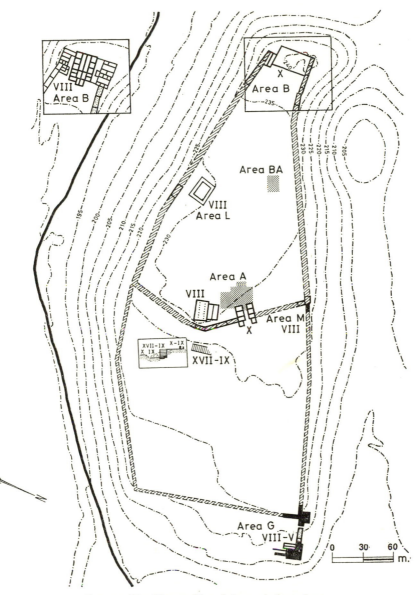

FIG. 27. The Upper City. Schematic key plan.

of the Tell and the large areas excavated, it is possible to deal
with the Upper City as a whole and describe its history period
by period. This will be done in the proper historical sequence,
starting with the earliest occupation. However, in order to
prevent interruptions and repetitions in the course of this treatment, the stratigraphy and main chronological conclusions in
each area will first be dealt with briefly. This will be done by

describing the remains and the strata from top to bottom, as uncovered by us. At this stage, only casual references will be made to the correlation between the strata of the Upper and Lower Cities. The latter problem will be discussed in detail at the end of the sequence-treatment. As with the Lower City, here too more space will be dedicated to the results which have not yet been published in full.

§ 2. AREA A[1]

Area A lies in the centre of the Tell just west of the edge of the big terrace which is about 3·5 m. higher than the area to its east. Garstang's 5 m. trench, cut on both sides of the monolithic pillars and extended to the east, was made here. It was found that Garstang cut through the four uppermost strata of this area, and most of our efforts in the 1955 season were concentrated in an area of about 1,500 sq. m. to the south and slightly to the north of his trench. The 1956 season was devoted mainly to reaching deeper strata, but the excavation extended further north in order to uncover the northern parts of the pillared building. Furthermore, a large trench was cut through the eastern slope of the terrace where the fortifications of the Iron and Bronze Ages were found.[2] In 1957 the main objective was the deepening of the previously excavated areas. The 1958 season was mainly dedicated to uncovering the deepest strata of the Bronze Ages. The narrow trench on the eastern slope was also widened, deepened, and extended (hence called the 'Big Trench').[3] In 1968 the area was particularly expanded west of its previous limits.[4] All told, Area A covered some 4,000 sq. m.

Except for some of the latest strata (discovered mainly in Area B) all the strata representing the occupational history of the site were found in Area A. The 'pegs' for fixing the absolute chronology of the main Israelite or Iron Age strata (XII–IV, II) found in this area were:

1. Stratum II. The graves contained Attic Ware as well as a silver coin[5] dated 400–332 B.C. Thus this stratum belonged to the Persian period generally and its latter part (450–300 B.C.) more precisely.

2. Stratum V contained the remains of the last Israelite fortified city, covered here, like the other areas, with heavy

---

[1] For detailed treatment of the results of the 1955 and 1956 seasons see *Hazor I*, pp. 9 ff.; *Hazor II*, pp. 1 ff. For plates of the 1957–8 seasons see *Hazor III–IV*, pls. II–XXX, CLIV–CXCVI.

[2] *Hazor II*, pl. 1.

[3] *Hazor III–IV*, pls. XXVIII–XXX.

[4] *IEJ* 19, 1969, pl. 1A.

[5] *Hazor II*, p. 32 and below § 3.

layers of ashes. There can be no doubt that this destruction should be attributed to the destruction by Tiglath-Pileser III in 732 B.C.

3. Stratum VI was found to have been destroyed by a violent earthquake which could be associated with the one mentioned in Zechariah (14 : 5) and Amos (1 : 4) in the days of King Uzziah, c. 760 B.C.

4. Stratum X, identified as the Solomonic city, and thus erected about the middle of the tenth century B.C.

5. Stratum XII represented the first semi-nomadic Israelite settlement, which was founded upon the debris of the last Bronze Age city. Thus, with the other strata squeezed in between the above well-dated strata and with the aid of the pottery, the dates of the Israelite strata seem to be well fixed, and the possible association of the less well-dated strata with historical events can be ventured. Thus Stratum VIII, distinguished by its powerful buildings and fortifications spread all over the area of the Upper City (unlike the more limited area of Solomon's city), should probably be dated in the times of Omri and Ahab. Strata IX (with its two phases) and VII are thus placed between Solomon and Omri and Ahab and Jeroboam II respectively. Stratum XI (found mainly in Area B) which represents an unfortified village must, on the other hand, be dated in the eleventh century. All this dating is of course corroborated by the pottery found in the various strata.

Thus, with the exception of Stratum I (Hellenistic) and III (Assyrian occupation in the seventh century) which were not represented in Area A, the stratigraphical skeleton of the Iron Age in Area A is as follows: XII—twelfth century; XI—eleventh century; X (with two local phases)—tenth century; IX (with two local phases)—end of tenth—beginning of ninth century; VIII–VII—ninth century; VI—first half of eighth century; V—destroyed 732 B.C.; IV—end of eighth century. Only in Areas A and L did we reach virgin rock and thus the whole sequence of occupation of the Upper City could be ascertained. It is regrettable, however, that the deeper strata were reached only in limited areas and although we have enough stratigraphical and pottery evidence for fixing and dating the sequence of the strata, with a few exceptions very little can be said about the actual layout of its buildings. Some confusion existed prior to the 1968 season as to the proper identification of the LB strata in Area A. This we now know to have been due to the enormous levelling-operation undertaken by Solomon's builders when they prepared the area for the building of the city-gate. Particularly we now know that the large orthostat building—of which only a small part was found in 1955–8—is not of the fourteenth century, as we assumed, but rather of the LB I period. Thus, some of the captions of the *Hazor III–IV* plates should be corrected.[1] Huge fortifications were found in the 'Big Trench' with good stratification, revealing the inner wall of the Upper City in MB II. Thus the following strata of the Bronze Ages were revealed in Area A: XIII—the last of the Bronze Age (LB III—and like 1A—of the thirteenth century); XIV— LB III (fourteenth century); XV—LB I; 'post XVI' (discovered in 1968)—end of MB II; XVI–XVII—MB II–CB; 'pre XVII' (discovered in 1968)—the beginning of the MB IIB settlement; XVIII—MB I; XIX—EB III (but post Khirbet Kerak Ware); XX—EB III (Khirbet Kerak); and XXI—EB II. The nature of these cities as evidenced in Area A and the other areas will be described later on. The above results show clearly that the Upper City or, more properly in this case, the Tell, was occupied in five distinct periods (EB, MB, LB, Iron, and Persian-Hellenistic); while the Lower City was occupied only in the MB–LB periods. In other words, at the beginning and the later periods, Hazor—normal in size—existed only on the Tell proper.

§3. AREA B

Area B occupies the western tip of the mound and a series of forts or citadels was revealed in most of its excavated strata. The area was eventually expanded east of the citadels as well, and by the end of the 1958 season a total of 2,500 sq. m. had been uncovered. Since most of the area had been occupied by the citadel, the finer points of the stratigraphy were obtained through the investigation of the smaller structures adjacent to it. The latest structure, partially excavated by Garstang, proved to be a citadel of the Hellenistic period; Stratum II contained a large Persian-period citadel, dated (as in Area A) with the aid of Attic Ware and a coin,[2] similar to the one found in Area A. In Stratum III we found a large citadel seemingly from the Assyrian or Babylonian occupation period. The remains of this stratum were found only in Area B, and the problems of its dating are discussed in great detail in *Hazor II*.[3] Its stratigraphical position is clear: after the latest Israelite settlement of

---

[1] These mainly concern pl. X, where in pictures 1–2 one should read 'Stratum XV' instead of XIV; pl. XI, 2, should read 'Stratum XV' instead of 'Strata XIII–XV'.
[2] *Hazor I*, p. 62.   [3] pp. 53–4.

Stratum IV and prior to the Persian Citadel of II, i.e. between
c. 700 and 400 B.C. The pottery tends to date it in the seventh
rather than the sixth century, but the evidence is not conclusive.
We found the poor remains of Stratum IV built over the destroyed citadel and fortifications of the last Israelite city (the
same was revealed in Area G—see below). The pottery is the
same as in the previous period. Thus, it seems that Stratum IV
represents an unfortified temporary settlement of squatters,
who returned to the area after the destruction of the city. The
Citadel of III is built *over* the remains of IV. Stratum V represents the last fortified Israelite city, and was found, as in Area A,
to be covered by a thick layer of ashes. There can be no doubt
that this conflagration is the result of the destruction by Tiglath-
Pileser III. This last phase actually belonged to a second phase
of V, i.e. VA, in which the whole area around the citadel underwent radical changes as a result of the strengthening of the
fortifications (probably in anticipation of the Assyrian onslaught)
—a phenomenon observed in Area G, too. Strata VI–VII were
observed mainly around the Citadel, the latter being in con-
tinual use. Stratum VIII, as in Area A, was occupied by a
massive citadel (the one reused in VII–V)—attributed on the
basis of Area A—its architectural elements (Proto-Aeolic capitals)
and the pottery—to the time of Ahab. Stratum IX was poorly
represented in Area B, in which the next dominant features are
the casemate fortifications of a Solomonic fort belonging to
Stratum X. Stratum XI was first, and mainly, discovered in
Area B in an excellent stratigraphical position: under the Solomonic fortifications and above the remains of XII. Its date in the
eleventh century was thus confirmed by both stratigraphy and
pottery. In Area B, as in A, the poor remains of the first Israelite
settlement of Stratum XII were found all over, above the debris
of the Bronze Age strata. Of the latter very little indeed was
found in undisturbed condition. Nevertheless enough floor- and
wall-fragments were discovered together with pottery to indicate that the area was occupied throughout the LB period.
Indeed it is most probable that in this period here, too, a fort or
a palace existed, to judge by the beautiful basalt ashlar and
orthostats incorporated in secondary use in the Israelite strata.
Its poor condition (it was built entirely of bricks) prevents us
from learning much of its plan. However, its interesting technique of construction will be discussed below in § 3. The excavations in Area B were stopped before penetration into the earlier
strata was ventured.

§ 4. AREA AB

This small area (which is sometimes called BA in our preliminary reports) stretched over 100 sq. m., and the main objective of excavating it was to clarify the stratigraphy of the Upper City in general and that of the MB II in particular.[1] On the whole the picture obtained here helped to corroborate the sequence of the Bronze Age and Early Iron strata; some isolated finds (graves of the MB II and a well-built storage-pit of Stratum XII) will be mentioned within their proper periods. One general remark concerning the layout of the Upper City should be made here. The dig in AB showed that throughout its history no great public buildings were erected there.

§ 5. AREA G

Area G, situated at the north-eastern corner of the Tell, was selected because of its proximity to the assumed site of the city-gates. Certain stratigraphic conditions, similar to those found in Areas A and B, and an abundance of pottery, enabled us to correlate most of the strata found here with those of A and B, although the area lies at quite a distance from them. The importance of the excavations here was that they offered further data concerning the extension of the Iron Age settlements and fortifications in the eastern part of the Tell, and revealed some of the MB II fortifications of the outer perimeter of the Upper City. Certain disturbed loci encountered during the excavations can now be explained as the results of Garstang's trenches dug there but unknown to us at the time.[2] The latest remains[3] found here belonged to the Persian period (Stratum II) covering most of the excavated area. A considerable amount of pottery (including Attic Ware) helps in dating the stratum.

The next stratum was identified easily with Stratum IV of Areas A and B. Some of its buildings (containing pottery of the eighth century) were built over the destroyed Israelite fortifications. Stratum V, the last Israelite fortified city, had all the characteristics of this stratum, including the thick layer of ashes covering some of its structures, particularly at the bottom of a large silo. Stratum V here, as in Area B, showed clearly two phases; the latest—VA—was manifested particularly by reinforcements of the fortifications and the blocking of a postern

---

[1] For plates of the results of 1958 in this area, see *Hazor III–IV*, pls. LVII–LIX.

[2] See above Chapter III, § 1, *b*—trenches β and τ.

[3] For plates of Area G, see *Hazor III–IV*, pls. LXXVIII–C. For the Persian remains see pls. XCIX–C and for the pottery, pls. CCLVII–CCLVIII.

in the city's wall. Remains of a large two-storey dwelling, with floors and reconstructions clearly representing Strata VIII–V,[1] enabled us to clarify the stratigraphy of the main Israelite occupation. The principal interest of the excavations, as far as the town-planning of Hazor is concerned, are the two major systems of city-walls. One of the walls, discovered in a trench against its northern face,[2] was found still standing up to 6 m. It was a solid stone wall, veering to the south on the edge of the most eastern terrace but one. The latter was further fortified by another wall. The remains of the houses (particularly the above-mentioned two-storey building), enabled us to conclude that this complex of fortification was first built in Stratum VIII, and gave us for the first time evidence that the Stratum VIII city was the earliest Israelite city to cover the whole area of the Tell. This question and the nature of the fortifications will be dealt with below.[3] The other system of fortifications found here belongs to the MB II period and is a fine example of a battered stone glacis and moat (Pl. IV*b*).[4] It represents the outer fortifications of the Upper City. In this area, except for trenches against the outer face of the glacis and some trial trenches, we did not penetrate below the Israelite strata. However, the soundings[5] have shown that the settlements of the LB periods had reached Area G as well, thus covering the whole area of the Tell.

§ 6. AREA L

This is the area in which the huge underground water-system of Stratum VIII was found. Since the stratigraphy of this area is closely related to the problem of the dating of this water-system and its uses and disuses in later periods, we would do better to discuss it in Chapter XIV, § 4, where the whole system is reviewed in detail. However, since in the course of excavations in the vicinity of the water-shaft—carried out in order to correlate the water-system with the city's strata—we cut through all the strata down to virgin rock, it is worth while saying a few words here about the general results obtained. The wide trench, cut north of the shaft, revealed that the sequence of occupation arrived at in Area A applied here too. Three strata of EB were found, with particularly rich Khirbet Kerak Ware. Similarly, the MB and LB strata were encountered in this trench, including some of the graves of the 'pre XVII' stratum.[6] Further to the

---

[1] See pls. LXXXI–LXXXII—showing all the phases of this building.
[2] pl. XXXIV, 3.   [3] § 7 and Chapter XII § 1, *c*; § 3; Chapter XIV.
[4] pls. LXXIX–LXXX.   [5] pl. LXXXVI, 3–4.   [6] See also Appendix, § 2.

south, a considerable segment of the Solomonic casemate-wall was discovered. This not only gave us additional data concerning its reuse in the Strata VIII–V periods, but proved that Garstang's so-called 'M.B.A. stone rampart' was in fact the Solomonic casemate city-wall.[1]

§ 7. AREA M

The stratigraphy of this area too, which lies in the middle of the northern edge of the Tell, will be better discussed with the problem of the Solomonic city-plan.[2]

§ 8. COMPARATIVE CHART OF THE STRATA OF THE LOWER AND UPPER CITIES

The results obtained in the dig of the Upper City enable us to correlate them with the strata of the Lower City. This can best be demonstrated by the following chart:

Periods	Upper City	Lower City	Remarks
Hellenistic-Israelite	I II III IV V VI VII VIII IX	No longer occupied	
Solomon	X		
Israelite	XI XII	Very few huts of Stratum XII	
LB III	XIII	IA	
LB II	XIV	IB	
LB I	XV	2	
MB IIC	'post XVI'		
MB IIC	XVI	3	Strata 'pre XVII' and 'post XVI' were not detected in Lower City
MB IIB	XVII	4	
MB IIA–B (transitional)	'pre XVII'		
MB I	XVIII		
EB II–III	XIX XX XXI	Not yet occupied	

[1] See *Joshua, Judges*, pl. XLIX (facing p. 196), and above Chapter III, § 1, *b* (the wall of trench ζ in Garstang's unpublished report).
[2] Chapter XII.

X

THE BRONZE AGE

§ 1. THE EARLY BRONZE AGE

THE small areas in which we struck EB strata do not enable us to say much about the EB cities, except that Hazor's earliest cities were erected in that period. In the Big Trench in Area A, where the massive wall of the MB II was found, no fortification of the EB was encountered. Several fragments of well-built EB houses were found under the MB wall, cut by its foundations.[1] This demonstrates that the EB fortifications were not built on that spot, although it is possible that they were in the vicinity. On the other hand, it is not improbable that the limits of the EB cities extend further to the east and up to Area G, and even slightly beyond. The large quantities of EB sherds found inside the earthen ramparts on the 'eastern spur' may indicate the existence of EB settlements not too far away, of which the debris was used as partial building-material for the ramparts.

The various soundings in Areas A (Pl. V*a*) and L revealed clearly three EB strata (XXI–XIX), which may have contained some further phases of floor-raising here and there. Too little of these buildings was found to reconstruct the house-plans; in Area L a well-built house was found with a plastered brick bench along the walls of a large room, together with an abundance of well-preserved Khirbet Kerak vessels. The use of plaster was visible also in Area A, locus 392,[2] and it is possible that the latter wall, too, was actually built in Stratum XX.[3]

The total absence of EB I pottery[4] indicates, *ex silentio*, that there was no settlement of any size in Hazor at this period. The earliest remains, founded on bed-rock (XXI),[5] seem to belong to the EB II, to judge by the only intact jar found there,[6] and by some of the other fragments.[7]

---

[1] *Hazor III–IV*, pl. XXVIII.   [2] *Hazor III–IV*, pl. IV, 2–4.

[3] In the caption to the above plate, we assumed that the plastered wall belonged to XIX and was built on stone foundations of Stratum XX. It is possible that both belonged originally to XX and were reused in XIX.

[4] pls. CLIV–CLVI, CXCII, CXCVII.   [5] pl. IV, 1, Locus 394b.

[6] pl. CLIV, 8. Cf. e.g. *Et-Tell* ('*Ay*), pl. LXXV: 1282.

[7] The three Khirbet Kerak fragments shown on pl. CLIV, 1–3, may, in all probability, belong to Stratum XX, as it seems now in the light of the 1968 season.

The EB Hazor reached its zenith in the EB III period. This is attested by the abundance of Khirbet Kerak Ware already found in 1955–8, but particularly in 1968, in both Areas A and M. The other material[1] fits in well with the Khirbet Kerak Ware. The end of the EB Hazor seems to fall within the EB III, but in what seems to be a 'post Khirbet Kerak' phase.

In 1968 a group of complete EB vessels was found above the remains of Stratum XX. This group belongs to Stratum XIX, and is the last evidence we have of the EB city.[2]

Thus Hazor serves as a further testimony to a densely populated Palestine in the EB II–III periods with its flourishing large cities spreading from Galilee in the north to the northern Negev in the south. At the same time, it becomes more and more clear that the Khirbet Kerak phase of the EB III represents in the northern and central parts of the country (as far south as Jericho and Tell Hesy), the acme of the EB cultures.

§ 2. THE MB I (EB–MB)

Nowhere in the excavated areas did we manage to locate an undisturbed locus of the MB I (called for convenience Stratum XVIII). On the other hand, the amount of sherds retrieved from the fill of later periods, as well as from the layers of debris between the EB strata and the MB strata, indicate quite clearly the existence of an MB I settlement in Hazor. The reasons for this state of affairs is either because the actual remains of this period were of a flimsy nature, or because the activities of later periods obliterated them. The truth of the matter lies, most probably, in the combination of the two factors. An additional cause is the fact that the MB I level, like those of the EB, was reached by us in limited areas only. Altogether, the picture of the MB I settlement is not unlike the situation in many excavated tells: an extensive settlement of semi-nomadic people dwelling mainly in huts or tents. The Hazor excavations do not add new data for the absolute dating of the MB I.[3] The most important types of the MB I pottery are represented by the sherds found, including

---

[1] See plates referred to on p. 119 n 4.

[2] See *IEJ* 19, 1969, p. 5. The group includes flat-based handleless metallic storage-jars and a tall-necked jug as well as a copper knife. The material will soon be published by A. Ben-Tor in a separate article. For recent discussion of the EB III problems, see J. B. Hennessy, *The Foreign Relations of Palestine During the Early Bronze Age*, 1967; A. Ben-Tor, 'Problems in the Early Bronze Age II–III in Palestine' (unpublished Doctoral Dissertation, Hebrew), Jerusalem, 1968, and Paul W. Lapp, 'Palestine in the Early Bronze Age', *The Glueck Festschrift*, 1970, pp. 101 ff.

[3] Unless of course if we identify the MB I Hazor with the Hazor mentioned in the Execration Texts (see above, Chapter I, § 2). However, this does not help much in the light of the

the 'Megiddo Tea-Pots',[1] the 'amphoriskoi' of the Ma'ayan
Barukh type,[2] the four-nozzled oil-lamps[3] and also the large
and deep bowls with ledge-handles.[4] On the whole one may say,
though, that this[5] represents rather the northern MB I cultures
than the southern—a fact to be expected.[6]

§ 3. THE MB II

The discoveries in the Lower City, showing that this large
city was established in the MB IIB period, clearly indicated that
the Tell was occupied at that period. More than that, it must
have been the Upper City or Citadel of the twin complex, since
otherwise the Lower City would have been at the mercy of who-
ever controlled the Tell. In fact the excavations in various areas
as indicated (A, B, G, L, AB) show quite clearly that the Tell
was densely populated and highly fortified during the MB II
period. Yet it is still not possible to ascertain with clarity whether
the first activities on the Tell coincided with those in the Lower
City, or preceded them to a certain extent. Two main Strata,
XVII–XVI, belonging to the MB IIB–C respectively, were
detected in most of the excavated areas, yet a certain amount of
sherds, which looked slightly older (say end of MB IIA or the
very beginning of MB IIB) was detected here and there and
ascribed in the *Hazor III–IV*, Plates, to Stratum XVII.[7] Solving
this problem was one of the main aims of the 1968 season.[8]

The renewed excavations in Areas A and in AB as well as
those in Area L failed to discover substantial MB II buildings
under Stratum XVII. Instead, meagre structures associated
with graves were found here and there, containing this MB IIA–
MB IIB transitional pottery. Unless we were unfortunate in our
choice of excavated areas, it seems to me at present that one has
to conclude that, prior to the erection of the large MB IIB City
(both Upper and Lower), there was some occupation which was

great divergence of opinion regarding the dates of the Posener Group. I would now retract
from my less-hesitant remarks concerning the relation between Stratum XVIII and the
Execration Texts, expressed in the preliminary report (*IEJ* 9, 1959, p. 78). For the latest
discussion of the chronological problems of the MB I see William D. Dever, 'The Middle
Bronze I period in Syria and Palestine', *The Glueck Festschrift*, pp. 123–63, and for
further bibliography. See also Appendix, § 2.

[1] pl. CLVI, 1–9.   [2] Ibid. 16–17.
[3] Ibid. 13.   [4] Ibid. 10–12.
[5] And many more which were found in the 1968 season.
[6] On the pottery of the 'northern groups', see Ruth Amiran, 'The Pottery of the Middle
Bronze Age I in Palestine', *IEJ* 10, 1960, pp. 204–25. The groups represented in Hazor are
'Group B' (the northern) and 'Group C' (the Megiddonian)—to use the most recent classification of Amiran (*Qadmoniot*, 2, 1969, pp. 47 ff. (Hebrew)).
[7] e.g. pl. CLVI, 18–25.   [8] *AOTS*, p. 262 n. 29.

confined to the Tell. In order not to upset the strata numeration already in use, we called this phase 'pre XVII'—a designation which I believe also conveys its transitory nature.[1]

Of the proper MB IIB–C cities we have considerable data, particularly concerning the fortifications and public buildings. Of particular importance is the discovery of the huge brick defence-wall found in Area A (see detail in Fig. 27), in the 'Big Trench' (Pl. IV*a*), some 12 m. east of the middle terrace. The trench showed that the terrace had been formed as a result of the strong eastward slope of the virgin rock. This was, of course, a convenient place on which to erect a defence-barrier. The brick wall is 7·5 m. thick and is built on a broader stone foundation[2] about 9·5 m. thick. Since this stands on the slope, its eastern face is 2 m. in height, while its western (inner) face is 1·2 m. and is founded on the natural rock. On the east its foundation is built over the EB structures mentioned above. The total height of the eastern face of the wall, as found, is about 5 m. The brick construction is very interesting indeed, as can be seen from the plates. The wall is built of three technical sections: outer, middle, and inner. The outer and inner sections are well-built of dark bricks with a sheath covering their outward faces, built of lighter bricks made of a limey material. The middle section or core is built with less care, of dark and light bricks. The outer face of the wall is further protected by a layer of plaster. Two layers of floors and structures were found east of the wall and contemporary with it. The top (probably Stratum XVI) floor is made of small well-spaced cobbles[3] and is limited in the south by a wall built at a right angle to the city-wall. It seems that the floor is part of a square or approach leading to a gate which most probably lies further to the north of the trench. The lower floor, which was the earliest connected with the wall (most probably Stratum XVII), was found about 20 cm. below the later floor. Near the wall, and parallel to it, we found a section of a fine drainage-system made of well-fitted clay pipes,[4] with draining-holes on their top part. It appears that, as in the later phase, here too there was an open square leading to the gate, the water from which, as from the city was drained through the pipes. It is worth remembering the elaborate draining-systems found in Areas F and N, and it is possible that the drainage-pipes eventually joined with the main gutters discovered in Area N. The function of this defensive wall, right

---

[1] See also Appendix, § 2.   [2] *Hazor III–IV*, pls. XXVII–XXX.
[3] pl. XXVIII, 3.   [4] pl. XXX.

across the width of the Tell, can be explained as the inner acropolis wall, protecting the most elevated point of the Tell. It is even possible that at this stage the Upper City proper was limited to that area only (see below). It is interesting to note that the building-technique of the brick wall is not dissimilar to that found in the 'core' of the earthen rampart in the 'eastern spur' of the Lower City, and a 'fort' in Area B to be discussed soon. The other element in the MB II fortifications lies further to the east in Area G.[1]

Here (Pl. IVb) under the Israelite fortifications was found a well-built stone glacis with a narrow and deep moat in front. The glacis is in fact a huge revetment-wall for a platform on which, most probably, a brick defensive wall was built. Most impressive in particular is the rounded corner protecting the northern and eastern part of the city. The glacis is made of medium-sized stones and is quite similar in appearance and function to the famous battered stone glacis at Jericho. The evidence of the stratigraphy and the few MB II sherds[2] found at the lowest point in the glacis and in some trial-trenches inside the city, offers sufficient proof for attributing this piece of fortification to the MB II period. However, we have no means at the moment of determining whether it was erected in Stratum XVII or XVI. If our previous tentative assumption concerning the brick wall in Area A is correct, one may conclude perhaps that the Area G fortifications were added in Stratum XVI, when the upper city extended eastwards, similar to the much later process in Stratum VIII (see below). This would accord also, to my mind, with the nature of its structure. The third element, which in a way may be associated with the MB II system of fortifications was found in Area B. Here foundations of what appear to be a large citadel or fort[3] were found. They are under the LB remains and covered most of the excavated area east of the Israelite citadel, extending westwards below the latter's foundations. They represent a strange, huge platform, built of bricks with rectangular 'rooms' filled deliberately with beaten earth. The walls between the 'rooms' are some 3 m. in thickness and they are built of the same type of bricks as the wall in the 'Big Trench' in Area A, the 'core' of the earthen rampart in the 'eastern spur', and the filled-in double-wall in Area K, all discussed earlier on. In fact, the similarity of this building-technique not only fixes its date but further explains its

---

[1] *Hazor III–IV*, pls. LXXVIII–LXXX.   [2] pl. CCXLVI, 2–16.
[3] *Hazor III–IV*, pl. XXXIII, 'Citadel 3351'.

object. The original western tip of the Tell, which was narrow and sloping, had to be turned into a wide platform, well-built to prevent its collapsing sideways. This caused the builders technical problems similar to the ones encountered in building the massive earthen ramparts. The filled 'rooms', although of an obvious constructional nature, may indicate the outlines and layout of the actual building erected above. Altogether, the 'platform' covers 13×10 m. of the excavated area with four filled 'rooms' in it, placed at even distances from one another. It is interesting that Sir Leonard Woolley noticed a strikingly similar building-technique in the Citadel at Alalakh.[1]

The whole area of the Tell so far excavated, revealed continuous well-built dwellings of both Stratum XVII and XVI, indicating dense occupation. The only other structure, obviously not of a private nature, was found in Area A.[2] Here, the northeastern corner of an enormous building was found. Unfortunately most of the building is buried under the Stratum VIII 'pillared building' (which we were reluctant to remove), and the western, unexcavated, area. However, enough was found to indicate the existence of a 'palatial' building of the MB II, which has no parallel in size in Hazor at this period, except by the 'Double Temple' in Area F. The thickness of the walls (2·3; 2 m., and even a 'double' wall of 3·7 m.) indicate perhaps that the building had two storeys. The foundations were dug deeply, reaching the natural rock. Two cobbled floors were laid down against the building in the north, both containing MB II sherds. On the lowest (Stratum XVII) a fine steatite 'Hyksos' scarab was found.[3] The building must have been part of the 'Royal Palace' which included also the 'Long Temple' discussed above. A fragment of an Old Babylonian tablet, containing parts of the Ḫar-ra = ḫubullu, was found in the dumps of the excavations in this area, and many have originated from this building.[4] The building may also have been used, in one way or another, in the later periods, but it was so thoroughly robbed then that not much can be said about it at present. All told, the impressive fortifications and public buildings, as well as the evidences of dense population, indicate that the Tell served as the Upper City or Acropolis of the Lower City during the MB IIB–C periods. The end of the MB II came as a result of a violent destruction. In the Lower City, as we have seen, the LB I City

[1] *Alalakh*, p. 167.   [2] *Hazor III–IV*, pls. V–VII, 'Building 387'.
[3] pls. CLVI, 29; CCCXVIII, 3.
[4] Soon to be published by Professor H. Tadmor. It contains items of measurements. See also Appendix, § 1.

was separated from the previous stratum by a thick layer of ashes. In the Upper City there is an indication of a short interval between the MB II City's (XVI) destruction and the rebuilding of the LB I City. In Areas A and B (and perhaps in AB too), several graves with late MB II pottery[1] were found dug into the ruined structures of the MB II, unrelated to any structure or with a floor above them. It may be assumed that this represents some squatters who came back for a while to the site, or that the Tell served as a burial place for people living in the vicinity. The full nature of this 'spasm' of a phase was realized by us only during the 1968 season, and we named it 'post XVI'.[2]

§ 4. THE LB I

The excavations of 1955–8 indicated quite clearly that the Upper City had been settled, like the Lower, in the LB I period, i.e. Stratum XV. This was attested mainly by the floors and fragmentary walls found in Area A, albeit much destroyed, and by the considerable quantities of LB I pottery,[3] including Bichrome[4] and Mycenaean II.[5] However, the full significance of the LB I highly developed culture in the Upper City was realized only in 1968, when we ascertained that the last phase of the Long Temple, with its orthostats in the entrance (Pl. XIIa) actually belonged to the LB I (Stratum XV) and not to LB II (Stratum XIV) as previously erroneously thought.[6] This conclusion dictates a re-evaluation of some of the other conclusions reached then concerning some of the structures, installations, and finds made in the area. The process is, however, extremely difficult, owing to the enormous levelling and looting there in the Solomonic period, but it is still in progress at this moment, and it would be rash on my part to offer a new interpretation before the fresh evaluation is completed. However, we can ascribe quite safely to this period the broken 'lioness orthostat',[7] which was found in the debris of the LB III stratum (Pl. XVIIIc). This orthostat is identical in style and technique with the one found in Area H, and with the orthostats forming the entrance to the 'Long Temple'. It may be assumed that it had once stood at the entrance to the court of the 'Palace-Temple' precinct, to which led a well-built staircase.[8] This may, of course, have been used in the LB II–III periods as well. There is still uncertainty

---

[1] *Hazor III–IV*, pls. XXXIV, 1–2, Burial 3314. [2] *IEJ* 19, 1969, p. 5.
[3] *Hazor III–IV*, pls. CLVII, and Area B, pl. CXCIX.
[4] pls. CLVII, 33; CXCVI, 18, and some more found in 1968.
[5] pl. CXCVI, 20, and a few more in 1968.
[6] See above, Chapter VII, § 4. [7] pls. XIII, 4; CCCXXIX.
[8] pl. XII, 5–6, where it is ascribed to Stratum XIV.

concerning the date of the huge underground water-reservoir found between the 'Long Temple' and the 'Palatial' building, originally ascribed by us to Stratum XIV. Possibly it was first made during the LB I (if not earlier). Because of this uncertainty, I shall describe it here, reserving the right to change my views in the final report.[1]

§ 5. THE LB II–III

The total destruction of the LB III City (Stratum XIII), was evident in all excavated areas. However, unlike the Lower City, where the area was never reoccupied and rebuilt and is thus better preserved, the remains of Strata XIV–XIII were found in many cases completely disturbed. This was due mainly to the constant robbing of the fine basalt ashlar and orthostats, found reused in most of the Israelite buildings. Furthermore, the one area in which we actually uncovered a larger area of these periods was Area A, precisely under and in the very vicinity of the Solomonic fortifications. The builders of the latter levelled the area, and while doing so, destroyed, and sometimes completely removed, the remains of the latest strata below. Indeed, were it not for the excavations of the Lower City it would have been quite impossible to get a clear picture of the Upper City in the fourteenth–thirteenth centuries, except to say (to judge by the abundant pottery) that the area was occupied in these periods. These remains[2] were found in all the excavated areas thus

---

[1] There is also uncertainty concerning some fragments of sculpture and inscription found in the 'Solomonic fill' and as building material in the Israelite citadel in Area B. These include the two fragments belonging to two different statues of Egyptian monarchs found in the fill of the Solomonic gate. Style-wise they could belong to either the XVIIIth or XIXth Dynasties (*Hazor III–IV*, pl. CCCXXIII). The other is a fragment of a red Nubian stele, found in the rubble of the Israelite Citadel in Area B (pl. CCCXVI, 1). Professor John A. Wilson, to whom I had shown the photograph (Pl. XXXV*b*), supplied (3 June 1959) the following remarks for which I am indebted and which I am happy to include here:

'There is nothing to be seen here except a normal Egyptian funerary prayer, of the type so common in Abydos or Thebes in the Middle Kingdom and the earlier part of the New Kingdom. The god of the dead, Ptah-Sokar-Osiris, is asked for mortuary offerings for the deceased. There is nothing of a historical nature, other than the negative fact that such an inscription would be most at home at Abydos, and thus is out of context in Asia. Dating criteria for such a standard formula are difficult. The formula was most used in the Middle Kingdom, but was repeated constantly in the New Kingdom. Perhaps all one could say is that it is most common from 2000 to 1750, common from 1750 to 1400, and less common later.'

Professor Wilson also supplied 'a probable rendering of the hieroglyphs [to be published in the Final Report] and a possible translation' which is as follows:

1. '[A boon which the King gives (to) Ptah-]-Sokar-Osiris, the Fore[most of the westerners].

2. [The Lord of Abydos, that he may give an] invocation offering bread, beer, cattle, fowl, cakes, . . .

3. . . . every good [and pure] thing . . . [to the spirit of So-and So justified].'

[2] It will be useless to enumerate here all the LB II–III pottery (including the imported Mycenaean and Cypriote Ware). This can be easily done by looking at the pottery plates, particularly those of *Hazor III–IV*.

attesting that the LB II–III cities covered the whole area of the Tell. The many orthostats found in the LB II–III debris[1] attest that the robbing of this fine building-material had already started in Strata XIV–XIII. Based on the discoveries in Areas C and H, we can imagine that some of Strata XIV–XIII buildings were adorned with orthostats, albeit in secondary use. The activities around the 'Long Temple' were already described earlier. Although the LB I Temple was definitely not restored, the LB II–III cult-installations and shrines found in the vicinity testify that the area was occupied. It is possible that certain parts of the 'palatial' building and its vicinity were in use. The enormous amount of LB II–III pottery found here corroborates this possibility.

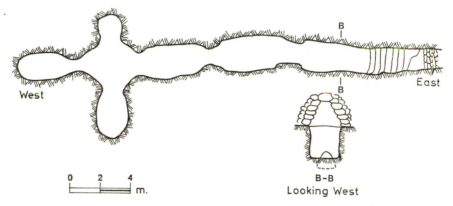

0 2 4 m.   B–B
                                Looking West

FIG. 28. Area A. The MB–LB underground water-reservoir.

One of the most impressive installations (Pl. XXII*b*) found to the north of the 'palatial' building is a huge underground water-reservoir (Fig. 28).[2] The top-most cobbled floors covered a channel with inlets which drained the water into the reservoir. We assumed at first that this, originally a MB II tomb,[3] had been converted into a reservoir during Stratum XIV. However, in the light of the 1968 discoveries it is possible that at least some of its elements may be ascribed to the LB I (Stratum XV) or the MB II. The problem is still being studied, but there is no doubt that the reservoir was reused in most of the subsequent periods, as is evidenced by the pottery found there and the rebuilding of its mouth with broken orthostats. There is no doubt that it served in fact as a reservoir and not as a means to reach

---

[1] pls. VIII, 2; XIV.   [2] *Hazor III–IV*, pls. XV–XVI.
[3] *IEJ* 9, 1959, p. 76. A somewhat similar underground water reservoir of the LB I period was recently discovered at Taanach (Paul W. Lapp, *BASOR* 195, 1969, pp. 31 ff; figs. 21–2).

underground water. This is attested by its plastered wall, nearly to its very entrance, by the channel leading to it, and by the fine basalt inlet built into its inner walls. The installation is about 30 m. long, and it consists of two parts: a large descending tunnel, hewn out of the rock and ending in a trefoil-shaped cave and, leading into the tunnel, a vaulted corridor with steps, some built and others cut into the rock. The reservoir has a capacity of about 150 cu. m. To fill it with an average rainfall of 500 mm. the cobbled-floor area would have to be at least 300 sq. m., and this is about the size of the area discovered. This reservoir must have served the occupants of the 'palatial' precinct.

XI

THE FIRST ISRAELITE SETTLEMENTS

§ I. STRATUM XII

THE destruction of the LB culture was total, and from now on the later history of Hazor is practically confined to the Tell alone. The earliest settlement of the Iron Age—Stratum XII— albeit the poorest in nature of the cultures found at Hazor, is perhaps the most important discovery for the solution of the complex problem of the biblical references to Hazor. In all the excavated areas of the Upper City the remains of this stratum are found above the ruined Canaanite city and below the later Iron Age strata. They clearly represent a settlement of semi-nomadic people, a settlement which cannot, in fact, be called a city. It has no city-wall and no public buildings; indeed no proper buildings were found at all. The nature of the remains may be divided into three main groups: foundations of huts or tents, cooking and similar installations, and storage-pits. The foundations are normally composed of one course of field-stones, laid either in circles or in other curved contours.[1] In several areas, particularly in Area A, ovens were found in the vicinity of these structures. They are made of the upper parts of upturned storage-jars, with a circle of stones around them. In two cases,[2] two phases of ovens were found. In one, both were made of upturned storage-jars (Pl. XXIVa), while in the other the lower phase was made of clay. The third group—the pits—is perhaps the most characteristic of this settlement. The excavated areas were literally strewn with these pits. In Area B, for example, 22 pits were found within an area of 25×15 m. It was very difficult at the start to comprehend their nature, since in many cases they were detected only through the different earth which they contained, or the typical pottery found intact deep inside the Late Bronze levels. Further difficulty was created (particularly in Area A) by the fact that the top parts of these pits were chopped off by the levelling-operations of the Solomonic stratum. A typical feature of these pits, when discovered, was a filling of

---

[1] *Hazor III–IV*, pls. X, 3; XVII, 4. The walls shown on pl. VIII, 1, may belong to Stratum XI (see below).

[2] pl. XVII, 2–3.

field-stones inside them.[1] This strange feature may now be explained in the light of a pit discovered in 1968 in Area BA. This
pit was found with its wall-lining intact. The lining is made of
field-stones, exactly of the type found in the filling, and therefore it may be presumed that the 'fillings' are nothing but the
stones of the collapsed lining. Many of the pits, which obviously
served as silos and storing-places for other vessels, contained
a considerable number of vessels, some of them found nearly
intact.[2] It may be emphasized once more, that the Stratum XII
remains were found in all the excavated areas of the Tell. Nevertheless it seems that some isolated tents or huts were erected in
very few localities in the by-now-ruined Lower City, as was
attested by the discovery of the pottery of Stratum XII.[3]

The pottery associated with the structures, pits, and installations of Stratum XII is basically different from that of the LB
and is most characteristic of the earliest phase of the Iron Age.
One of the most prominent features of this culture are big
storage-jars or pithoi.[4] They have a tall neck with a ridge at the
base; they are elliptical or egg-shaped with a pointed base.
Unlike the LB pithoi they are sometimes provided with two loop-
handles, normally below their shoulders. Many of them show
marks of rope-impressions around their belly, obviously a result
of the potter's efforts to 'hold them together' before they were
put in the furnace.[5] The pithoi have some similarity to Albright's
so-called *collared-rim* found in many sites in South Palestine.[6]
Another typical vessel is the bowl,[7] as a rule large, with round or
sharp carination and no ornamentation. The cooking-pot is
typical of the Early Iron pot found throughout the country:
carinated, round-bottomed, and without handles. Of importance
for dating is its rim, a derivative of the triangular rim of the
LB but much thinner, longer, and normally concave. Finally
one should mention several pyxides,[8] all derivative of previous
Mycenaean pyxides, but by now typical of the Early Iron period.

It is important to stress some of the pottery characteristics in
view of the problems to be discussed below.

---

[1] pls. XVII, 1; XXXVI, 1–3.

[2] pl. CCI.

[3] See above, Area K, Chapter VI, § 1, and Area P, ibid., § 2.

[4] pls. CLXVII–CLXVIII.

[5] For discussion of these pithoi and the other types of pottery from Stratum XII of Hazor,
see Ruth Amiran, *Ancient Pottery of the Holy Land*, Jerusalem, 1969. See the chapter dealing
with Iron I pottery (pp. 193 ff.) under storage-jars, bowls, pilgrim-flasks, and the pyxis.

[6] *BASOR* 56, 1934, pp. 1 ff., and see below.

[7] pls. CLXIV; CCI, 1–8.

[8] pl. CCI, 26–8, as well as a fine pyxis found in 1968 in Area BA.

§ 2. STRATUM XII AND THE ISRAELITE OCCUPATION

The pottery found in Stratum XII is the same as that found in the small Iron Age settlements in Upper Galilee by Aharoni,[1] and there can be no doubt—taking into account all the factors together—that Aharoni is correct in seeing in these settlements the earliest efforts of the nomadic Israelite tribes to settle in a more permanent way. Aharoni, following the approach of Alt and Noth, saw in these settlements the evidence of the so-called 'peaceful infiltration' which *preceded* the destruction of the Canaanite cities. Observing correctly the Iron Age nature of the pottery, but following Mazar's suggestion that the Battle of Deborah preceded the fall of Hazor as recorded in Joshua 11, he concluded that the great Canaanite city of Hazor was destroyed by the Israelites at the end of the twelfth century, i.e. a generation or so after the date of the upper Galilee settlements.[2]

The discovery of the same culture in Stratum XII, above the destroyed LB Canaanite city, poses a serious challenge to the above theories. The *chronological* sequence of Strata XIII and XII, is clear. The former is LB and thirteenth-century while the latter is twelfth-century Iron Age.[3] The attempt to overcome the stratigraphical and ceramic difficulties by dating the upper Galilee pottery to the thirteenth century, is against all archaeological evidence.

If the settlements in Galilee *preceded* the fall of Hazor, then the latter should have occurred sometime well into the twelfth century—a conclusion decisively negated by the results of the excavations which point clearly to LB III as being thirteenth-century.[4] The settlements in Galilee as well as Stratum XII represent the same situation: the settlement of the semi-nomadic Israelites *after* the fall of the Canaanite cities. Thus, even those who suggest (in the light of the Hazor excavations) dating Deborah to the thirteenth century[5]—a date which encounters

---

[1] *The Settlement of the Israelite Tribes in Upper Galilee* (Hebrew), Jerusalem, 1957, pls. IV–V, and figs. 4–5.

[2] For literature see above, Chapter I, § 5, p. 10 n. 4.

[3] See the comparative material assembled by Ruth Amiran in her book (see above, p. 130 n. 5). This material (including parallels from Megiddo VIIA–VI) also challenges another assertion, i.e. that this pottery is exclusively Israelite in the *ethnical* sense as well. It seems to me that a more correct way to explain the nature of the pottery would be to say that the pottery is typical of Iron Age I pottery in Palestine, *including* that of the Israelites. For a bold treatment of this question see M. Weippert, p. 130 (see above, Chapter I, p. 10 n. 4). Even Ruth Amiran—who accepts the 'ethnical' interpretation—had to admit that it encounters difficulties (p. 233). The latest effort of Aharoni (*The Glueck Festschrift*, 1970, pp. 263 ff.) to prove that Megiddo VI was Israelite rather than Canaanite, does not carry much conviction on the basis of its material culture. (See below Chapter XIII, § 3, *a*.)

[4] See above, Chapter VIII, § 3.   [5] e.g. Mazar and Rowton.

great difficulties—must then conclude that the Iron Age settlements are later.[1] An additional important conclusion is, that, after the fall of the LB Hazor and before the Solomonic activities, a proper city did not exist on the mound of Hazor.[2] This means that there was no Jabin, king of Hazor, in the time of Deborah.[3] Thus it confirms the theory suggested long before the excavations—that the historical source concerning the Deborah–Sisera Battle is contained in the Deborah Song (Judges 5) which does not mention Hazor at all, and the mention of Jabin in the prose version (Judges 4) must be attributed to a later editor, who tried to ascribe the historical background to the Battle of the Valley of Jezreel.

§ 3. STRATUM XI

Interesting remains of Stratum XI were found in Area B. Stratigraphically, they are clearly placed above in the tops of the Stratum XII pits, but below the foundation of the Stratum X casemate-wall.[4]

In the south-east part of the excavated area, there existed a structure of an obvious cult-nature (Fig. 29).[5] In the north (partially covered by the casemate-wall), there was an enclosed area (3283) of about 5 × 4 m. Its southern half had a bench-like structure. The south-western bench was made of a large, crudely shaped basalt slab. In the south-western corner of the enclosure a jug full of bronze votive objects was found (Pl. XXIV*b*) lying just under the floor.[6] South of this enclosure lay a well-paved area (3275) with well-placed flat field-stones. On it, two broken incense-stands were found,[7] as well as beads and votive arrowheads.[8] West of 3275 and 3283, another paved area (3729) was found, limited on its western side by four stone pillars.[9] In this area several small objects were found:[10] a scarab, some worked

---

[1] The results of the excavations are so clear-cut that they do not even allow the possible blurring of the issue by a terminology which uses 'late thirteenth or early twelfth century' to define the date of the fall of Canaanite Hazor. In retracting from his previous date (late twelfth century) for the fall of Hazor, Aharoni writes now (see above, p. 131 n. 3, p. 263): 'These considerations also point, therefore, to the late thirteenth or early twelfth century as the probable date for the great battles in the north ... and fits the destruction of Canaanite Hazor (Stratum XIII) at *approximately* [My italics—*Y.Y.*] the same time'. For a detailed criticism of Aharoni's concept of Hazor and the Conquest, see my comments in *Studies in the Book of Joshua* (Hebrew), The Ben Gurion Biblical Circle, Jerusalem, 1960, pp. 234 ff. A most recent discovery at Tell Dan of a 'Hazor XII' pithos with Philistine vessels inside it, further clinches this problem. Cf. A. Biran, *Hadashot Arkhiologiyot* (Hebrew), 39, 1971, p. 7.

[2] See below the discussions of Stratum XI.

[3] Unless we accept a thirteenth-century date.

[4] *Hazor III–IV*, pls. XXXVII–XXXVIII; XXXIX, 1.

[5] pl. XXXVIII, 1. The 'Looking south' caption should be corrected to 'Looking west'.

[6] pl. XXXVIII, 3–4.   [7] pl. XXXVIII, 2.   [8] pl. CCIV, 10; 18.

[9] pl. XXXVII, 1; 5.   [10] All are shown on pl. CCIV.

haematite weights(?), a bone-inlay and two mutilated bronze needles, all similar to the objects found in the jar and in Locus 3283. To the east of 3283 remains of a wall were found with traces of paving (3307). On the latter lay an upper and lower mill-stone,[1] as well as two fragments of yet another two incense-stands.[2] The nearly complete incense-stand[3] found on 3275 is of

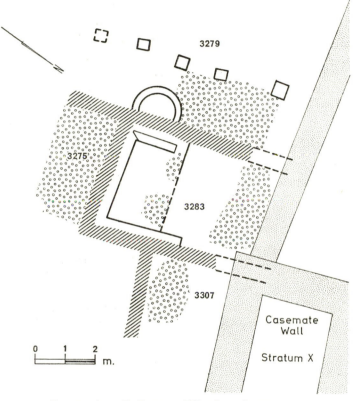

FIG. 29. Area B. Stratum XI—the cult-structure.

particular interest, since it is very similar indeed to the incense-stands from Megiddo VI.[4] Most enlightening were also the votive objects found in the jar which may have been a foundation deposit.[5] Most conspicuous and important is a bronze figurine of a seated male deity with a coned helmet (Pl. XXIVc). The hole in his left palm indicates that he was holding a weapon.[6]

[1] pl. XXXVIII, 5.   [2] pl. CCIV, 3–4.   [3] pls. CCIV, 1; CCCXLV, 11.
[4] H. G. May, *Material Remains of the Megiddo Cult*, Chicago, 1935, pl. XX, and Ruth Amiran (above, p. 130 n. 5), pp. 302–6.
[5] All shown on pls. CCV; CCCXLV–CCCXLVII.
[6] Perhaps the crumbled bronze wire—pl. CCV, 9. On this figuring, see Orah Negbi, *The Canaanite Metal Figurines in Palestine and Syria* (unpublished doctoral dissertation, Hebrew), 1963, ii, p. 78, no. 1413.

This must have been a warrior deity as attested to by the nature of the other votives found in the jar: a sword, two javelin heads with the javelins' butts, an arrowhead, as well as a lugged axe.[1]

The above-mentioned objects (incense-stands and the bronze votives) leave no doubt that the whole structure served as a cult-place, although its exact nature is difficult to assess. It looks like a chapel or a high place of which one reads quite often in the Bible, particularly in the period of the Judges. It is similarly difficult to say without reservations that it was Israelite, although this is quite probable, since Stratum XI follows Stratum XII and is followed by the Solomonic Stratum X. Its date, based on the stratigraphy and the pottery, seems to be somewhere in the eleventh century, most probably in its second half. The remains of Stratum XI, as mentioned above, were found in Area B. Nevertheless it is possible that this settlement occupied some other parts of the Tell.[2]

Whatever the case, it is clear that the remains represented a small unwalled village,[3] to be replaced by the well-fortified Solomonic city of Stratum X.[4]

[1] On the nature of these weapons and their parallels in the Iron I, see my discussion in *Enc. Miqrait* (Hebrew) v, 1968, pp. 931 ff.

[2] Some of the walls found in Area A and assigned to XII may actually belong to XI. When the Stratum XII was excavated in Area A, we were not yet aware of the existence of Stratum XI. See particularly pl. VIII, 1; 3 ('wall of Stratum XII'). Note 11 in *Hazor II*, p. 3 should be modified accordingly.

[3] Obviously not representing a city of an alleged Jabin in the times of Deborah.

[4] The assertion (*The Glueck Festschrift*, p. 264) that there is a gap in Hazor between Stratum XII and Stratum X must be a mistake.

XII

THE SOLOMONIC PERIOD

§ I. AREA A

a. Stratigraphy

THE first discovery of the Solomonic city was made in Area A. Here too, the remains were more substantial than in the other excavated areas. The discussion of the Solomonic period, therefore, will centre mainly on the discoveries in this area,[1] and the finds in the other areas will be presented in the following sections. The identification of Stratum X with Solomon's city was obtained as a result of many factors: the stratigraphy, which showed Stratum X to be the first Iron Age city above the remains of Stratum XII (and XI in Area B), but below the monumental remains of Stratum VIII (ninth century); the pottery, which was identical with other tenth-century strata in other excavated Tells, and above all the biblical passage (1 Kings 9:15)[2] which states that Hazor was built by Solomon together with Gezer and Megiddo. The discovery of a city-gate (Fig. 30), identical in plan with the Solomonic gate at Megiddo (and that of Gezer—see later) clinched the identification of Stratum X as representing the Hazor of Solomon's times. The main remains of Stratum X were the fortifications—the casemate-wall and the city-gate (Pls. XXIII, XXV*a*). They were built in Stratum X, and in them we distinguished only one floor, with a meagre amount of pottery belonging to the original use of the wall. Inside the city, on the other hand, a substantial building was found, which although erected in Stratum X, had been rebuilt several times, *all* before Stratum VIII. The changes in plans and the raising of its floors enabled us to distinguish in it four phases designated XB–XA and IXB–IXA. On these floors a considerable amount of pottery was found, which is presented in the pottery plates of *Hazor III–IV* according to the various phases.

[1] The data presented here concerning the finds of the seasons of 1957–8, are drawn mainly from the material presented by Y. Aharoni for the text volume of *Hazor III–IV*, the plans prepared by the late I. Dunayevsky, and personal observations. The descriptions of the finds of 1956 are to be found in *Hazor II*, pp. 1 ff., of which portions are incorporated in the present discussion.

[2] See above, Chapter I, § 5, *c*.

In the following discussion we shall begin with the fortifications and conclude with a detailed description of the sub-phases and their chronology.

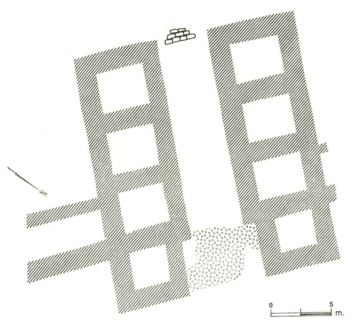

FIG. 30. Area A. Stratum X—the Solomonic city-gate.

b. The casemate-wall

The casemate-wall was found just on the border of the main terrace of the Tell (see also Fig. 27). In fact, it was the main cause of this terrace. Its first segment appeared in the deep section made by Garstang east of the pillared building. It is the 'enclosing wall at the foot of the slope', in his unpublished report.[1]

Altogether we have completely excavated four and partially two casemates.[2] The line of the wall runs generally north to south, apart from two obtuse angles to fit the line of the wall to both the topography and to the direction of the city-gate. The casemates are 8–10·5 m. long (see also Fig. 31). The outer wall is 1·5–1·6 m. thick, the inner wall 1·1 m. thick and the partitions between the casemates are 1 m. thick. The space between the wall (i.e. the inner width of the casemates) is 2·4–2·5 m. Each of the casemates has an entrance located in a corner near one of the partitions. The rooms have earthen floors only, which are about 30–40 cm. above the wall-foundations. The latter were dug to

[1] See above, Chapter III, § 1, b.   [2] *Hazor III–IV*, pls. II–III.

a depth of 0·30–1 m. (according to the terrain) and were laid in many cases directly on the floors and walls of the previous strata. Remains of bricks in debris indicate that the upper part of the wall was brick-built—a fact corroborated also by the horizontal finish of the top of the stone-foundations. Similar casemates were found also in Areas B, L, and M (Fig. 27). Along the inner wall of the casemate-wall, and between the building further to the west and the city-gate, a paved street was found,[1] with a drainage-channel running close and parallel to the wall. This was probably the gate's street or square to use biblical terminology.[2] This pavement, like the building to be described later, was raised several times—a raising which nearly corresponded to the main phases observed in the building.[3] All the pavements were built on to the casemate-wall.

c. The gate

In the northern part of the excavated area, at a point about one-third of the Tell's width from the northern edge, we found the city-gate. The gate consists of six chambers (Fig. 30), three on either side of its passage, with square towers in front. These are slightly narrower than the chambers thus creating an entrance-porch 6·1 m. wide. The total outer length of the gatehouse is 20·3 m. (the northern half) and 20·8 m. (the southern half); its width is 18·2 m. The actual passage is 4·2 m. Most of the gatehouse is built into the city and only the two towers protrude outwards from the casemate-wall. Of the actual gate only the foundations were preserved, up to the level of the passage-paving made of crushed chalk. The depth of the foundations varies from west to east. The foundations of the southern tower, for example, are 2 m. deeper than those of the innermost chambers. In fact, the whole passage slants from west to east. The inner threshold, which is made of reused LB orthostats,[4] is 2 m. higher than the cobble-paved entrance-hall. The reason for this is the high debris of the orthostats Long Temple which lay just beneath the gate, thus accentuating the slope. In order to minimize the steep slope into the city, the gate builders carried out enormous levelling-operations (as we ascertained in 1968) eradicating the LB Strata, and sometimes even the MB, just to the west of the gate. The debris was dumped to fill the

---

[1] Ibid., pl. XIX.

[2] *RV*: 'the broad place at the gate of the city' (2 Chron. 32: 6).

[3] Three pavements were observed: XB, XA, and IXB. In IXA no new pavements were added but some installations were built on it.

[4] *Hazor III–IV*, pl. XVIII, 2.

areas between the deep foundations in the eastern part of the gate.

The paved entrance, too, slanted steeply eastwards and south-wards, indicating perhaps that the approach to the gate was not straight but rather angular or curved. This area has not, as yet,

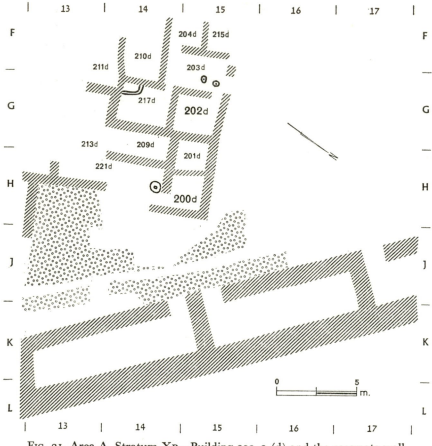

FIG. 31. Area A. Stratum XB—Building 200-2 (d) and the casemate-wall.

been excavated and therefore we do not know whether there was another external gate or any other structure in front of this city-gate.

d. The moat

Another important element in the Solomonic fortifications is a wide and deep dry moat or fosse, which was cut east of the casemate-wall.[1] The existence of this moat and its rough dimensions, were discovered as a result of the 'Big Trench',

___
[1] Only mentioned in *Hazor II*, p. 2.

which we cut along some 50 m. to the east of the casemate-wall.[1] The trench indicated that the Bronze Age floors east of the casemate-wall were cut slanting eastwards[2] up to the thick MB II brick wall. On the paved MB II floor in front of the brick wall, fragments of fallen bricks were found[3] and above it

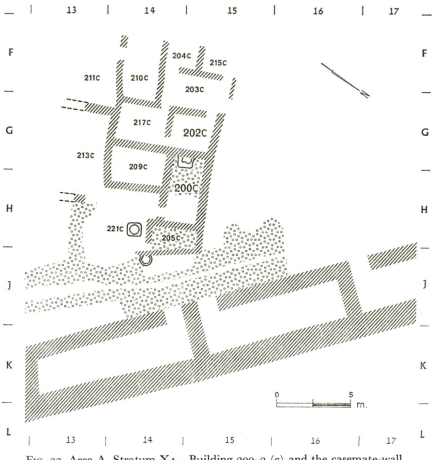

FIG. 32. Area A. Stratum XA—Building 200-2 (c) and the casemate-wall.

slanting layers of fill, which contained Iron Age pottery, later than that of Stratum X. It is clear that this deep area was not filled during the Solomonic period (see also detail in Fig. 27). The fill does not resemble a wash, and it was our impression that it was deliberate, most probably done in Stratum VIII, after the city expanded eastwards and the Solomonic wall was in ruins. Above the fill we found fragments of walls with pottery of Strata VIII and VII.

[1] See above, Chapter IX, § 2.   [2] *Hazor III–IV*, pl. XXVIII.   [3] Ibid., pl. XXIX, 3.

The MB II paving was destroyed at about 14 m. east of the brick wall. Obviously this area was part of the deliberate cut of the moat. On the other hand, further to the east remains of MB and LB reappear delineating the eastern border of the moat. The moat appears, therefore, to have consisted of a slope: from the casemate-wall to the top of the brick wall, the brick wall itself, and a cut below it. The rough measurements of this formidable moat were about 10 m. in depth and 45 m. in width.

§ 2. AREAS B AND L

In Area B, too (Pl. XXVIIIa), a considerable part of the Solomonic fortifications was exposed (cf. Fig. 27).[1] Six casemates were found in the north and four in the south. Their general layout and measurements were similar to those of Area A. The stratigraphy here, too, was clear: they lay below Stratum VIII and above Stratum XI. There is enough evidence to indicate that in Stratum X, as in the earlier and later periods, there was here a fort or a citadel. Twenty metres east of the western end of the casemates, a thick wall (1·50 m., like the thickness of the outer wall of the casemate-wall) was built at a right angle to the inner wall of the casemate-wall. This wall continued southwards for about 5 m. but was then cut by the foundations of the citadel of Stratum VIII. About 2·5 m. from the casemate-wall, a fragment of a thinner wall (about 1 m., like the thickness of the inner walls of the casemate-wall) was found built onto the above in a westward direction, and at right angles. Since on the western tip of Area B we found only one wall, the above remains indicate the possibility that the whole western tip was a fort or a storehouse with long parallel rooms about 20 m. in length. This building was further protected in the south, where the casemate-wall joined it. Here we found something like a keep, 15 × 10 m., with two parallel narrow spaces, most probably a staircase.

The reconstruction of the plan of the whole complex is possibly similar to some section of the fortifications of Zinjirli.[2]

In Area L (Pl. XXIX), to be described later, two casemates were found, again of the same layout and dimensions.

§ 3. THE SOLOMONIC CITY LAYOUT—AREA M

The above facts indicated quite clearly that the Solomonic city occupied only the western portion of the mound. The gate

---

[1] *Hazor III–IV*, pls. XXXIX–XLII.

[2] Conveniently, see Frankfort, *The Art and Architecture of the Ancient Orient*, fig. 82, p. 170.

had been built in the centre of the Tell, while the adjoining casemate-wall stretched from north to south across the width of the mound. Furthermore, casemate-fortifications were found in the western part in Areas B and L. In Area G, on the other hand, a section of solid wall was found with Stratum VIII–V buildings, indicating that the Solomonic city did not expand to that point. Although our conclusions seemed based on solid facts, there remained a theoretical possibility that the gate and adjoining casemate-wall had formed only the inner fortifications of an acropolis, and that yet another wall existed further to the east, but not as far as Area G. This was indeed the suggestion of Dr. K. M. Kenyon.[1] It was too serious and basic a problem to be left unanswered, one way or another. Although, as will be shown, Kenyon's suggestion proved wrong, I am indebted to her for raising it and thus compelling us to further our investigation. In 1968 we opened a new area—M—on the north side of the Tell, north of the Solomonic gate, for the specific reason of clarifying that point (Fig. 27).[2] This site was fixed at the theoretical meeting-point of the line of the city-wall, on the northern edge of the Tell, and the estimated prolongation of the casemate-wall at about 55 m. north of the gate. Here we could expect a conclusive answer as to whether indeed the casemate-wall of Area A, upon reaching the northern side, turned west in keeping with the perimeter of Solomon's city as we had previously conceived. If, however, the wall turned both east and west (forming a T-shaped casemate-wall), it would clearly indicate that the casemate-wall attached to the gate belonged only to the acropolis. The site selected covers nine squares, totalling some 225 sq. m. We began by cutting a trench from west to east in order to find the continuation of the north to south casemate-wall. The wall was found exactly along the straight line conjectured according to the direction of the casemate-wall section, immediately adjacent to the south of the gate. The casemate-wall found here (one complete casemate and a portion of another) was precisely of the same dimensions as that of Area A (Pl. XXV*a*). Parts of the wall had been uprooted in antiquity, most probably after the city expanded eastwards in Stratum VIII. In other places clear evidence of earthquake destruction was visible—most probably that which destroyed the city of Stratum VI. Near the inner

[1] K. M. Kenyon, 'Megiddo, Hazor, Samaria and Chronology', *Bulletin of the Institute of Archaeology*, University of London, 4, 1964, p. 144: 'It must, however, be remarked that they [the Solomonic defences—*Y.Y.*] probably represent the defences of an acropolis or royal quarter rather than of a town.'

[2] *IEJ* 19, 1969, pp. 5 ff., from which some portions of the following description are taken.

wall, some paving was found with a drainage-channel, like the one found in Area A.

Once the direction of the wall had clearly been established, we cut a wide north to south trench, i.e. perpendicular to the former trench and to the conjectured northern city-wall. The results were clear and provided definite answers to our query: the casemate-wall turned only to the west. Moreover, east of the corner of the casemate-wall, we discovered the solid offsets and insets wall of Stratum VIII (Pl. XXV*a*), built onto the corner of the casemate-wall. The actual layout of the corner and the method of joining the solid wall to it is of interest. The original corner was well planned and the northern casemate, i.e. the last before the corner, is built in an obtuse angle to the inner wall of the northern casemate-wall. Thus the actual corner was built with a west to east casemate of the northern wall. The Stratum VIII wall joins the casemate-wall, not in the very corner but rather 1 m. south of it (Pl. XXV*b*), thus forming an offset. The actual corner was reinforced and most of the older casemate was built inside it (or filled) to the width of the new wall. This method of partially filling the old casemate-wall, was observed in other areas as will be described in Chapter XIV. It was clear then that the Solomonic city was confined to the western portion of the Tell only, and its total area was about 26,000 sq. m. (6·5 acres).

§ 4. THE SUB-PHASES AND CHRONOLOGY

To conclude this chapter about the Solomonic city, the nature of the sub-phases of Strata X and IX must be discussed. This is essential since the evidence has not been published, although pottery is presented in *Hazor III–IV*. This situation has put some scholars in a handicapped position in discussing the stratigraphy and pottery of Hazor at this period, and its relation to other sites.[1] As mentioned above, no phases were noticeable in the casemate-wall floors, but a clear raising of the paved street and square were clearly detected. However, the pottery presented in *Hazor III–IV*,[2] comes solely from well-stratified floors found in a building (200–2) situated some 5 m. west of the casemate-wall. The building itself (with all its phases) was found sealed off by the cobble-floors of the pillared building of Stratum VIII. In

[1] See in particular the exhaustive study of K. M. Kenyon (see above, p. 141 n. 1; p. 147 n. 11) and her justified remark: 'The bulk of the Stratum X material is published in *Hazor III–IV*, of which the plates but not the text have appeared; the distinction between XB and XA is, therefore, not yet clear.'

[2] pls. CLXXI–CLXXVI.

fact the sunken rectangular areas of the floor corresponded to the plan of rooms of this building.[1]

The first and main phase of the building corresponded to the original period of the casemate-wall as was attested by the lowest level of the cobble-floored street or square, lying between the building and the wall (Pl. XXVII*b*). Its walls, still preserved to some 2 m. in height, were reused with additions and with new floors in most of the subsequent phases, of which we could observe four. The lowest two resembled each other in plan, and therefore we called them X<small>B</small> (the lower) and X<small>A</small>. The same applied to the upper two which we designated IX<small>B</small> (the lower) and IX<small>A</small>. Wherever the plans of the rooms remained more or less throughout, we retained the same locus number, but attached a Latin letter to designate the phase. Thus, the lowest phase was marked in *Hazor III–IV* with the letter 'd' and the upper one with 'a':

$$\text{Locus 202a} = \text{IX}_\text{A}$$
$$\text{Locus 202b} = \text{IX}_\text{B}$$
$$\text{Locus 202c} = \text{X}_\text{A}$$
$$\text{Locus 202d} = \text{X}_\text{B}.$$

Of all the pottery presented in the plates, it is obvious that only that emanating from loci determined by the letter 'd' should be ascribed to the oldest Solomonic period.[2]

Since there can be no doubt about the dates of the basic phase, X<small>B</small> (*c.* middle of the tenth century), and that of Stratum VIII (second quarter of the ninth century), phases X<small>A</small> and IX<small>B</small>–IX<small>A</small>, are squeezed within a period of about sixty years. Both the similarity between some of the pottery types and the variants are to be explained by this short chronological difference in time between the phases. The thick layer of ashes terminating this group of phases may be attributed to the campaign of Ben-Hadad King of Aram in 885 B.C.[3] The following is a short description of the four phases in Building 200–2, illustrated with the help of the plates in *Hazor III–IV*.[4] The building in its original phase (X<small>B</small>), was composed of two units with a common wall: unit 200 to the east and 202 to the west. Unit 200 is composed of three square or rectangular rooms (200d, 201d, and 209d) and a court (213d–221d) in the south-east corner. The walls are built from small stones but are

[1] See below, Chapter XIV, § 2.   [2] Coming, of course, from its latest occupation.
[3] *Hazor II*, p. 37 n. 217. I find it futile to speculate on the possible causes responsible for the changes in the various phases where there is no clear archaeological or historical datum.
[4] pls. XIX–XXIII and here, Figs. 31–34.

carefully laid in a very straight line. In the court, three ovens and a bin were found. In Unit 202, three rooms (202d, 203d, 217d) were completely excavated, and parts of a further four rooms were uncovered (204d, 210d, 211d, 215d). In these rooms, too, many ovens and bins were found. The relatively few vessels

Fig. 33. Area A. Stratum IXʙ—Building 200–2 (b) and the casemate-wall.

found here are of an ordinary nature (cooking-pots, bowls, juglets, store-jars, etc.), and testify that this building (the two units) served as a dwelling.

The number of the small rooms, and the position of the building near the wall and the gate, suggests perhaps that it served as barracks. In the next phase (Xᴀ), Unit 200 (Fig. 32) was expanded eastwards and an additional room (205c) was built. The two previous rooms (200d–201d) were formed now into one larger room (200c) and a new room (205c) was added to its west. Room 209d was enlarged to the east. The western unit (202) underwent no changes except for a new floor about 40 cm. above those of Xв.

In phase IXв (Fig. 33), again, more changes are noticeable in the eastern unit. Only room 209c retained its plan (now

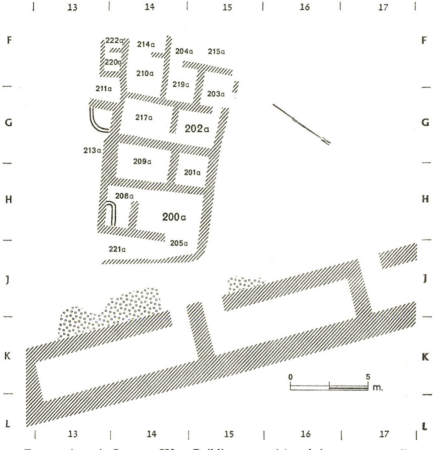

Fig. 34. Area A. Stratum IXᴀ—Building 200–2 (a) and the casemate-wall.

called 209b). Room 200 was again redivided into two rooms (200b and 201b). In the court a room (208b) was built, and the remainder (218b), with a cobble floor, may have served as a small court. The western unit (202) now underwent some changes. Room 203c was divided into two cubicles (203b–219b); so, too, was room 211c, which now consisted of two smaller rooms 211b and 220b.[1]

[1] An interesting find was made in this Stratum, in Room 217b—a room in the western building, which was hardly changed in the four phases, except for the raising of its floors. It is a terracotta figurine (*Hazor III–IV*, pl. CLXXVI, 24). In the preliminary report (*IEJ* 8,

In phase IXA (Fig. 34), again, the main changes affected the eastern building 200. Rooms 200b, 205b, and 218b were enlarged into a large room or court, 200a. In the western building, 202, only minor changes took place: the entrance between 217a and 219a was blocked and Room 220b was re-divided into two minor rooms, 220a and 222a. The detailed description of the changes which took place in this building are furnished in order to explain why these four phases were grouped into two main strata. It will also help, I hope, those students who wish to study more closely the pottery of Strata X–IX according to the loci in which it was found.

1958, p. 3) I referred to it as a 'stylised head of a horse', but I believe now that it represents a bull's head. The wedge-like mark on the forehead is found on many bull-head figurines in various periods. Of particular interest is the 'circle and cross' emblem between the ears. This is remarkably similar to the emblems found in the Orthostat Temple in Area H, both on the incense altar and on the deity's breast (see above, Chapter VII, § 2, *e*). There too the deity's animal was the bull. We may interpret the terracotta figurine as representing Hadad's bull. See here, Pl. XIX *c*.

XIII

HAZOR, GEZER, AND MEGIDDO IN THE TIMES OF SOLOMON AND AHAB

§ 1. GENERAL REMARKS

IN order to evaluate fully the significance of the Solomonic fortifications discovered at Hazor, and the subsequent changes which took place there in the times of Ahab, we have to digress for a while from Hazor and examine the situation at Gezer and Megiddo. The reason is the oft-mentioned passage in 1 Kings 9: 15 which clearly indicates that, together with Hazor, Solomon built Gezer and Megiddo. It should be noted that the passage does not specify the exact nature of these three cities, whether they were built as chariot-cities or garrisons. However, the mention of these three cities is inserted in the flow of the narrative to explain the reason for the forced labour which the king levied in order to build his main architectural achievements: the House of the Lord, the King's Palace, the fortifications of Jerusalem 'and Hazor, Megiddo and Gezer'. The next verse (16) explains that Gezer was given to Solomon by the Egyptian Pharaoh, but says nothing about Megiddo and Hazor. We can take it to indicate that the latter two sites had been in Solomon's possession. The strategic positions of the three cities, dominating the main lines of communications in the land, are quite clear, and one can take it that here, more than anywhere else, Solomon's military engineers were responsible for the planning of the fortifications. These cities were the key to the whole defence-system of the country. When the excavations of Hazor began, the existence of Solomon's gate at Megiddo had been known. The similarity of the plans of both gates, even more than before, posed the question of the Solomonic fortifications at Gezer.

§ 2. GEZER

Gezer was excavated by Macalister at the beginning of the century, when archaeology was still in its infancy. Moreover, Macalister served as his own administrator, architect, and recorder, which renders the evaluation of the results of his

excavations one of the most difficult problems in Palestinian
archaeology. Some compensation, however, may be found in
his detailed three-volume report,[1] which is rich in drawings and
accurate descriptions. He did not observe in Gezer any casemate-
wall, or city-gate attributable to Solomon, but the discoveries
in Megiddo and Hazor induced me to re-examine his report.
It was gratifying to identify in his plans[2] a casemate-wall and
even a structure similar to Solomon's gates at Megiddo and
Hazor.[3] Macalister had marked these structures 'Maccabean
Castle' (Fig. 35), mainly because of their Hellenistic pottery and
a Greek inscription discovered in the area. Since only the
western part of the gate had been discovered, and since, to be
fair, the gates of Megiddo and Hazor were yet unknown, he
failed to realize the full significance and nature of this complex
of fortifications. The plans of the casemate-wall and the gate
were not only identical with those of Hazor, but were, for all
practical purposes, of the same dimensions (Fig. 36). The
lengths of the gate-house were 19 m. at Gezer, 20·3 m. at Hazor,
and 20·3 m. at Megiddo. The widths of the gate-house: 16·2, 18,
and 17·5 m. respectively. The total width of the casemate-walls
at Hazor and Gezer is 5·4 m. In addition, the dressing of the
ashlar in the gate-jambs and the method of laying the headers
and stretchers were all rather similar to those of Megiddo. The
above facts left little doubt that the 'Maccabean Castle' was
indeed part of the Solomonic fortifications. Fortunately, we
need no more rely on the resemblance of outward features only.
The site of Gezer is now being excavated on behalf of the Hebrew
Union College. For several seasons, beginning in 1964, the site
of the 'Maccabean Castle' has been examined and excavated,
and the results established their Solomonic date beyond any
doubt: 'the sealed pottery from the floors and the make-up
below was characteristic red-burnished ware of the late 10th
century B.C. Solomon did indeed rebuild Gezer!'[4] The existence

---

[1] R. A. Stewart Macalister, *The Excavation of Gezer*, vols. i–iii, London, 1912.

[2] Vol. i, p. 104.

[3] The following description touches upon the main points only. For a detailed treatment
of the subject, see Y. Yadin, 'Solomon's City Wall and Gate at Gezer', *IEJ* 8, 1958, pp. 80–6.

[4] William G. Dever, 'Excavations at Gezer', *BA* 30, 1967, p. 61; see further, idem, 'Ex-
cavations at Gezer, 1964–1967', in *Jerusalem Through the Ages*, the Twenty-fifth Archaeological
Convention of the Israel Exploration Society, Jerusalem, 1968, pp. 26 ff., 'Gezer—A City
Coming to Life' (Hebrew), *Qadmoniot*, 3, 1970, pp. 57 ff.; 'Gezer—A Palestinian Mound
Re-excavated', *Raggi*, Zürich, 8 (3), 1968, pp. 65 ff. and figs. 5–6. See also, Hebrew Union
College's 'News Letters' of 28 February 1969, concerning the 1968 seasons: '. . . the clearance
of the western half of the Gate, begun in 1967 season, was virtually completed. . . . An area of
narrow lanes and fragmentary building complexes, contemporary with the founding phase of
the Gate, were revealed just inside the gateway. Overlying this was a substantial destruction

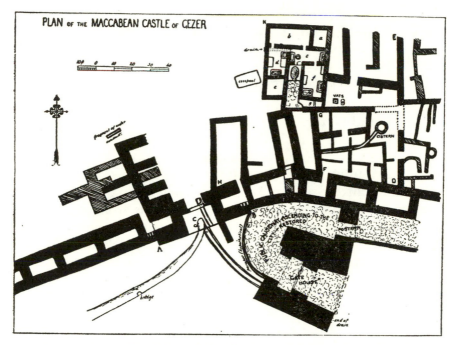

Fig. 35. Gezer. The Solomonic fortifications—'The Maccabean Castle'.

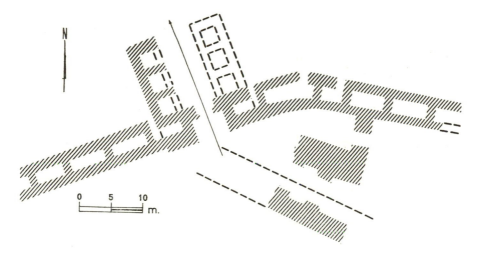

Fig. 36. Gezer. Reconstruction of the Solomonic fortifications.

of casemate-walls both at Hazor and Gezer made the re-exam-
ination of the situation at Megiddo unavoidable.

§ 3. MEGIDDO[1]

a. *The problem and the stratigraphy*

Despite the absolute similarity between the gates of Hazor,
Megiddo, and Gezer, there was an apparent difference regarding the city-walls associated with them. While in Hazor and
Gezer the walls were of the casemate type, the Megiddo wall
(325), attributed by its excavators to Solomon (Fig. 37), was
quite different; a solid wall, with 'insets' and 'offsets', both
interior and exterior. There was no doubt, from the stratigraphical point of view, that this wall was contemporary with
the famous stables (Fig. 39), also attributed to Solomon. It was
hard to accept the suggestion[2] that Megiddo was fortified in a
special way because it was a chariot city,[3] while Hazor and
Gezer had only been store cities. It is axiomatic that the strength
and character of a wall is determined by the tactics, strength,
and siege-craft of the enemy against whom it is erected. Gezer
in the south and Hazor in the north, could theoretically have
been fortified against two different potential enemies, yet both
had the same type of fortifications. The possibility that in
Megiddo, too, the Solomonic fortifications were of the casemate
type, had to be examined. In fact, the results of the Megiddo
excavations were perplexing, as far as our subject is concerned,
for other reasons as well. Despite the methodical and systematic
excavations of the Chicago Oriental Institute in 1925–39, quite
a number of stratigraphical problems remained without satis-
factory solution, mainly because of the changing directorship of
the expedition, which impaired their continuity.[4] As far as our
subject is concerned, the foremost problem can be defined as

---

level with quantities of pottery attributable to the late 10th/very early 9th century B.C.
horizon, perhaps evidence of the raid of Shishak, *ca.* 918 B.C. . . .' See now also, W. G. Dever,
H. D. Lance, G. E. Wright, *Gezer I*, Jerusalem, 1970, p. 5.

[1] For a detailed discussion of the Megiddo problems and the results of my short digs there,
see my article, 'Megiddo of the Kings of Israel', *BA* 33, September 1970. Portions of the present discussion are incorporated there.   [2] Y. Aharoni, *BASOR* 154, 1959, pp. 35 ff.
[3] For a recent bold, but not entirely convincing, effort to explain these structures as store-
houses or barracks, rather than stables, see James B. Pritchard, 'The Megiddo Stables: A
Reassessment', *The Glueck Festschrift*, 1970, pp. 268 ff.
[4] The following publications are referred to in the present discussion: G. Schumacher,
Tell el-Mutesellim, i, Leipzig, 1908; P. L. O. Guy, 'New Light from Armageddon', *Oriental
Institute Communications* (= *OIC*) no. 9, Chicago, 1931; Robert S. Lamon and Geoffrey M.
Shipton, *Megiddo I, Seasons of 1925–34*, Chicago, 1939; Gordon Loud, *Megiddo II, Seasons of
1935–39*, Chicago, 1948; Herbert Gordon May, *Material Remains of the Megiddo Cult*, Chicago,
1935.

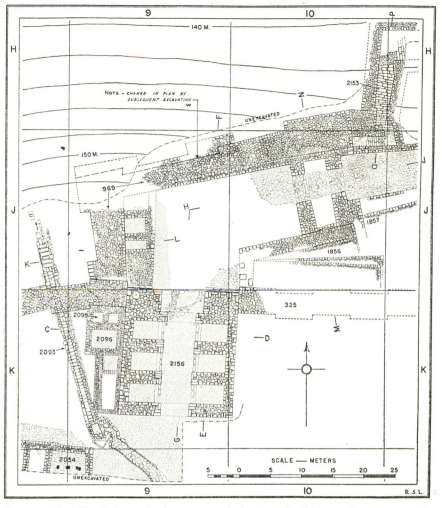

FIG. 37. Megiddo. Solomon's city-gate, and the 'associate' city-wall—325, as published in *Megiddo II*, fig. 105.

follows. The main buildings attributed by the excavators to the Solomonic period were discovered in Stratum IV from the top, which they were compelled (see below) to call Stratum IVA. This stratum included the two stable complexes,[1] the southern (1576) and the northern (407, following the number of one of its halls). There was no stratigraphical doubt that the stables were contemporary with the offsets/insets wall. Since the latter was attributed to Solomon, it followed that so should the stables be. Below this stratum, another Iron Age stratum was found, which they called Stratum V. However, further excavation made it

---

[1] *Megiddo I*, pp. 32 ff., 41 ff.; Guy, *OIC*, pp. 37 ff.; *Megiddo II*, p. 116.

clear that in fact they had struck two strata and not just one.
Since, by that time, they had designated the next stratum VI,
they were compelled to designate the two strata under the
stables VA (the upper) and VB. Beneath these was Stratum VI,
which also turned out later to consist of two strata, VIA (the
upper) and VIB. Under the latter, the earliest Iron Age
Stratum (VIIA) was discovered, with its famous ivory treasure,
and inscriptions of Rameses III and Rameses VI. This stratum
established the earliest possible date for Stratum VIB, in the
second half of the twelfth century.

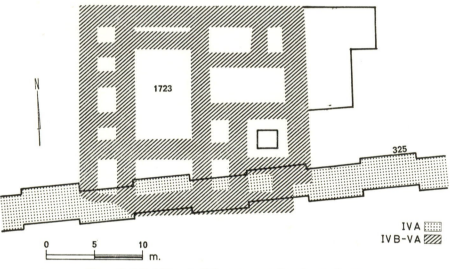

FIG. 38. Megiddo—building 1723 under city-wall 325.

The great complication in attributing Stratum IV to
Solomon arose still earlier, as the result of a surprising discovery
on the south side of the Tell, east of the southern stables. Here
a building (1723),[1] a palace or fort, was discovered, measuring
22 × 20 m., built of ashlar, and similar in style to the Solomonic
gate (Fig. 38). It became clear to the astonished excavators that
the so-called Solomonic offsets/insets wall (325) had been erected
on the ruins of that palace. Moreover, even west of the palace,
a huge, well-conceived structure (1482)[2] had been discovered.
Its west part was under the foundations of the southern stable
complex, so it too preceded the stables and the adjacent wall.
These structures were marked *Stratum IV*B. The excavators
were left with two alternatives—neither of them logical—to
explain these facts: the first that the palace had been built at the

[1] *Megiddo I*, pp. 11 ff.   [2] Ibid., p. 9.

beginning of Solomon's rule, before the city was fortified, at which stage it had been a single structure on the Tell, serving perhaps as the governor's residence. Later, the palace, and structure 1482, which were built on the edge of the mound, were demolished by Solomon's engineers, when they built the offsets/insets wall. The second alternative was that the palace had been built by David only to be destroyed by Solomon. Both these explanations assumed that Solomon himself destroyed the two grandest Israelite structures existing in Megiddo.

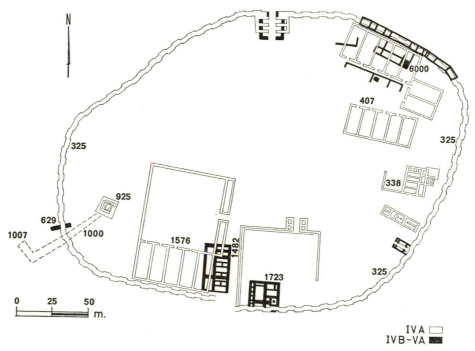

FIG. 39. Key plan of Megiddo in Strata IVA; IVB–VA.

Albright and Wright contributed much to solve these difficulties.[1] They proved that not only the palace, but many other buildings, attributed by the excavators to Stratum VA, should have been ascribed to Stratum IVB. Thus Albright and Wright introduced a new stratum, which they called 'IVB–VA'. They too, however, were compelled to assume that the palace and the other buildings were built in David's time.

It became clear to us that the stumbling-block in attributing the offsets/insets wall to Solomon was not only its difference

[1] For a summary of their views, and bibliography on the subject, see G. Ernest Wright, 'The Discoveries at Megiddo, 1935–1939', in *The Biblical Archaeologist Reader*[2], Garden City, N.Y., 1964, pp. 225 ff., and there n. 15 on p. 240.

from the Solomonic walls at Hazor and Gezer, but also its
stratigraphy.

b. *The 1960 and 1966–1967 excavations*

In order to clarify these problems, I went to Megiddo briefly
in 1960 (13–15 January, and again for a few days later in the
month). I selected an area in the northern side of the eastern
half of the Tell, east of the 'Schumacher Trench', and area
DD of the Oriental Institute excavations. Here the offsets/insets
wall (325) had not been removed by the excavators and was well
preserved. This brief dig brought about interesting finds, of
which the most important was the discovery of a second palace,
also built of ashlar like the Solomonic gate, with a casemate-
wall on either side—all built under the offsets/insets wall and
the adjacent stables complex (Fig. 40). Further, two short

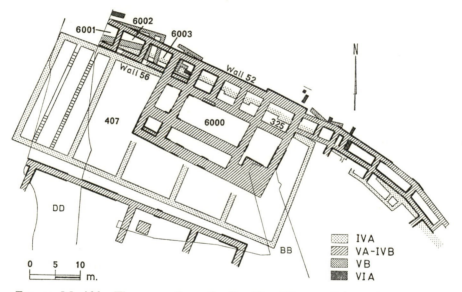

FIG. 40. Megiddo. The excavations of 1960; 66–7. The new Solomonic palace and
the casemate-walls. Note the position of Strata VB; VIA.

seasons of excavations[1] (a few days in August 1966 and the end
of March to the beginning of April 1967) helped to clarify all the
stratigraphical problems, as well as the date of the Megiddo
Water-System.

c. *The 'New Palace'—6000*

We became aware of the existence of the new palace (which
we numbered 6000) even before we began the dig in 1960.

---

[1] See *IEJ* 16, 1966, pp. 278 ff.; 17, 1967, pp. 119 ff.

The already excavated outer face of the offsets/insets wall here, showed that what seemed to be the lower part of the foundations of the wall was actually built in a straight line (without offsets and insets) measuring 28 m. (wall 52). This fact was not recorded in the excavators' report. While the city-wall itself had been constructed of field-stones, or small dressed stones, this stretch of wall was built of ashlar, some of which had margins dressed in the manner of Solomon's gate and the southern palace. This stretch of ashlar wall stopped abruptly in a straight and perpendicular line, at its western end. At that point, the ashlar blocks were particularly large and well-dressed, and laid in the header-stretcher fashion, similar to that of the six-chambered gate. It immediately became clear that the stratigraphical situation here is similar to that of the southern palace (1723). The subsequent peeling off of the foundations of the offsets/insets wall not only revealed the walls of this building which extended into the city, but showed quite clearly that the building was built under the stables, too.

The building is rectangular in shape, its length from east to west is about 28 m. and from north to south about 21 m., occupying a built-up area of 600 sq. m., slightly more than the southern palace. The building's front was to the south; on its north (at the edge of the Tell) it had five rooms, while the east and west sides had elongated halls. Its south-east corner must have had a tower, and the south-west corner a square room. Its plan proves that it resembles greatly the so-called *bit-hilani* of Zinjirli and sites on the Syrian coast. This type of building served as a ceremonial palace. This additional proof of Phoenician influence on Solomon's building-activities is of great interest. Meanwhile, it became clear that Stratum IVB was composed of no isolated palace, but of a series of monumental buildings, all of the Solomonic period. Careful examination of the remains under the stables revealed an important technical phenomenon which helped us not only to locate another large structure of the same period, south of Palace 6000 (Fig. 40), but also to comprehend why the earlier Megiddo excavators had failed to locate some of the structures of this magnificently built city. South of the palace, across a rather wide street, we discovered remains of a large structure resembling the building-style of the other IVB–VA structures. However, except for a few places in which the lower stones were preserved, we noticed that elsewhere, where stones were missing, beautiful beaten chalk floors were revealed, stretching practically to the assumed line of the walls, then abruptly stopping. It became evident that most of the beautiful ashlar stones of structures IVB had been pulled out and removed. No doubt, this was done mainly by the builders of the stables. This explains the fact that a number of stones bearing the same mason's marks were discovered in both IVB and IVA.

The stratigraphical attribution of the new palace (6000) and the large structure to its south, in relation to the offsets/insets wall and the stables, is clear enough if one counts the strata from top to bottom. The wall and the stables belong to Stratum IVA, while the newly discovered buildings, lying immediately below, belong to Stratum IVB. It was imperative, though, to prove that such attribution is correct too, if counted from bottom to top, since theoretically it might be argued that the discovered buildings, even though they lay beneath the stables and the wall, might not belong to IVB, but to an earlier period or stratum. To ascertain this point, we excavated in several places under the floors of the palace, in the hope of hitting the remains of the huge conflagration of Stratum VIA, which were evident all over the Tell; and this indeed occurred. Beneath the palace floor (Fig. 40), but above the unmistakable remains of VIA, we came across relatively poor walls, which obviously belonged to VB. Thus it was corroborated that the palace did indeed belong to IVB–IVA, by counting either the top downwards or the bottom upwards.

d. The casemates

The discovery of Palace 6000 was a very important link in the clarification of the Solomonic stratum and its character, but the main problem had been the city's fortifications during that period. The section selected for excavation was east of Palace 6000 (Fig. 40). After carefully peeling off the foundations of the offsets/insets wall, we hit a fill of earth and field stones, and immediately beneath it a casemate-wall of which a stretch of 35 m. in length was uncovered. The casemates in this section are built of moderately thick walls (external wall about 1 m. thick), with an average distance of 2 m. between them. They are made of field-stones as a foundation for a brick wall. The length of the ordinary casemates is about 7 m., but where the wall turns at an obtuse angle towards the palace, there are two smaller casemates. The casemate-wall here is less strong than the one at Hazor, which is easily understandable, since the slope here is much higher and steeper, and in fact, it is impossible to attack the city from this side. One problem had still to be solved. Since we uncovered the casemate-wall in sections, we realized that its foundations lay on the burnt layer of Stratum VIA. Although we could attribute it (counting downwards) to Stratum IVB, one could argue that the casemate-wall was in fact part of Stratum VB, having been built on VIA. In that case, the wall had been integrated into and reused in the IVB fortifications. This problem was carefully checked and solved in 1967. The walls of Stratum VB building were discovered beneath the casemate-wall and above the burnt layer of Stratum VIA (Fig. 40)[1] Thus the circle closed.

From the start of our excavations, we discovered a wall-top made of ashlar stones and constructed mainly of headers, which appeared west of Palace 6000 in a level below that of the offsets/insets wall and the stables. That wall had already been uncovered by the previous excavators, but it was not marked on their plans.

After excavating the area, a series of casemates was discovered here, too. Altogether, we uncovered two complete casemates (6002–3) and half of a third (6001). It was not possible to check the situation further to the west because here Area DD of the Megiddo excavators began, which was but an extension of the Schumacher Trench. However, by examining the plans of the Oriental Institute excavators,[2] it is possible to reconstruct the remainder of that casemate, and even discern the traces of a fourth casemate.

We do not know what Schumacher discovered, and nothing can be learnt about this from his publications, but there seems to be no doubt that these casemates continued westwards to the gate. It is difficult to know whether casemates were found by the previous excavators in the section between those found by us and the gate, but it is feasible that the wall in this particular section was deliberately demolished by the builders of the offsets/insets wall, for its stones. From this particular portion, dug by us, a very slanting slope begins, as far as the gate, and it is conceivable that when the offsets/insets wall was built, the

---

[1] Incidentally, the floors of VIA were not only covered by a thick layer of ashes, but contained also a wealth of typical pottery, including the famous 'beer mugs' of the decadent style, ascribed by Trude Dothan (*The Philistines and their Material Culture* (Hebrew), Jerusalem, 1967, p. 125), to the third phase of the Philistine culture, i.e. the second half of eleventh century. In one of the rooms we found a cache, containing many ivory spindle whorls and several bronze and iron objects, as well as jewellery—all attesting to the high technical standard of the Stratum VIA Philistine-Canaanite culture. For a detailed description of this cache, see, *Qadmoniot*, 3, 1970, pp. 47 ff., and the *BA* 33, 3, September 1970, pp. 77 ff.

[2] *Megiddo II*, fig. 414, square K 12.

earlier wall could not serve to support it, and the whole area had to be reorganized.

Excavations below the floors of the casemates revealed that the poorly built Stratum VB had not been fortified by a special wall, and certainly had no city-gate.

The interesting feature of the Solomonic fortifications is that the palaces and forts were built on the edge of the mound, and their external wall (with their rooms/casemates) served as part of the city-wall. The casemate-wall properly joined the palaces from both ends. A similar phenomenon was observed, as mentioned, in Area B of Hazor, in Stratum X. This is surely an economical way of building the fortifications.

e. The gates

Once it has been proved that the Solomonic city had not only a gate but also a city-wall, an attempt should be made, even briefly, to clarify the complex problem of the Megiddo gates in the Iron Age. The problem is not easy, not only because most of the gates and especially the wall adjacent to them were removed by the excavators, but also because the said area had been excavated by two separate excavators and some important details do not figure in their records. Our proposal to solve the complex problems of the gates might best be served by reviewing briefly the developments of the Megiddo fortifications in the period preceding and following Solomon.

Since the offsets/insets wall was the only one to last to the end of Megiddo in the Iron Age,[1] and since, on the other hand, post-Solomonic gates were discovered in various strata, it was assumed rightly that the new gates had from time to time been integrated into that wall. As for the Iron Age strata below the Solomonic gate, in Stratum VIIA the magnificent six-pilaster (or four-chambered) Bronze Age gate continued to exist. In Stratum VIA, a small but well-constructed gate was found directly under the Solomonic gate (Fig. 41). The Megiddo excavators assumed that the gate of VIA continued through VB, but had no facts to substantiate the assumption. In a check we made in 1967, we ascertained that no gate existed in the VB city, a fact which fits in well with its unfortified character. Above the ruins of Solomon's six-chambered gate, P. L. O. Guy[2] (the excavator of the stables) discovered two additional gates. While unearthing the remains of the older of the two, Guy

---

[1] The city of Stratum II was unwalled, for a large fort was discovered which had been partially built above the offsets/insets wall; see *Megiddo I*, p. 83, fig. 95.
[2] *OIC* 9, pp. 25 ff.

thought it should be attributed to Solomon, because it was bound to the offsets/insets wall, which he had ascribed to Solomon. However, in the 1935–6 campaign under Loud, the six-chambered gates had been found and rightly ascribed to Solomon.[1] Guy's gate was therefore attributed by Loud to Stratum III, the last fortified city. Then a new difficulty arose,

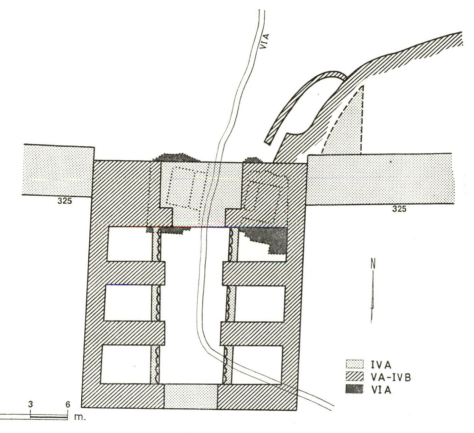

FIG. 41. Megiddo—city-gates, Strata VIA–IVA.

when it was established without doubt that this gate (500) comprised in fact two gates, which from the stratigraphical-technical viewpoint belonged to separate periods and had different plans. Since both gates could only be ascribed to Stratum III, the earlier of the two was labelled gate IIIB and the later gate III (Fig. 42).[2] As it was impossible to ascribe them to one single level from the historical viewpoint, the strange conclusion was reached that in fact only one gate—III—existed, while IIIB was taken to be a misconception, a mistaken

[1] *Megiddo II*, pp. 46 ff   [2] *Megiddo I*, pp. 74 and fig. 86.

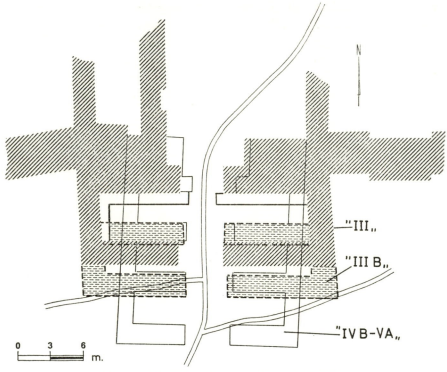

FIG. 42. Megiddo—city-gates, Strata IVᴀ–III.

beginning abandoned in due course in favour of the gate III
plan. With the discovery of the casemate-wall, it seems that
the difficulties can now be overcome:

   (i) The six-chambered gate (Solomon)—casemate-wall—
      Strata IVʙ–Vᴀ.

  (ii) The four-chambered gate (IIIʙ)—offsets/insets wall—
      Stratum IV main phase (ᴀ).

 (iii) The two-chambered gate (III)—offsets/insets wall—
      Stratum III.

It is possible that, when the offsets/insets wall was first built
(after Shishak's destruction), it was still leaning on Solomon's
gate, except that its level had had to be raised (temporarily
designated IVᴀ1). This leads us to the main discussion of the
nature of Solomon's gate and its stratigraphy. The Megiddo
excavations assumed that the magnificent construction, mostly
of well-dressed ashlar, was only the gate's sub-structure or
foundations.[1] This view was mainly based on the fact that the
lower level of the gate is much lower than the foundations of the

---

[1] Robert S. Lamon in *Megiddo II*, pp. 46 ff.

offsets/insets wall, and the 'lack' of an earlier city-wall to be associated with it. This assumption has one great stumbling-block, namely that not only were the chambers discovered to be filled-up and bordered by secondary walls of field-stones block-ing them off towards the gateway, but that even the gate's entrances, external and internal, were blocked by thick support-ing walls made of field-stones.[1] Had the builders really planned the position of the gate, which was discovered as a mere foundation, they would certainly have built it differently, incorporating the supporting and revetment walls into the structure. Moreover, they would certainly not have built the foundations of well-dressed ashlar, but of drafted stones with bosses, as is the case in Samaria and other places.[2]

So it seems that the original structure was not a foundation, but the actual gate associated with the casemate-wall. When the offsets/insets wall was joined in the higher level, its builders had no alternative but to block the gate and raise its level. Accord-ingly the Megiddo excavators were bound to find a lower pavement, associated with the gate's original phase. This pavement, I believe, is the road made of well-pressed chalk, discovered by them, which leads towards the lower courses of the six-chambered gate.[3] Since the excavators assumed the gate-structure to be but a foundation, they attributed that level to Stratum VB, which, as was now ascertained, had neither fortifications nor gate. In fact, the lower courses, partly covered by the road, are the very foundation-courses of Solomon's gate, and not of the nonexistent gate of VB.[4]

f. The water-systems

The last subject of the Israelite Megiddo to be discussed is the date of the famous Megiddo water-system. This is of such importance for the history of Megiddo and for the understanding of our discoveries in Hazor, to be related in the next chapter, that it will be treated in greater length. One of the most interest-ing and spectacular structures discovered by the Megiddo excavators in the south-eastern edge of the Tell was labelled by

---

[1] Ibid., figs. 105-6, 108, 111.

[2] Kathleen Kenyon, too, has challenged the excavator's assertion. Her shrewd remarks are worth quoting although she has not pressed this point any further: 'Indeed in the photo-graph, *Megiddo, II*, Fig. 108, the masonry underlying the indicated pavement level [the upper and only one according to the excavators—*Y.Y.*] is not of the type found in foundations at Samaria, and mason's setting-out lines are only found there on the dressed superstructure.' *Archaeology in the Holy Land*[3], p. 250 n. 1.

[3] *Megiddo II*, figs. 89, 91-3, 97, p. 57.

[4] So Kenyon, ibid.

M

them Gallery 629.[1] This Gallery is only a narrow passage (Fig.
43), slightly over a metre in width, leading from the city outwards towards the south-western slope of the Tell, at the bottom
of which the well-known spring-cave exists. The walls of this
passage are actually revetments, and only their internal faces
are well built. They are constructed of exceedingly well-dressed
ashlar, laid pedantically 'header and stretcher' fashion. The
discovered walls stood up to 2 m. high. One may assume, as the

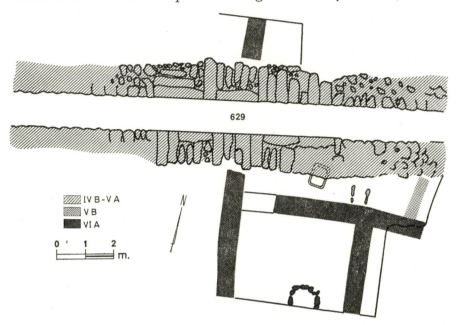

Fig. 43. Megiddo—the 1967 excavations near Gallery 629.

excavators did, that the passage was covered and camouflaged
and led towards the spring. Stratigraphically speaking, the
passage is immediately under the offsets/insets wall, and for
that reason it was assumed that the Gallery had been built
before Solomon. Since it was impossible to ascribe this magnificent structure to the relatively poor strata of the eleventh century,
it was attributed to Rameses III, namely Stratum VIIA.
Fixing the Gallery's date was a point of departure for R. Lamon's
brilliant study of the dating of the famous water-shaft (925) and
tunnel (1000). The upper point of the shaft was cut through
layers of accumulation of the earlier strata, and its walls here
were lined with stone. To achieve its main purpose, namely
water-supply in time of siege, it was necessary to block the cave-

[1] On this, and the water-system, see Robert S. Lamon, *The Megiddo Water System*, Chicago,
1935.

opening from the outside, so as to prevent the enemy from poisoning or blocking the spring-water. The cave's entrance was, indeed, discovered to be blocked by a wall of huge stones. At first, the excavators of Megiddo sought to determine the date of the shaft-quarrying through the identification of the latest stratum through whose ruined layers the shaft was dug. This indicated that the highest stratum to be affected contained pottery of LB fourteenth–thirteenth centuries. The excavators could not check the conditions above that stratum, since the higher strata collapsed in antiquity together with part of the stone lining of its walls. They concluded that the shaft was cut later than the fourteenth–thirteenth centuries. The discovery of a man's skeleton inside the cave—taken to be a guard—and, therefore, of the period before the blocking of the cave, together with pottery of the twelfth century, led to the assumption that the cave's blocking, and therefore also the quarrying of the shaft and tunnel, were executed in the middle of, rather than before, the twelfth century. Lamon rightly assumed that the Gallery's function was to make the spring accessible before the quarrying of the tunnel and shaft. Hence, in his opinion, the Gallery was made in the first half of the twelfth century. Having ascertained that the offsets/insets wall was not Solomonic, there was no further reason to assume that the Gallery preceded Solomon. On the contrary, the Gallery's stratigraphical position was identical with that of the structures of Stratum IVB, the palaces, the city-wall, etc. Moreover, the manner of its construction and stone-dressing matched to a surprising extent the construction methods of that stratum. Since the exact dating of the Gallery is of paramount importance for the dating of the water-system, we decided, in 1967, to check the assumption of the new date through excavation. The method was simple enough: since it was obvious that the Gallery had been dug into previous strata, we selected a square adjacent to the Gallery on its south, and began to excavate it thoroughly. Our purpose was to determine the uppermost strata damaged by the Gallery's quarrying.

This trial-dig (Fig. 43) was very successful indeed. We succeeded in descending to Stratum VIIA, and discovered the whole array of strata familiar from other areas, and even in enriching the pottery repertoire of some. It became definitely clear that the Gallery's quarrying damaged both Strata VIA and VB. Thus the Gallery was squeezed in, stratigraphically speaking, both when counting from top to bottom and when counting from bottom to top: it was built in Stratum IVB. Had we needed further proof for the attribution of the Gallery to Stratum IVB, we now had it accidentally. Since the excavation of the Gallery by the first excavators of Megiddo, some of its stones had come loose, and fallen to the ground. On overturning one such stone, we noticed that it bore a mason's mark, identical with marks discovered in the Stratum IVB structures, and in secondary use in Stratum IVA.

Once the date of the Gallery was established—and following Lamon's sound relative-dating—it follows that the water-system (shaft and tunnel) are later than Solomon and must have been cut in the first half of the ninth century, in the reign of Omri's house, most probably by Ahab.[1] Before returning to Hazor and its post-Solomonic strata, it is important, I believe, to emphasize the fact that Ahab's Megiddo (as we shall see in Hazor), built on top of the Solomonic ruins, was quite different in character and plan. It was not just an administrative city, with palaces for its governors—but a well-fortified city, with stables and a water-system for times of siege: it became a typical—to use a biblical terminology—siege-city, i.e. a city capable of withstanding prolonged siege.

[1] While examining the Israelite strata, we checked an additional find of the earlier excavators, the so-called 'pedestrian approach' (*Megiddo II*, figs. 123-4). It turned out, on further excavations, to be an approach *from* the city to another water-system, apparently connected with the other spring of Megiddo discovered near the Jenin–Haifa road. For further details, see *IEJ* 17, 1967, pp. 119 ff.

XIV

AHAB'S HAZOR—STRATUM VIII

§ I. THE CITY'S PLAN AND FORTIFICATIONS

THE city of Stratum VIII is entirely different from that of Strata X–IX in layout, area, character, public buildings, and installations. It has now become a strongly fortified city, with mighty walls, strong citadel, public store-houses and, above all, a huge underground water-system, capable of sustaining the city through a long siege. The most salient contrast with the Solomonic city is the fact that the Stratum VIII city covers the whole Tell, doubling its built-up area. The main evidence for this expansion comes from the excavations in Area G,[1] at the extreme east end of the Tell (see above, Fig. 27). The oldest Iron Age stratum to have been discovered here was Stratum VIII, where a double system of fortifications was found: the main new city-wall embracing the eastern half of the Tell, and a sort of 'forward bastion' protecting the extreme eastern terrace, which included the main city-gate. The city-wall (10540–7) is solid, 3 m. thick, with offsets or insets in its outer face at unequal distances.[2] It is built of large and medium-size field-stones, and its upper portions were built of bricks. The north-east corner of the wall[3] is built of ashlar blocks with drafted margins of the typical ninth-century Israelite style found at Megiddo and Samaria. There is a considerable difference in altitude between the Stratum VIII buildings found within the wall (217·7 m.) and those found outside it (213·9 m.). This indicates that the city-wall here served also as a retaining wall of the main eastern terrace. The solid wall of Stratum VIII was traced with the help of trial soundings all along the eastern and southern sides of the Tell. Thanks to the excavations of Area M, we now know that this solid wall was built on to the corners of the previous Solomonic casemate-wall. From these corners westwards (that is, in the former Solomonic city area), the old casemate-walls were reused. In many cases, they were filled and turned into a

---

[1] For plates, see *Hazor III–IV*, pls. LXXVIII–C. The following description is partially based upon the field report prepared by Trude Dothan and I. Dunayevsky.

[2] pl. LXXXIV, 3 and below, Fig 49, on p. 183.   [3] pl. XCI, 2.

solid wall,[1] and sometimes the entrances of the casemates were blocked.[2]

Within the north-eastern corner of the wall a well-preserved two-storey house was found. The good stratification of this building (cf. Pl. XXXIVa), which had been rebuilt several times,[3] helped to establish that the solid wall was indeed built in Stratum VIII, together with the earliest phase of the building (Building 10060).[4] The strategic position of the house, as well as its dimensions (8 × 8 m.), indicate perhaps that it was the house of a commander.

The forward bastion (below, Fig. 53 on p. 191)

The narrow eastern terrace, which lies further to the east and below the solid wall of Stratum VIII, was further protected by a series of fortifications. The northern part of this system was excavated in its entirety, while only parts of its eastern side were uncovered. Two towers protected the northern edge: one on its western side (10014)[5] and the other on its north-eastern corner (10029).[6] The screen-wall between the towers, as well as that in the eastern edge, is a double wall, or a casemate-wall. The casemates are different from those of Stratum X: they have no entrances, the space between the walls varies from section to section, as does the size of the casemates themselves. They may be looked upon as constructional casemates rather than casemates in the true sense of the word. The upper parts of the wall were built of bricks, remains of which were found all over the area. Tower 10029 is right-angled in shape, and its 'arms' protrude, offsets-wise, out of the walls to about 1·3/1·1 m. The tower is built on the earlier MB II stone glacis, which serves as its foundation.[7] A well-built drainage-channel[8] (10507) is built through the tower and terminates with a basalt outlet, made of Bronze Age pieces in secondary use.[9] Tower 10014 protrudes nearly in its entirety out of the wall, to the north. Its main function, it appears, was to protect the postern-gate which lies east of it. The tower's stone foundation is rectangular (10 × 8 m.), while the brick upper structure (preserved to a height of 1·2 m.), is rounded in its north-eastern and north-western corners.[10] East of the tower there was a small gate

---

[1] For example in Area B, *Hazor III–IV*, pls. XXIX, 2; XLI, 1–2.
[2] Ibid., pls. XL, 3–4; XLII, 1.   [3] Ibid., pls. LXXXI–LXXXIII.
[4] Ibid., pl. LXXXI, 1.   [5] pls. LXXXVIII, 2; LXXXIX, 3–4; XC, 1.
[6] pl. XCIII, 2.   [7] pl. XCV, 1.
[8] pl. XCIII, 2–4.   [9] pl. XCIV, 1.
[10] pl. LXXXVIII, 2.

(10067), its jambs as well as its inner faces built of well-dressed ashlar, typical of the Israelite ninth century.[1] This gate (or postern: 1·5 m. wide) was obviously not the main entrance to the city. It must have been a 'service entrance' to the 'forward bastion'. The nature of the buildings in the later period (a great silo and store-rooms, see below) indicates perhaps that also in Stratum VIII the bastion was self-maintained in certain aspects. Technically, the 'forward bastion' was built after the solid wall of Stratum VIII, but it seems to us—based on soundings near the foundations—that it was during the Stratum VIII period.

§ 2. THE PILLARED BUILDING (AREA A)

The central part of the city (Area A) was dominated by a large public structure (Pl. XXVI*b*), characterized by two rows of monolithic pillars (Fig. 44).[2] The northern row of nine pillars was uncovered by Garstang.[3] Of the southern row, six pillars were found *in situ*, as well as a fragment of a fallen pillar. Another fragment of a pillar was found in an Arab building in the same area. Based on the number of shelves between the pillars, we can assume the number of pillars in the southern row to have been ten. The pillars were square and roughly dressed; their average height was 2 m. Only one, the second from the east in the northern row, was perforated by a round hole. The pillars were sunk about 0·5 m. under the floor, and the burnt layer of Stratum IX ran under them. Between the pillars were shelves (or cells) built of two rows of rubble-stones. Inside the shelves, storage-jars and kraters were found. On the floor a single-handled bowl was found, of the so-called 'grain-cups' type. The two rows of pillars stand in the middle of a large rectangular hall (20·7 × 13·5 m.) stretching from west to east, with only one entrance in its north-western corner. To the north of the pillared hall, two long halls were found (Pl. XXVII*a*), joined by an opening on the western side. Both halls are paved and in several places the paving seems to have sunk in accordance with the plan of the earlier buildings under the pavement (Pl. XXVII *b*).[4] The entrance to both halls was from a single opening in the west, next to the entrance of the pillared hall. There is thus no direct connection between the two elements, but they are structurally joined and a corridor or narrow alley runs between them, showing that they are two wings of the same building.

[1] pl. XCII.

[2] For a detailed description of the pillared building, see *Hazor I*, pp. 11 ff.; pls. III–IX and plan on pl. CLXXII; *Hazor II*, pp. 6 ff.; pls. IV–V, and plan on pl. CC

[3] See above, Chapter III, § 1.   [4] See above, Chapter XII, § 1.

Garstang thought that the pillars belonged to a stable, but our excavations found no evidence for that. On the contrary, the nature of the vessels found in the building rather indicates that the building served as a store-house. The well-paved northern halls and their narrow plan suggest perhaps that they were used to store grain in bags or similar containers. The store-house

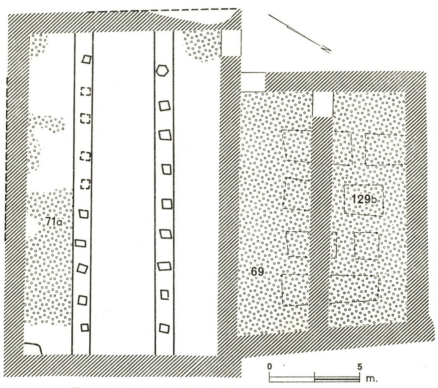

FIG. 44. Area A. The pillared building of Stratum VIII.

theory is strengthened by the fact that the whole area around the building was used for storing too. Thus the casemates of the old Solomonic wall (now out of use as a defensive wall) were still being used for storing. This is evidenced by the large quantity of pottery found in them, including many storage-jars. Similar structures (sometimes with and sometimes without pillars) were found at Beth-Shemesh,[1] Tell Abu Hawâm,[2] and recently in Beer-Sheva,[3] Tell es-Sa'idiyeh,[4] and other places. Nevertheless, it seems that the Hazor building was the biggest of its kind yet found. Two phases were detected in the building. About 0·4 m. above the original floor of the pillared hall and

---

[1] *Ain Shems V*, pp. 68 ff.   [2] *QDAP*, 4, 1934, pl. IV.
[3] *IEJ* 19, 1969, p. 246.   [4] *The Glueck Festschrift*, p. 272.

the two adjacent paved halls another floor was discovered. The top floor was ascribed by us to Stratum VII. In this stratum the pillared building was in use, more or less as in the previous Stratum VIII. But greater changes were detected in the vicinity of the building. Most of the casemates went completely out of use, and in many parts around the pillared building ordinary dwelling-houses appear to be the rule. A row of workshop-like rooms was built here too. The general impression was that the area lost some of its public character and became a residential quarter. Stratum VII was utterly destroyed by fire, perhaps by the Aramaeans at the end of the ninth century. The character of the following city, Stratum VI, was completely different in nature. Four fragmentary Hebrew inscriptions, on jars, were found in Stratum VIII. Although not much can be read in them, they are highly valuable from a palaeographic point of view because of their early date.[1]

§ 3. THE CITADEL (AREA B)

The whole of the western tip of the Tell was occupied by a large citadel or fort, with its ancillary buildings (Pl. XXVIII*a*).[2] This citadel, first built in Stratum VIII, was reused with minor changes until the fall of Hazor in VA. It is a rectangular building (25 × 21·5 m.) of symmetrical plan (Fig. 45) with its central wall (3551) as an axis running from west to east. However, the arrangement of the inside doorways divides it, as it were, into two uneven parts: a closed block in the south-west corner, with only the doorway between Room 3136 and Hall 3092 leading into it. The second part is a row of interconnected rooms, north and east of the above block. All the outside walls of the citadel and three of the main inner walls are 2–1·9 m. thick. Most of the rest are 1·4 m. thick; all the walls are constructed with large, well-laid stones on both faces of the wall, with a filling of stones and earth within. The four corners of the citadel and the door-jambs are of ashlar. There is proof that all the citadel walls were plastered inside and outside. All the doorways are made at wall-ends and have only one built door-jamb. The door-sills are generally raised in comparison with the floor-levels in the rooms. These sills are peculiar in that the door-jambs, like the walls, go down below floor level. The space left in each doorway up to sill- and threshold-level, was filled in only after all the citadel

---

[1] See *Hazor II*, pp. 70 ff., pls. CLXIX–CLXX.

[2] For a detailed description of the citadel and the other buildings, see *Hazor II*, pp. 43 ff.; for further plates see *Hazor III–IV*, pls. XLIV–LIII.

walls had been built. The structure as discovered represents the basement of the building. The staircase discovered in the north-west corner leads to the upper floor.[1] As mentioned, some of the walls are very thick (2 m.) while the rest are thinner. If we assume that the thin walls are merely partitions dividing the basement into units, and that they did not continue up to the

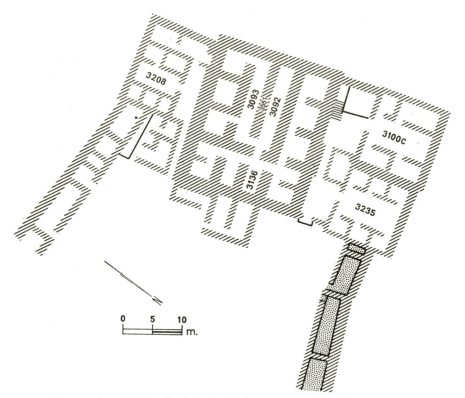

Fig. 45. Area B. The Citadel, the filled casemate-wall and the ancillary buildings—Stratum VIII.

top floor, we get a plan arranged on the principle of the 'four-roomed house'. The inner part (Halls 3092, 3093) comprised an enclosed courtyard surrounded by rows of rooms on three sides. The main entrance to the citadel was through the long corridor (or courtyard) to its north which led directly to the staircase. The corridor is flanked on the south by the northern wall of the citadel, and on its north by the twin administrative buildings[2] to be described below. The actual entrance to the corridor, from the east, was built in monumental fashion adorned by a porch consisting of pilasters crowned by Proto-Aeolic capitals (Pl.

[1] *Hazor II*, fig. 2 on p. 53.   [2] *Hazor III–IV*, pl. XLVI.

XXVIII*b*). The latter were found in front of the corridor, in secondary use, forming the two walls of an oven[1] in Stratum VII; together with them, we found the monolithic[2] lintel, 2·4 m. in length, of the monumental entrance. One of the capitals bore a relief on one side only—like most of the Proto-Aeolic capitals found elsewhere[3]—while the other bore reliefs on both sides.[4] This meant that one of the capitals crowned an attached pilaster, while the two-faced one stood upon a free-standing pillar. The remains of the bases found in the entrance[5] fit these measurements exactly. The base adjacent to the northern wall of the citadel belonged to the pilaster with the one-sided capital, while the other one in the middle of the entrance belonged to the free-standing pillar. The distance between the two bases also corresponds to the length of the monolithic lintel.

South of the entrance, in the middle of the eastern façade of the citadel, there was a square building with two rooms which looked like a tower or a redoubt. At a later stage this tower was enlarged and rebuilt with beautifully dressed ashlar.[6] On the north and south (3208) sides of the citadel, just bordering the slopes, there stood a number of buildings, all built according to a uniform plan. These belonged most probably to the governor's household and administrative staff. The two buildings (3100–3235) in the north,[7] are similar in plan: a square building (13 × 13·7 m.; 12·6 × 12·3 m.) with two rows of rooms flanking a court.[8] These buildings excel not only in symmetry, but in other features as well: all their walls are of equal thickness—about 1 m.—except the northern (outer) wall which is 1·5 m. thick. All the corners, as well as the door-jambs, are built of ashlar, similar to those of Area G. Like the citadel, here too the doorways are all placed at the end of the wall, so that each has

---

[1] Ibid., pl. XLVIII.

[2] Described erroneously as a pillar in pl. XLVIII (ibid.), 4, and in *IEJ* 9, 1959, p. 79.

[3] On another capital with reliefs on both sides, see H. G. May, *Material Remains of the Megiddo Cult*, Chicago, 1935, p. 11.

[4] *Hazor III–IV*, pls. CCCLXII–CCCLXIII.

[5] Ibid., pls. XLIV, 1; XLVI, 1; XLVII, 4.

[6] Ibid., pl. LII. Since this enlargement (Building 3188) was technically later than the main building of the citadel, we ascribed it to Stratum VII. However, since Stratum VII was a period of decline, I now think that this extension was perhaps made during a later phase of Stratum VIII. The beauty of the stone-work definitely tallies with the achievements of the builders of Stratum VIII.

[7] 3100c, 3235. *Hazor III–IV*, pl. XLVI, 1. See also *Hazor II*, plan on pl. CCIV, showing these buildings at a later stage.

[8] Very similar to the group of buildings in Samaria, adjacent to the long halls, where the famous *ostraca* were found. The only difference between the Samaria buildings and those of Hazor, is that at Samaria the buildings have one common wall, while in Hazor they are built back to back, each building with its own wall. See *Harvard Excavations at Samaria 1908–1910*, 1924, i, pp. 114–17; ii, Plan 5. Cf. also *Hazor II*, pp. 53 f.

but one door-jamb. The public character of these buildings and
their direct connection with the citadel are further manifested by
the fact that, when at a later period (VA) part of their areas had
to be sacrificed in order to make room for a defensive wall, two
additional buildings (of the 'four-roomed' type) were constructed
in front of the citadel.[1] The whole area of the citadel had no
defensive wall: the outer walls of the structures served as such.
The previous casemate-walls, now partially filled and reused,
reached the north-east and south-east corners of the complex,
and thus formed one continuous line of defence.

The whole series of Stratum VIII buildings shows a high
standard of architecture and grandeur, which is equalled only
by the contemporary buildings of Samaria and Megiddo IVA.

§ 4. THE WATER-SYSTEM (AREA L)[2]

a. General

The problem of water-supply to Israelite Hazor in times of
siege intrigued us from the start. The three soundings at
Megiddo proved the famous water-system to have been of the
ninth century, approximately the period of Hazor VIII. The
similarity—from historical and archaeological points of view—
between the two cities, indicated clearly that a similar water-
system should exist also in Hazor. The main effort of the 1968
season was dedicated to solving this problem. The only spot
where the expected vertical shaft of such a system could have
existed was the southern part of the mound (see Fig. 27), where
a large, shallow depression existed. Moreover, at the southern
foot of the mound, along Wadi Waggâs, springs abound to this
day. The experience of the excavations at Megiddo, Gibeon,
and Gezer taught us that the most difficult problem in excavating a water-system of this sort is to determine the date of its
construction; the dating of its final use is naturally easier. We
therefore decided, right from the start, to obtain a clear picture
of the plan and stratification of the structures *adjacent* to the
depression. With the aid of these data, we should then be able
to ascertain which of the strata had been cut through by the
hewers of the shaft, and which structures and strata were
contemporary with it. The proximity of the shaft to the edge of
the mound meant that a good starting-point for fixing the
stratigraphy would be the Solomonic casemate-wall, which must

---

[1] See below, Chapter XV, § 3.
[2] See *IEJ* 19, 1969, pp. 12 ff. Considerable parts of the description—with additions—are .
incorporated here.

have existed here too. A long trench of one square (5 m.) was opened, from north to south, just off the centre of the depression and tallying with the excavation-grid. After many difficulties the water-shaft was indeed found there (Figs. 46–7). At the very beginning of the work, though, it became clear that there were no proper structures in the depression up to the time of the abandonment of the mound. The whole area was filled with silt containing considerable quantities of late pottery (including Persian, Hellenistic, Byzantine, and late Arab). It appeared that, following the abandonment of the shaft and its almost complete blocking, the depression had been used as a pool to store rain-water at two main phases (most probably, Persian and Hellenistic). The centre of the depression, in the upper phase, had been crudely and lightly paved with field-stones. Furthermore, the sides of the depression were lined with a sloping terrace on the west, north, and east, while in the south the old city-wall served as additional support. A similar use of an abandoned water-shaft as a water-collection pool was found at Megiddo.[1] In the lower phase, a number of terrace-like structures, almost circular in shape and made of small field-stones, were built around the deepest point of the depression, as if meant to facilitate the drawing of the water collected there; jars could be placed in these terraces, which were found in two levels at least, one beneath the other. Considering the fact that during a rainy year these terraces could have been covered with silt, it is not necessary to conclude that these two levels indicate two proper strata, although it is, of course, possible.

b. The water-system

The original water-system was discovered beneath the two levels mentioned above (Pl. XXIX); it was clogged with the debris of the fallen supporting walls and the silt swept down from the slopes into the shaft, probably upon the destruction of Stratum V. The water-system consists of three elements: the vertical shaft, the sloping tunnel, and the entrance-structure.

1. The shaft

The shaft consists of two parts: the upper part which was cut through the strata of the Tell, and the lower which was quarried out of virgin rock (Pl. XXX). The upper part measures some 19 m. from west to east and 15 m. (on the average) from north to south. Its depth from the top of the mound is about 10 m.

---

[1] *The Megiddo Water System*, Chicago, 1935, p. 37.

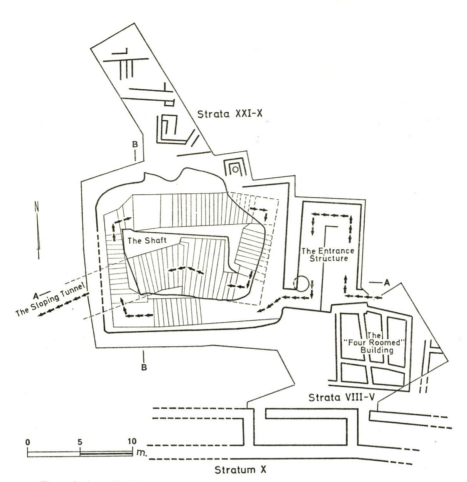

FIG. 46. Area L. The water-system and the adjacent buildings and sections.

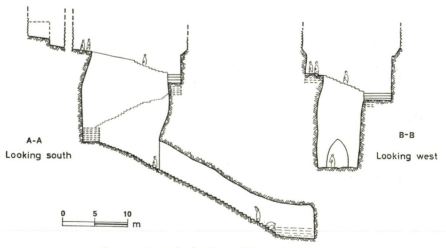

FIG. 47. Area L. Sections of the water-system.

This part was revetted by huge supporting walls, built mainly on the south and the west sides, where the virgin rock was relatively lower owing to its natural south-westward inclination. The supporting walls were well preserved up to a height of 4 m., mainly in the corners. Three of the shaft's corners are right-angled, while the north-west is rounded. The supporting walls are built on a ledge cut into the rock and in part resembling a foundation-trench. The depth of the rock-hewn part of the shaft is 19 m. on the average, and the total depth of the shaft is some 30 m. The dimensions of the hewn shaft (about 16 × 13 m. at the top) diminishes as one descends. The descent is effected by means of a rock-cut staircase, reaching, at times, 3 m. in width. The first flight of stairs is on the southern wall (11 stairs plus sloping ramp); the second is on the western wall (14 steps); the third on the northern wall (22 steps) and the fourth on the east wall (10 steps). The fifth begins again on the southern wall, but then widens and takes up the entire width of the shaft, until it merges (after further narrowing and slight change of direction) with the staircase of the tunnel. This part contains 23 steps, some reaching 6 m. in width, the width of the shaft at this stage. The exaggerated width of the stairs suggests the possibility that water was perhaps drawn by pack-animals descending and ascending simultaneously.

2. *The sloping tunnel*

The tunnel-entrance (Pl. XXX), pointed in shape and 4·5 m. in height, is at the bottom of the shaft, on the west side. The tunnel was found blocked by hundreds of fallen boulders from the revetment walls (Pl. XXXI), but its inside was found emptier as one descended. The tunnel is of the same width as the entrance, about 4 m., but it narrows slightly (to 3·2 m.) about 9 m. from the entrance, only to widen again. The end part of the tunnel—which is in fact a sort of pool, is 5 m. in width. The length of the tunnel is 25 m., and its direction is west/south-west. The tunnel descends for about 10 m., until the average water-level is reached. The end part of the tunnel—the pool (Pl. XXXIIa)—has an additional depth of about 2·2 m. The rock-cut steps (35 in number) were covered with a thick layer of plaster which protected the soft stone, while the last 8 steps, which are occasionally covered by water when the level rises, are built of basalt slabs (Pl. XXXIIb) and of broken orthostats in secondary use. The total depth of the shaft and tunnel (down to the surface of the water) is about 40 m.

The direction of the tunnel came at first as a surprise, since we expected to find it to the south in the general direction of the springs. However, the deliberate and planned position and direction of the tunnel indicate that the engineers possessed sound geological knowledge. It is obvious that they anticipated encountering the water-level—the same as that of the springs— even within the perimeter of the Tell. Cutting the tunnel directly towards the springs would have had the disadvantage of placing part of it beyond the extent of the mound. Moreover, the length of the tunnel would have had to reach some 100 m. Finally, a situation might have arisen in which the slope of the rock could have precluded cutting through it. By digging westward, on the other hand, all these obstacles were overcome.

3. *The entrance-structure*

The approach to the shaft (Pl. XXIX) was from the south-eastern corner, near the edge of the mound. The entrance-structure was carefully planned so as to minimize the length of slope from the level of the city to the top of the quarried shaft. The entrance-slope comprised two ramps—one from the south to the north and the other, after a landing, from north to south. The former (10 m. in length including the landing) was built on a deliberate fill, the top of which consisted of a crushed yellowish, chalky stone. This ramp was originally supported on the west by a revetment-wall separating it from the second ramp. On the east it was bounded by a revetment-wall which simultaneously served as the outer supporting wall of the entire approach-structure. In order to diminish the slope of the second ramp, which began on the level of the highest rock to the north, the rock here was quarried to some depth, from north to south. Thus, a vertical scarp was effected on the west side, on which the western wall of the approach-structure was then built. Later, that area too was filled with layers of crushed chalk, until the desired slope was attained. The slope of the upper ramp is 2 m., and that of the lower is 2·7 m. Access to the entrance-structure, and exit from it towards the shaft, were built of large ashlar, similar in style to that found in the citadel of Area B. In one of the doorposts, there was a large basalt orthostat in secondary use. The entrance-structure shows many signs of repair of its revetting walls. While quarrying the rock in preparation for the second ramp, the builders encountered an earlier, bottle-shaped cistern. They cut its 'neck' off and filled up the top. This fact is most important also for the determination

of the date of construction of the water-system, since a considerable quantity of intact LB vessels was found sealed off in the
cistern.

c. The date of the water-system

The dating of the final use of the water-system is determined
by the latest object discovered at its bottom. The large number
of vessels and sherds, typical of Stratum V, found in the debris
along the whole depth of the shaft, indicates that it continued
in use until Hazor was destroyed in 732 B.C. The real problem
was to determine the date of the quarrying and construction of
the water-system. From the northern part of the 5-m. trench,
it became clear that all the strata of the Bronze Age were cut by
the builders of the shaft. It was also verified that, in this particular spot, the natural rock sloped southward; because of this,
most of the buildings in all periods were terraced. In some of the
MB structures, drainage-channels were found descending
towards the southern side of the mound. A similar phenomenon
was discovered in the structures of the LB, below the entrance-
structure. One may, perhaps, assume that the slope was exploited
in the periods prior to the construction of the water-system, as a
convenient passage towards the many springs at the foot of the
mound. It is even possible that a 'water-gate' existed here,
through which the drainage-channels passed out of the city.

The decisive point in answer to the question of the absolute
date of the water-system was found in the southern section of
the trench, between the casemate-wall (Pl. XXIX) and the top
of the built shaft. It became clear that the uppermost layer cut
by the builders of the shaft belonged to Stratum X. Here we
found a building of Stratum X (immediately below it we
discovered installations of Strata XII–XI, as well as of the LB II–
III strata, with an intact vessel) of which the northern part was
cut. The plan and orientation of the building indicated that the
cutting did not result from collapse after the system had been
abandoned, but rather from the actual digging of the shaft.
This established that the earliest date to which the water-shaft
could be ascribed was post-Solomonic. One can, therefore,
relate it to Stratum VIII, the period in which the entire mound
was rebuilt, refortified, and turned into a city for siege. Confir-
mation of this conclusion was gleaned also from the dressing of
the ashlar of the entrance-structure and from the fact that a
'four-roomed' building, found near the entrance, originated in
Stratum VIII.

The discovery of this enormous water-system and its dating in the first half of the ninth century B.C. evoke a picture similar to that emerging from the redating of the Megiddo water-system. One can assume that from the beginning of the ninth century B.C., when the Aramaean and Assyrian menace to Israel and the neighbouring countries became apparent, defensive measures generally increased, and fortifications in particular were strengthened[1] to withstand a long siege.[2]

---

[1] This period witnessed the substitution of casemate-walls in city defences (but not in isolated forts or the acropoli of cities) by more solid walls. Cf. Y. Yadin, *The Art of Warfare in Biblical Lands*, London, 1963, pp. 289 f.

[2] On the date of the Gezer water-tunnel, see my note in *BA* 32, 1969, p. 70, and William G. Dever's reply, ibid., pp. 71 ff. On the possible interpretation of certain passages in the Mesha inscription in the light of the water-shaft discoveries, see my remark in *IEJ* 19, 1969. p. 18.

XV

THE LATER PERIODS

§ I. STRATUM VI (JEROBOAM II)

a. Area A

THE destruction of Stratum VII in Area A had been total and the pillared building was not reconstructed (Fig. 48). In fact, new blocks of houses were built on its debris, changing the nature of the area from public to residential. While the northern row of pillars remained untouched and served to support the roof of a newly erected court, the southern row had either been uprooted or its pillars were embedded in the floors and walls of the new structures. Instead of the casemates, which were still partially used as store-rooms in Stratum VII, the area is now covered with small rooms, some on the ruined casemates, some to their east, and some attached to the new building and facing east towards an alley. They look like a row of shops and workshops. The buildings themselves are amongst the nicest found so far in the Israelite periods, and testify to the prosperity of the citizens of Hazor. This fact is further corroborated by the objects found in the houses, which includes fine ivory vessels. Of the several houses discovered in Area A, two in particular merit special description.

1. Building 2a[1]

Building 2a (Pl. XXXIIIa), located south-west of the previous pillared building, is the most beautifully planned and preserved building among the Israelite structures at Hazor. In fact, it represents the finest example of the Israelite 'corner-court pillared house' of that period ever found in Palestine. The house consists of a large (9 × 8 m.) court (81a) and a series of rooms on its western and northern sides. The eastern part of the court was covered by a roof supported by six well-dressed square stone pillars. Three of these were found still *in situ*. The floors of both the uncovered and covered parts were made of well-placed cobble and flat stones. The entrance to the court (and the house) was from the south. It is located in the middle

---

[1] Shown on the plan of *Hazor II*, pl. CCII, but not described there, since its excavation terminated in the 1957 season. For plates, see *Hazor III–IV*, pls. XXIV–XXVII.

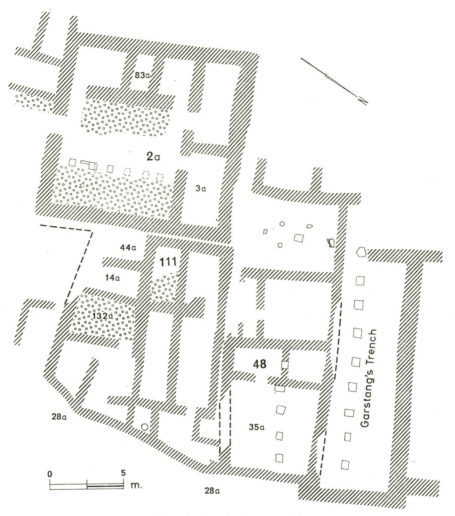

FIG. 48. Area A. Stratum VI.

of the south façade of the building and built with ashlar jambs.[1]
South of the entrance, remains of stairs were visible, connected
to a series of rooms. It is possible that through these rooms one
could reach the roof or second floor of the building. The two
northern rooms are elongated, and their long side faces the
courtyard, from which they were entered. There are signs that
during the period of Stratum VI, alterations were made in some
parts of the building. Thus, the entrance to Room 3a was
blocked, and several installations were added to it and to the
nearby court. These included a big oven and a stone with a
circular crevice.[2] In the room proper, a well-plastered basin, or

[1] pl. XXV, 5.　　　　[2] pl. XXVI, 1, Locus 188.

pool, was found and its whole floor was covered with fine plaster.[1]
All this indicates that at a certain time, part of the house was
turned into a workshop or industry of unclear nature. Of the
three rooms in the west, the small central room (83a) had no
entrance but an abundance of vessels, including many storage-
jars.[2] The room seems to have served as a store-room and it is
possible that the entrance to it was from a higher hatch, which
is not preserved. The house was severely damaged by an earthquake; all the walls and pillars were tilted southwards. In all
the rooms, as well as in the western part of the court, huge
blocks of ceiling plaster were found[3] sealed off by the floors of
Stratum V, which were built 1·5 m. above the floors of Stratum
VI.[4] The reason for this is that, although the walls of Stratum VI
were still standing after the earthquake, they were so tilted that
only their tops could be used, and even those only as a base for
the new foundations. The earthquake which destroyed Stratum
VI seems to be the one referred to in the Bible, which occurred
during the reign of King Uzziah (c. 760 B.C.).[5]

2. Building 14a—The house of Makhbiram[6]

This building was nicknamed by us 'The house of Makhbiram', after an inscription: 'belonging to Makhbiram' (Pl.
XXXVe)[7] incised on a storage-jar found in it. The house, which
is partially a restored Stratum VII house, is squeezed between
two houses, and had a narrow façade with shops overlooking
the alley (28a on the plan). Behind the shops, there was a paved
yard (132a) which led to the house's only two rooms, built one
behind the other. The assemblage of vessels and objects in the
various parts of the rooms indicates their functions. In the yard
we found cooking-pots, a basin, a basalt bowl, and six basalt
millstones: four bottom and two top ones. Obviously the daily
preparatory cooking was done in the yard. The richest collection
of finds was in the two rooms of the house itself, where most of
the household ware and family utensils were found. Opposite
the doorway, in the outer (eastern-14a) room, we found an oven
made of the upper part of an upturned storage-jar encircled by
small stones. This same room had deep bowls, kraters, juglets, a
decanter, a pilgrim-flask, a stand, and a lamp, and in its corners
many storage-jars, some slender and small for liquids, and some

---

[1] pl. XXVII, 1.   [2] pls. XXVI, 2; CLXXXI–CLXXXVIII.
[3] pls. XXV, 4; XXVII, 1.   [4] pl. XXVI, 4.
[5] See above, Chapter IX, § 2.   [6] Hazor II, pp. 20 ff.; plan on pl. CCII.
[7] For another inscription found in the same house, see Pl. XXXV f; Hazor II, p. 73,
inscription 6.

ovoid; one of these bore the inscription mentioned above. This
room seems to have served as the main living-room. The innermost room (44a) must have been the bedroom. Although here,
too, one pithos, two storage-jars, and two cooking-pots were
found, the main find of the house—an ivory cosmetic spoon—
lay in a heap by the doorway together with three juglets and
some iron tools. The ivory cosmetic spoon,[1] although it could,
generally speaking, fall within a certain well-known category,[2]
is nevertheless an unusual piece without exact known parallels.
The spoon (Pl. XXXVI*b*) is divided into handle and bowl,
taking up three-quarters and one-quarter, respectively, of its
total length. The decoration of the handle consists of inverted
palmettes, curving upwards. This type of palmette is known from
the Samaria, Arslan-Tash, and Nimrud ivories. The back of the
bowl is carved in the shape of a woman's head; a dove on each
side of the bowl appears to be caught up in the woman's locks.
The spoon must have been a costly object and, although it is
inferior in workmanship to some of the ivories known from
Samaria, Arslan-Tash, and Nimrud, it is one of the few of its
kind to be found, not in palaces, but in a private house, in this
case that of a relatively flourishing merchant at Hazor. That
this artistic object was not unique in Hazor at that period is
attested by a carved bone handle (Pl. XXXVI*a*), probably of a
mirror, which belonged to Mrs. Makhbiram's neighbour and
was found in the courtyard (35a) of House 48, 8 m. to the north.[3]
The relief on its convex side shows a creature with four extended
wings, two on each side; the hands are outstretched sideways to
grasp the open volutes of a 'tree of life', carved on the flat side
of the bone. In several aspects it resembles a similar object found
at Nimrud in the south-east palace, which is dated by Barnett[4]
between the late ninth and late eighth centuries, a period
exactly appropriate to our find.

b. Area G

The prosperity and building-activities of the Stratum VI city
are well manifested, too, in Area G.[5] Three of the more important structures, in addition, of course, to the Stratum VIII city-
wall which continued to be used, merit description.

[1] *Hazor II*, pls. CLXVII–CLXVIII.   [2] Ibid., p. 35.
[3] *Hazor I*, pls. CL–CLI.
[4] Richard D. Barnett, *A Catalogue of the Nimrud Ivories*, London, 1957, p. 52, pls. XLVI–
XLVII.
[5] For plates of Stratum VI, see *Hazor III–IV*, pls. LXXXII; LXXV; LXXVII, 1.

1. *Building 10037c*

This building (Fig. 49) is built over the ruins of the Strata VIII–VII house (Pl. XXXIV*a*), in the north-east corner of the wall (10540–7). In this phase the house by far surpasses its predecessors in its architectural elements. A part of the house is

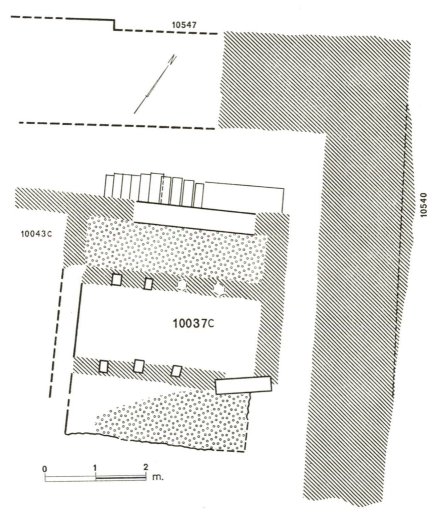

FIG. 49. Area G. Building 10037c of Stratum VI.

now divided by two rows of pillars into three units (not unlike Stratum VIII) of which the northern and the southern have paved cobble-floors. The pillars (four in each row) are monoliths and reach 1·4 m. in height. Their size and square shape resemble closely those of Building 2a in Area A. West of these three long units there was a wide north-to-south room (10043c), which we excavated only partially. This house obviously belonged to the classical 'four-roomed house' type. Along the northern wall of the house there was a flight of well-dressed stone steps, of which ten were still found *in situ*.

It can be calculated that the whole flight originally consisted of sixteen steps. Since the height of each step was 15 cm., one may assume[1] that the total height of the room (the height of the stairs minus the thickness of the ceiling) was about 1·6 m.— which also tallies with the height of the pillars plus the horizontal columns. This is a rather low room, and it may therefore be assumed that the lower floor was used by cattle, while the actual living-rooms were on the second floor, which was built of bricks.

2. *Storehouse 10030c*

In the north-eastern corner of the 'forward bastion', there was a structure consisting mainly of two long (12 m.) yet narrow (1·6–1·8 m.) rooms. The plan of this structure differs basically from all the other private houses and resembles that of a store-house. Its position in the 'forward bastion' suggests that it served that part of the fortifications.

3. *Silo 10034*

It seems that the centre of the storage-structures (which in Strata VIII–VII was in Area A) was at that time moved to Area G. In addition to that particular storage-structure, most of the centre of Area G was now occupied by a huge rectangular (12 by at least 12 m.) silo, 3–4 m. deep. The silo was dug in the ground and its walls were revetted by small and medium-sized field-stones. The total capacity of this silo was about 400 cu. m., and it was therefore a public silo, like its contemporary in Megiddo III. It was only partially excavated.

c. *Area B*

The citadel in Area B continued to be in use, although much of the grandeur of Stratum VIII was by now gone. The monumental entrance with its Proto-Aeolic capitals, reused as an oven in Stratum VII, had not been restored and the capitals remained buried below the floor of the open area in front of the citadel, and no effort was made to retrieve them. While the twin buildings in the north were restored, the courtyard, or corridor, between them and the citadel was reduced in size.

---

[1] All these observations and calculations are based on the material submitted for *Hazor III–IV*, by the late I. Dunayevsky.

In its midst, several rooms or enclosures were built, in which ovens and other installations were found.

The general impression of Stratum VI was of prosperity on the one hand, and some negligence in maintenance of the few remaining, or restored, public buildings, on the other. The destruction wrought by the earthquake was quickly repaired and the next city represented by Stratum V is very similar indeed in character to that of Stratum VI.

§ 2. STRATUM V (KING PEKAH)

a. General

Stratum V—the last Israelite fortified city—was rebuilt immediately following the destruction of City VI by the earthquake, and in many areas the layout of its houses did not much differ from that of the previous stratum. Because of this similarity, and as most of this stratum has already been described in great detail in *Hazor I–II*, it will be dealt with here rather briefly. The brevity, however, should not give the false impression of a poor city. Indeed, it was as prosperous as the previous one and quite a lot of new building-activities took place. These activities were particularly noticeable in the sensitive areas (from a strategic point of view). In Areas B and G, we noticed clear reinforcements of the fortifications, which occasionally necessitated realignment of some of the buildings in the vicinity. This phase in Stratum V, was marked by us as VA, and thus the original V became VB. There can be little doubt that all these changes were effected in order to meet the looming threat of the Assyrian invasion, which ultimately brought down the city, and caused the end of Hazor as a fortified city.

b. Area A

The area preserved its residential nature, and most of the buildings of Stratum VI were restored, albeit with minor interior changes (Fig. 50).[1] The street (locus 28) on the eastern side of the quarter remained (with a raised floor of course, as was the case in the other buildings), with rows of shops and workshops flanking it on both sides. While most of the changes in the houses affected their interior, some houses were enlarged at the expense of neighbouring structures. These changes are dealt with in *Hazor I–II*. One might mention here Building 1 (111 in Stratum VI)[2] in which the effects of the final destruction by the Assyrians

---

[1] *Hazor I*, pp. 17 ff., *Hazor II*, pp. 29 ff.   [2] *Hazor I*, plan on pl. CLXXIV.

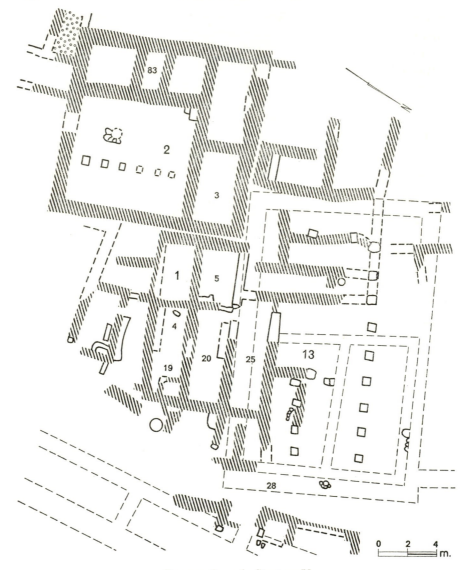

FIG. 50. Area A. Stratum V.

were most noticeable (Pl. XXXIII*b*).[1] This building is situated
between the House of Makhbiram in the south, and Building 13
(Building 48 in Stratum VI) in the north. It was of the pillared-
type with a courtyard divided by the pillars into two parts
(20, 4+19). Two of the rooms (1, 5) in the west belonged to the
original building of Stratum VI, but a new room (25) to the
north was now added to the building. In Stratum VI the area
of this room was included in Building 48, and it seems that

[1] *Hazor I,* pl. VI–VII.

Building 1 grew at the expense of the house to its north. The latter in turn expanded northwards, in the area which, in Strata VIII–VII, contained the northern row of pillars in the pillared building. In all the buildings of Stratum V, but particularly in Building 1, a thick and very conspicuous burnt layer was found.

c. Area B

1. Stratum V_B

The citadel (Fig. 51) continued to be used, and again the changes in Stratum V_B were mainly noticeable in the ancillary buildings to its north and south. These buildings, too, were basically those which were originally built in Stratum VIII and reoccupied and restored in Stratum VI.[1] Both the northern buildings (now numbered 3100b—the western; and 3067b—the eastern) underwent similar changes, obviously as a result of one general plan; many of the doorways were narrowed[2] and the original large court, between the two rows of flanking rooms, was further divided into two unequal parts by a row of pillars set in a low wall. The floor of one part of the redivided court was paved with a cobbled floor. The paved area is the narrower of the two and it may be assumed that it was roofed. Clearly the court was divided at the same time as the doorways were narrowed, for otherwise the row of pillars would have partially blocked the doorway in its original width. Of the many additions in the main corridor or alley, between the citadel and the two northern buildings, one should note in particular Structure 3103b.[3] This structure is built in the space between the stairs of the citadel, the southern wall of Building 3100b and the western wall of the corridor. It is almost square (4.5×4.6 m.) and a row of pillars divides it into two equal parts. The whole structure looks like an additional store-unit built in the most protected area of the corridor.

2. Stratum V_A[4]

As was indicated above, the characteristic features of Stratum V in Area B are the fundamental changes which were made there by the reorganization of the system of fortifications.

One should remember that the citadel in Area B and its surroundings were, until V_B, the only place in the entire city without a city-wall. This was so mainly because the area is

---

[1] *Hazor II*, pp. 44 ff   [2] Ibid., pl. XIX, 3.   [3] Ibid., plan on pl. CCIV.
[4] Ibid., plan on pl. CCV, and pp. 47 ff.

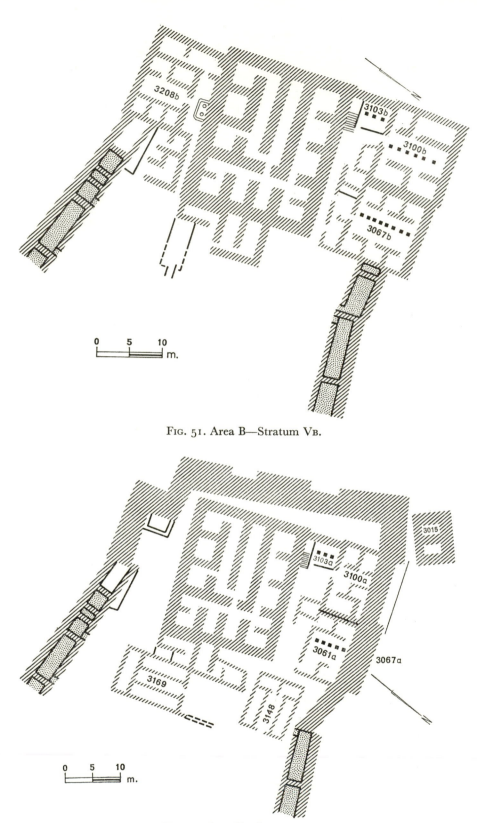

3208b

3103b

3100b

3067b

0 5 10
m.

Fig. 51. Area B—Stratum Vв.

3015

3103a

3100a

3061a

3067a

3169

3148

0 5 10
m.

Fig. 52. Area B—Stratum Vа.

naturally protected by the steep slopes as well as by the thick
walls of the citadel itself. However, the complex of the joint
buildings in the north and south (built up to the very slope)
must have been considered at a certain time as an insufficient
defensive barrier. This may explain, why, when the enemy's
threat increased, it became imperative to strengthen the fortifications in this area by an additional city-wall and tower, and
why this wall had to be made at the expense of the ancillary
buildings. The new city-wall encountered in VA is built with
alternate offsets and insets in its outer face. Some of these,
particularly in the corners, assume the character of a real
bastion, capable of providing a good base for flanking fire. The
average thickness of the wall at the offsets is 5 m. and at the
insets 3·5 m. The wall was built of stone foundations with a
brick top-work. As mentioned earlier, the building of the wall
in the north and south cut off about 40 per cent of the existing
ancillary buildings: it did not eliminate them altogether, but the
reduced area had to be reorganized. The changes effected are
clearly shown on pl. CCV in *Hazor II*. Of particular interest is a
tower (3015) erected in the most strategic spot of the area, the
north-western tip.[1] It is rectangular (10 × 7·5 m.) and consists
of two chambers. The thickness of the walls varies from 1·5 m.
on the side facing the city, to 2·25 m. on the other, more
exposed, sides. The purpose of the tower and its isolated position
may perhaps be explained by the topographical features of this
corner of the Tell: the bluff was too narrow for the city-wall to
be built to the limit of its slope, but owing to the strategic
importance of its position, dominating both the western and
northern approaches, the building of a tower at this point was
imperative.

Another interesting feature, which is a direct outcome of the
changes introduced in VA, is the building of two new structures,
east of the citadel.[2] Both of these buildings are of the 'four-
roomed' type. One (3148) is built a few metres east of the main
entrance to the citadel and its own entrance was in the east.
It measures 10 m. from east to west and nine from north to south.
The three long units are separated by rows of pillars built into
low walls, and the fourth unit is further divided into two rooms.
The other building (3169) is similar and is built in front of the
south-east corner of the citadel, with its entrance in the north.
It measures 13 m. from north to south and 9 m. from west to

---

[1] *Hazor I*, pp. 33 ff.
[2] See the air photograph in *Hazor III–IV*, pls. XXXI–XXXII.

east. Its fourth unit (in the south) is undivided and consists of a rectangle, 7·5 × 2 m. (inner measurements). It is almost certain that these two buildings were erected in order to offset the considerable loss of area in the northern and southern buildings caused by the building of the city-wall. The whole area of the citadel and the adjacent buildings was covered with a very thick layer of ashes, testimony to the terrible conflagration which destroyed Hazor Va in 732 B.C.

d. Area G

Area G, too, was reconstructed (Fig. 53) after the destruction of Stratum VI[1] and its buildings, generally speaking, follow the plans of the previous stratum with raised floors and minor changes. Building 10037b was reconstructed, but one of its fallen pillars was left as it was, and covered by a stone wall instead. The two most conspicuous remains of the last phase, Stratum Va, were the postern-gate (10067b) and the big silo. The gate was cunningly blocked and camouflaged.[2] The outer face of the blockage (Pl. XXXIVb) was stone-built, while the inner face was brick (Pl. XXXIVc). This must have been done in the face of the Assyrian threat, and it could be ascribed to Stratum Va also on stratigraphical grounds.

The bottom of Silo 10034[3] was completely covered with a very thick layer of ash (some of it very fine) indicating that the town was taken when considerable amounts of grain were still in the silo. As mentioned above, the date of the destruction of Stratum Va can be determined with the help of 2 Kings 15: 29, as 732 B.C. The signs of the terrible destruction manifested in all the excavated areas were still 'fresh' when uncovered, and the next occupants did not trouble to clear the debris.[4]

§ 3. STRATUM IV (STILL ISRAELITE)

The next phase in Hazor's history is evidenced by very poor structures, built above the ruined citadel or on top of the city-

---

[1] See *Hazor III–IV*, pls. LXXXII, 2 ff.   [2] Ibid., pl. XCII.   [3] pl. LXXXV, 2.
[4] Of the objects found in the debris of Stratum V, two, in particular, merit mention, both from Area B. One (*Hazor I*, pl. CLV) is a finely carved ivory pyxis, similar in style to objects found in the North-West palace at Nimrud (Barnett, *The Nimrud Ivories*, pls. XVI–XLI). The motif contains a 'cherub' and a kneeling figure flanking a 'tree of life' (for a detailed discussion of the pyxis, see *Hazor I*, pp. 41 ff.). The other is an elegantly scratched (after firing) inscription (Pl. XXXV d) on the shoulder of an ovoid store-jar, which was found in the debris of Stratum Va (*Hazor II*, pls. CLXXI; CLXXII;). The first word is clearly *lpqḥ*, i.e. 'belonging to Peqah'. The second seems to me to be *smdr*, which could indicate the contents of the jar: wine made of tender grapes (see ibid., p. 73 f., for a detailed treatment of this inscription, and for the opinions of Aharoni and Amiran who would like to read the second word *smrh*, a hitherto unknown name).

wall. The pottery associated with these structures[1] is for all
practical purposes, identical with that of V, and one can assume
that only a short period had lapsed between the two. In Area B,[2]
fragments of walls were found above the debris of the citadel,
and south of it, above the buildings of VA. In the north, however,
the buildings of VA, with minor changes, were still used. Here
and there additions and floor-raising indicate some changes
effected during Stratum IV.[3]

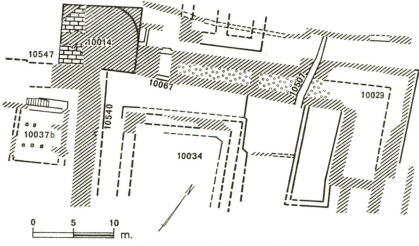

FIG. 53. Area G—Stratum V.

In Area A, a few walls, entirely different in layout from their
predecessors—were found above the debris of Stratum V. Not
much could be learnt from them, except that the settlement of
Stratum IV had occupied this area, too.[4] The most conspicuous
remains were found in Area G.[5] Here several buildings were
found actually constructed above the city's fortifications, thus
indicating that this settlement was bereft, not only of a citadel,
but of fortifications as well. We may therefore assume that
Stratum IV represents a short-lived effort by the Israelite
inhabitants to renew the settlement destroyed by Tiglath-
Pileser III.

§ 4. STRATUM III (ASSYRIAN)

The remains of Stratum III were found in Area B only
(Fig. 54);[6] in fact, the only structure belonging to this period is

---

[1] *Hazor II*, pp. 59 f; *Hazor III–IV*, pls. CCLIV–CCLVI.
[2] *Hazor II*, plan on pl. CCVI.   [3] Ibid., p. 58.
[4] *Hazor I*, plan on pl. CLXXV.   [5] *Hazor III–IV*, pls. XCVII–XCVIII.
[6] For a detailed discussion of this stratum, see *Hazor I*, pp. 45 ff. and plan on pl. CLXXVII.
For additional structures as well as a schematic plan of the citadel, see *Hazor II*, fig. 3, p. 62.
The following description is a summary of the treatment of the above.

a large citadel occupying the whole of the western bluff. Since
the building was of a clearly military nature and belonged to
the period between, say, *c.* 700 B.C., and 400 B.C. (see below), it
may be assumed that the citadel constituted an isolated fort
serving the military administration of the occupational forces:
Assyrians or Babylonians. The building is distinctly separated
from the previous strata and was planned and built at one go.

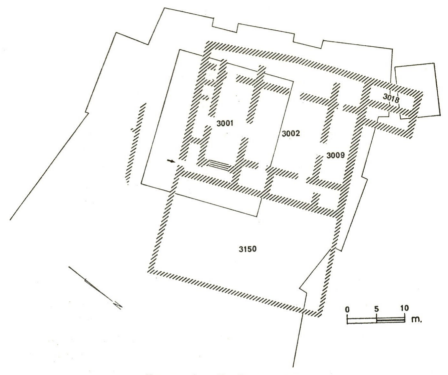

FIG. 54. Area B—Stratum III.

It is rectangular (30 m. from north to south and 25 m. from west
to east) with a dominating central (3002) square courtyard
(12 × 12 m.), enclosed on three sides by a row of rooms and halls
and on the fourth, south, side by a double row of rooms. In the
west, north, and south the rooms (or halls) were long, corresponding in length to the sides of the court; each corner of the
court had a small, almost square room. Adjacent to the north-
west corner we found the remains of a tower (3018) consisting
of two long rooms. Although the tower is partially built above
the tower of Stratum V, there is in fact no relation between the
two, either in plan or in orientation. Nevertheless, both were
erected for the same tactical reason. East of the citadel, there

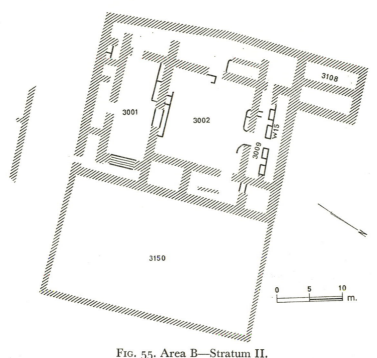

FIG. 55. Area B—Stratum II.

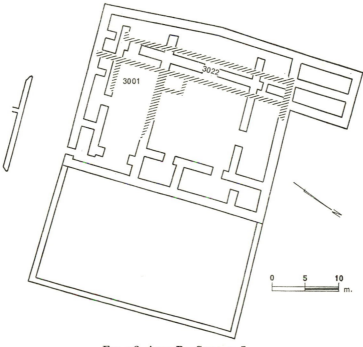

FIG. 56. Area B—Stratum I.

was a large enclosed open court (3150) which was nearly the size of the citadel itself.[1] The walls were composed of two faces of undressed stones, and the space between them was filled with field-stones of various sizes, some very large. Mud-clay filled the joints between the stones and courses, and amounted to at least one-third of the material used in the wall. All the door-jambs were built of large, smoothly tooled ashlar. The entrances were well planned; those leading from the courtyard to the rooms were 2·5–2·1 m. wide and all others were only 1·4–1·1 m. wide. The entrances to the southern rooms (store-rooms) were very narrow, just 70 cm. The main entrance to the citadel was through a narrow door in the south-east corner of the building, leading through a very wide (3·5 m.) entrance to the southern long hall (3001) and then into the main central court. Since the building was reoccupied, with alterations, in the subsequent period, no objects of the original citadel were found on the floors, and therefore it is very difficult to date the building accurately. From some of the pottery found in the original drainage, and other material in the fill, it can be attested that the building is definitely pre-Persian, the date of the following stratum. Thus it was built between c. 700 (the date of Stratum IV) and 400 (the date of Stratum II), with the probabilities nearly even between the seventh and sixth centuries. In other words, it may have been built either by the Assyrian or the Babylonian forces. The similarity of this building's plan to that of the Assyrian buildings at Megiddo III (Buildings 1052, 1369), may perhaps tilt the scale in favour of the first alternative.

§ 5. STRATUM II (PERSIAN)

a. Area B

The remains of this stratum were found in Areas A, B, and G, as well as in the vicinity of Hazor, within the grounds of Kibbutz Ayeleth Ha-Shahar. The most important of the remains were found in Area B, where the citadel of Stratum III was reused (Fig. 55)[2] as a whole with some alterations and additions made by the occupants of Stratum II to the building's interior, to suit their needs. The previous building was thoroughly cleaned out by the new settlers and the loci of Stratum II lay directly on the original floors. Only in very few places, such as under the walls added at that time, and under the newly built

---

[1] See fig. 3, on p. 62 in *Hazor II*.
[2] *Hazor I*, pp. 54 ff., and the plan on pl. CLXXVII.

enclosures, did a thin accumulation belonging to Stratum III remain.

The changes introduced into the building were:

1. The partition of the building into two blocks or residential units. This was effected by blocking off the southern entrance (from hall 3001) to the main central court (3002).

2. The reduction in size of some of the entrances or the blocking off of others.[1]

3. The conversion of some of the large halls around the central court into smaller units, by means of partition walls.

4. The addition of small chambers and enclosures.

Amongst the changes, one should mention in particular those which took place in the northern long hall (3009). Here a kind of wall (W 15) with 'enclosures' and niches was added, dividing the hall lengthwise into two long narrow rooms with a passage in between. The wall consisted of five 'enclosures' with three niches between them. In every niche a few vessels—either juglets, loom-weights, or broken jars—were found. It seems that the building lost much of its military nature; it looks more like a large farmhouse. On the other hand, the possibility cannot be excluded that this building may now have been occupied by soldiers with their families.

The date of the Stratum II—the Persian period—was ascertained with the help of the numerous vessels found in the building and the date of the final destruction of the building was fixed by a silver coin, a silver stater of Tyre, 400–332 B.C.[2] In addition, two Attic lamps, found in the building, are to be dated in the first half of the fourth century B.C. and in the second half of the same century, respectively.[3]

b. Area A

Most of Area A was occupied at this period by a large cemetery.[4] The vessels, including Attic Ware found in the

[1] Marked by hatched lines in the plan referred to in the previous note.

[2] For a similar coin found in Area A, see below.

[3] The locus (3043) in which one of the lamps was found is rather strange; it is a crack in the jamb of the north wall entrance. There can be no doubt that the lamp (and the juglet found there) belonged to Stratum II (see *Hazor I*, p. 55 for detailed discussion). D. Barag, in a most interesting article ('The effects of the Tennes Rebellion on Palestine', *BASOR* 183, 1966, pp. 6 ff.), suggests that Stratum II in Hazor (together with many other remains of the Persian period) was destroyed as a result of a rebellion against Persia, which took place around 340 B.C. Because of that he suggests (ibid., n. 16) that the finds from locus 3043 should be attributed to Stratum I. The similarity between the finds made here and those in the other areas, precludes, in my opinion, such a conclusion. On the other hand, the dating of the objects could fall within the dates suggested by D. Barag for the destruction of Stratum II.

[4] *Hazor II*, p. 32; *Hazor III–IV*, pl. XXVII, 5–7; CXC–CXCI. Many more graves containing fine glass and metal vessels were found here in 1968.

graves, were identical with those found in Area B and Area G (see below). Here, too, a coin was found of exactly the same type as that found in Area B.[1]

c. Area G[2]

The whole of the excavated area of Area G was covered with buildings of Stratum II. This fact showed that the settlement of Stratum II was not confined to the fort in Area B (with its cemetery in Area A), as we concluded after the first season, but rather expanded to the whole area of the mound. The remains belong to at least five large dwellings which look like farmhouses. The main area of the terrace was occupied by a large building with a court (10003)[3] and paved rooms.[4] In the courtyard, four Bronze Age orthostats were found, serving now as a base for wooden columns. Another impressive building was found to the west of the above building. One of its rooms (10006)[5] had walls 1 m. thick. In a series of rooms further to the west a considerable quantity of pottery was found.[6]

d. Ayeleth Ha-Shahar

The settlement of Stratum II, apparently consisting mainly of farmers and landlords, expanded even beyond the limits of the Tell. Remains of several buildings of this period were discovered also within the area of Kibbutz Ayeleth Ha-Shahar.[7]

§ 6. STRATUM I (HELLENISTIC)

The remains of this stratum were found only in Area B. In fact it seems that at this period there was no settlement in Hazor but for an isolated fort dominating the western tip of the mound.[8] The walls of Stratum I were visible above the surface, and were partially excavated by Garstang. But only a few walls have survived. The builders of the Stratum I fort executed considerable levelling and filling operations, and the foundations of the Stratum I building are built above the stumps of the walls of the previous building. The principal remains were of the western part of the building (Fig. 56); they consist of a long and narrow

[1] *Hazor II*, p. 32 and pl. CLXVI, 16.
[2] *Hazor III–IV*, pls. XCIX–C.   [3] Ibid., pl. XCIX, 2.
[4] pl. C, 1; Paving 10000.   [5] pl. XCIX, 1.
[6] pl. C, 3–4. For other objects found in Area G, see pl. C, 5–6. These include two sickles.
[7] *Bulletin of the Department of the Antiquities of the State of Israel* (Hebrew), 5–6, 1957, pp. 19–20 (reported by P. L. Guy). On the buildings from the Persian period at Hazor (Stratum II) and other localities in Palestine, see E. Stern, *The Material Culture of Palestine in the Persian Period*, doctoral dissertation (Hebrew), 1969, pp. 11 ff.
[8] *Hazor I*, pp. 63 ff., and plan on pl. CLXXVIII

hall (3022) in the west, and another hall (3001) running from west to east, at right angles to the long hall. It must be assumed that the fort in Stratum I was also composed of a central court-yard surrounded by halls and rooms, but it was relatively poorly built and, from the little that survives, the exact plan cannot be ascertained.

The precise dating of Stratum I is a very difficult problem. One fact is sure: it is later than the fourth-century Stratum II. The small amount of Hellenistic pottery found here indicates the general period of the stratum, the third or second centuries B.C. There may even be a connection between the existence of this fort and the passage from I Macc. 11, which mentions the plain of Hazor in the battles between Jonathan and Demetrius.[1]

[1] See above, Chapter I, § 6, a.

XVI

THE HISTORICAL AND ARCHAEOLOGICAL
DATA: CONFRONTATION

Now that all the historical and archaeological data relating to
Hazor have been presented, we can attempt a confrontation
between the two. This confrontation is based on the fact that the
historical data are absolute, while the archaeological material—
due to objective and subjective limitations—is not always as
definitive as we might have wished. On the other hand, certain
archaeological evidence is absolute by its nature, although we
lack an historical source related to the same period. Surveying
all the data which have been presented in the previous chapters,
it seems to me that it can be grouped in five categories:

(a) Absolute corroboration between the two sources.
(b) Apparent contradiction between them.
(c) Probable correlation.
(d) Correlation with sources which do not refer directly to
    Hazor.
(e) Problematic.

Under group (a) one should include those cases in which the
date of both sources is absolutely certain. This would include:
(1) Stratum XV (Lower City—Stratum 2)—LB I which still
existed in the times of Thutmosis III. (2) Stratum XIV (Lower
City—Stratum IB)—LB II, fourteenth century B.C. which
corresponds to the El-Amarna period. (3) Stratum X—the
Solomonic city (1 Kings 9: 15). (4) Stratum VA—Destruction in
732 by Tiglath-Pileser III (2 Kings 15: 29).

Group b. Strata XII–XI and Judges 4.

Group c. (1) Stratum XVII (Lower City—Stratum 4)—the
Mari Documents. (2) Stratum XIII (Lower City—Stratum IA)
—Joshua 11; Rameses II—Papyrus Anastasi I. (3) Stratum I—
1 Macc. 11: 67.

Group d. (1) Stratum VIII—Ahab. (2) Stratum VI—
destruction as the result of the earthquake in the time of King
Uzziah, c. 760 B.C. (Zechariah 14: 5; Amos 1: 4).

Group e. The Execration Texts—Strata XVII—'pre XVII'.
Other strata were dated on purely archaeological evidence.

The essence of the evidence at our disposal is summarized in the following table which also concludes our survey.[1] Nobody is more aware than the writer of how much is still lacking in our knowledge of the history of Hazor and of the possible erroneous interpretations we have given some of the facts. Yet at the same time, I believe, the table demonstrates that we are today in a much better position to grasp the problems and define them. If I have succeeded at least in so presenting the material, then the foundation for the future research and study of the history of the 'Head of all those kingdoms', has been laid.

[1] See also Appendix.

TABLE OF THE HISTORICAL AND ARCHAEOLOGICAL DATA

Stratum	Archaeological period and/or date	Historical source or period	Remarks	Upper/Lower City
XXI	EB II			Upper
XX–XIX	EB III			Upper
XVIII	MB I			Upper
'Pre XVII'	MB IIA(?)–MB IIB	(Execration Texts?)		Upper
XVII	MB IIB—18th–17th cents.	The Mari Documents	Foundation of the Lower city	Upper and Lower
XVI	MB IIC—17th–16th cents.		Destruction at end of the MB II	Upper and Lower
'Post XVI'	MB IIC transitional		Graves in the ruined city	Upper
XV	LB I—16th–15th cents.	Thutmosis III	Pottery includes Bichrome Ware; probable introduction of orthostats	Upper and Lower
XIV	LB II—14th cent.	The El-Amarna documents	Pottery includes Mycenaean IIIA. Possible destruction by Sethi I	Upper and Lower
XIII	LB III—13th cent.	Joshua 11	Pottery includes Mycenaean IIIB. Total destruction of Upper and Lower cities. Evidence of fire	Upper and Lower
XII	Iro nI—12th cent.	First Israelite settlement. Apparent contradiction with Judges 4	Semi-nomadic settlement corresponding to similar settlements in Upper Galilee	Mainly Upper
XI	Iron I—11th cent.	Pre-Solomonic	Limited settlement (with no defences) with a sanctuary	Upper
XB	Iron I—c. 950 B.C.	Solomonic city—1 Kings 9: 15	City confined to the western part of the Tell. Casemate-wall	Upper
XA	Iron I—end of 10th cent.		See Chapter XII, § 4	Upper
IXB–A	Iron II—early 9th cent.		See Chapter XII, § 4; possible destruction by Ben-Hadad, 885 B.C.	Upper
VIII	Iron II—9th cent.	Ahab	City reorganized and refortified to include the whole area of the Tell. The water-system	Upper
VII	Iron II—9th cent.		Signs of decline	Upper
†	Iron II—first half of 8th cent.	Jeroboam II.; Zech. 14: 5; Amos 1: 4	Destroyed by an earthquake	Upper
VB	Iron II—second half of 8th cent.	Menahem		Upper
VA	Destroyed 732 B.C.	2 Kings 15: 29	Reorganization of fortifications; Destruction by fire	Upper
IV	Iron II—end of 8th cent.		Unfortified small Israelite settlement. Squatters	Upper
III	Early 7th cent.	Assyrian	Mainly a citadel—Assyrian garrison(?)	Upper
II	Persian—4th cent.		Citadel; some farmhouses; graves	Upper
I	Hellenistic—3rd–2nd cents.	1 Macc. 11: 67	Isolated citadel	Upper

APPENDICES

§ 1. *The identification of Hazor with Tell el-Qedaḥ established*

While the present book was in the press, my attention was called to the existence of a cuneiform tablet said to have been found at Hazor. This provenance is borne out by its contents, which have so far been subject to a preliminary inspection only. Full publication must await intensive study of the original,[1] which it is hoped will not be too much delayed. It can, however, already be stated on very good authority that the tablet records a litigation involving real estate in Hazor ([URU] *Ha-ṣú-ra*) and another town, conducted in the presence of the king, and adjudicated by the king under penalty of a heavy fine for contesting his decision in the future. The text appears to be of (late) Old Babylonian date, with relatively few departures from standard Old Babylonian orthography and grammar.

The importance of this find to the study of the history of Hazor is clear:

(*a*) although there was hardly any doubt of the identification of Hazor with Tell el-Qedaḥ, this find clinches it decisively. Thus Hazor becomes one of the very few Biblical cities whose identification has been confirmed by written documents found on their sites (e.g. Gezer, Beth-Shean, and Arad);

(*b*) the fact that the ruler of Hazor was called 'king' in the Mari and the el-Amarna documents (cf. Chapter I, 3; 4, *b*) is again attested by this document;

(*c*) the discovery of a document with such a clear archival character, written on the spot, is—together with the ḪAR-ra = *hubullu* fragment (cf. Chapter X, 3, p. 124), as well as the clay model of the liver (cf. Chapter VII, 2, *c*, p. 82)—further proof of the existence at the court of Hazor of experienced scribes and gives grounds for hope that one day the archive of cuneiform texts of the kings of Hazor may be located.

§ 2. *New data concerning Hazor in the MB II period*

An accidental discovery made at Hazor after the manuscript of the present book had already been completed, deserves special discussion, since it has, I believe, important bearings on some of the problems discussed above,[2] i.e. the nature and date of the first MB II settlement in Hazor.

On 4 January 1971, a rock-hewn burial-cave was accidentally discovered by a team employed by the National Parks Authority in reinforcing the southern flight of the rock-cut steps of the water-system,[3] in which a crack had been observed along the shaft face. It was decided

---

[1] For various reasons this is beyond my control at the present moment.
[2] Chapters I, 2–3; VIII, 2; X, 3; XVI.   [3] See above, Chapter XIV, 4 and Fig. 46.

to bore a horizontal hole into the rock and fill it with concrete. While drilling, the workers hit a cavity at about one metre from the shaft face. The cavity, which turned out to be a rich burial cave, was subsequently excavated by the writer and Mr. Y. Shiloh. It became clear that the drilling party had hit the *back* of the cave, which had obviously just been missed by the hewers of the original shaft. The cave's original entrance was found still blocked by its slab, and the cave itself virtually free of dust and debris. About 150 vessels, mostly complete and intact, were found mainly alongside the walls. Remains of between seven and nine skeletons were found, most of them pushed to the side, the skeleton of the last burial lying intact in a crawling position.

The discovery of this extremely large collection of vessels of the 'pre XVII' phase of occupation[1] and the position and nature of the burial cave shed much light on this phase at Hazor, and therefore merit a more detailed description, before the conclusions based on the discovery are presented.

The large variety of the vessels confirms conclusively that this phase should be placed roughly within the MB IIB period, contemporary with Tell Beit Mirsim's E and Jericho's groups I–II, with some additions and modifications. None of the exclusively MB IIA pottery is represented in the cave, while considerable numbers of vessels are exclusively MB IIB. At the same time, quite a number of pots still preserve some of the MB IIA traditions. Aside from the pottery, two daggers were found of typical MB IIB, as well as a spearhead, two toggle-pins, and some beads.

The position of the cave, too, seems to confirm our earlier conclusion that at that phase the settlement was still unfortified, and the population used to bury their dead inside the settlement—even in rock-cut caves.

The rectangular chamber with its rounded corners, measures some 4·5 metres from north to south and about 3 metres from west to east. The entrance is located in the middle of the southern end, i.e. further down the southern slope of the mound. The approach to the entrance— from which three steps led into the cave—was made from the outside, through a shaft or a descending cave, which is now completely covered by later debris. The shaft, or descending cave itself, could not have been too deep, due to the slope of the natural rock face. The size of this shaft cannot be ascertained, but to judge by the size of the cave, should be about 2×2 ms. Adding to these measurements about 1 m., for the width of the actual entrance, a total of about 7–8 metres is reached for the length (from south to north) of the burial complex. From the excavations at area A,[2] we know that the 8–9 metre-thick Stratum XVII city-wall, had to exist also in the southern edge of the Tell; its most natural course would be roughly under the foundations of the Solomonic casemate-wall.

If this assumption is correct, then the entrance to the cave must have

---

[1] Chapters X, 3; XVI.   [2] Chapter IX, 2–3.

been *under* the foundations of this wall, i.e. the 'pre XVII' phase preceded the building of the MB II defences.[1] The date of the 'pre XVII' phase seems to be roughly the middle of the eighteenth century, plus 2–3 decades. This means that this phase falls within the XIIIth dynasty, and marks a transitional period, which heralds the fortified cities of the MB IIB.[2] It seems to me now most probable, that the Hazor mentioned in the Execration Texts[3] should be identified with the 'pre XVII' settlement.

These conclusions led me to re-examine the situation in the other excavated MB II sites in Palestine. This was imperative, in view of the confusing views, still current, regarding the nature of the MB IIA cities. On the one hand some scholars still claim, from time to time, that even the earthen rampart fortifications should be dated to MB IIA.[4] On the other, even K. Kenyon in her shrewd discussion of the MB IIA period[5] was forced—with much reluctance and against her better judgement—to conclude that some cities (Tell Beit Mirsim and Megiddo) were already fortified in the MB IIA.[6]

As for the claim that the earthen ramparts and *terre pisée* defences were first built in the MB IIA, only little has to be added here.[7] The results of the excavations at Tell Dan, where MB IIA and even MB IIB strata were found under the earthen rampart,[8] and the situations at Hazor, prove conclusively that at least the largest known and excavated cities of this nature were erected in the MB IIB. The other cases on which the contrary claim is based,[9] are not yet fully published and it is therefore difficult to reach an independent opinion. Nevertheless, it seems that even in these cases, MB IIA settlements existed prior to the erection of the defences.

The two sites in which huge MB IIA fortifications were allegedly discovered, are Tell Beit Mirsim and Megiddo. This is the reason for statements concerning the MB IIA, such as the following: 'Thus, it is probable that a process of building fortified cities on sites which had previously known only open villages had already begun, *particularly at strategic points on important highway junctions*'[10] [my italics—*Y.Y.*].

---

[1] Even if we are somewhat mistaken in our calculations, it is quite clear that the entrance to the cave would have been in a most awkward position in relation to the city-wall.

[2] Cf. also Miss D. Kirkbride, *apud*, *Jericho II*, London, 1965, pp. 582–3. In fact, this phase could be designated MB IIB1.

[3] See above, Chapter I, 2 and the chart in Chapter XVI.

[4] For example, most recently, J. Kaplan in the *Publications of the Tel-Aviv-Jaffa Museum of Antiquities*, 3, 1969, p. 13. Such views were rightly rejected by P. J. Parr's survey in *ZDPV* 84, 1968, pp. 22 ff. However, even Parr, although with some reservations, ascribes some of the earlier fortifications to the MB IIA.

[5] *CAH* (revised edition of Vols. i and ii), Vol. ii, Chap. III, Fasc. 48, 1966, pp. 4 ff.

[6] Ibid, pp. 30; 38. Cf. also her article in *Levant*, 1, 1969, pp. 25 ff., in which these views are further modified.   [7] See also n. 4 above.   [8] See Chapter VIII, 2.

[9] Yavne-yam (see Kaplan, op. cit., above n. 4), p. 13; *IEJ* 19, 1961, pp. 120–1; Tell Poleg, see R. Gofna, *RB*, 72, 1965, pp. 552–3; See now, idem., *Enc. of Arch. Exc. in the Holy Land*, p. 601. See further n. 2 on p. 207.

[10] B. Mazar, *IEJ* 18, 1968, p. 72. Kenyon follows the same line, but obviously with much more scepticism and caution: 'Only at Megiddo and at Tell Beit Mirsim is there as yet evidence of walled towns at this stage, and in neither case is it conclusive' (above n. 5, p. 38).

Now, Megiddo, because of its geographical position, is definitely situated on a 'strategic spot'; but what 'justification' could there be for Tell Beit Mirsim, lying as it were 'far from the madding crowd'?

Before dealing with these two apparent exceptions, it is worth while to survey, albeit briefly, the situation in some of the strategically important sites of the country:[1]

Ras el 'Ain. The situation in this highly strategic city—the classical site of the MB IIA pottery—is very instructive: The MB IIA pottery was found mainly in graves (Level II), stratigraphically, lying clearly *under* the MB IIB fortifications. Thus the MB IIA settlement was unwalled![2]

Jericho. Poor, open settlements in MB IIA; first fortified settlement in MB IIB.[3]

Schechem. An unwalled MB IIA settlement; first fortified in MB IIB.[4]

Tell el Far'ah (North). Poor, unwalled MB IIA settlement with tombs inside the city. The same situation exists in the early phase of the MB IIB (not unsimilar to Hazor's 'pre XVII'). The first fortifications— MB IIB.[5]

Gezer. Small, unwalled MB IIA settlement (oral communication by Dr. W. G. Dever—July 1971); first fortifications in later phases of MB IIB–C.[6]

Tell el 'Ajjul. In this important site, where MB IIA pottery found in the 'courtyard cemetery', is often quoted as a classic case, the situation is the same: a poor, unwalled settlement in the MB IIA and the first fortifications are of the MB IIB–C.[7]

These most important and strategic sites of Palestine demonstrate quite clearly that in MB IIA the settlements were open, with no fortifications whatsoever. To this rather impressive array one may add the results from other sites, which show either the same picture, or indicate that in the MB IIA there existed no settlement at all:

Tell Nagilah. No city in MB IIA. First settlement and fortifications— MB IIB.[8]

[1] Cf. also the survey of Kenyon (op. cit., p. 203, n. 5) and Parr (op. cit., p. 203, n. 4).

[2] J. Ory, *QDAP*, 6, 1937, pp. 99 ff; see particularly the plan in Fig. 2. This situation throws some doubt on the claim that at Tell Zeror, some 30 kms. further north on the coastal plane, the fortification system of the brick walls belong to the MB IIA (K. Ohata and M. Kokhavi, *IEJ* 16, 1966, p. 275). The last volume of the final season (*Tel Zeror III*, Tokyo, 1970, K. Ohata, ed.) sheds very little light on this question. We shall have to wait until all the pottery is published with clear indication to what was found in the fills, and the exact location of the loci. Nevertheless, the very good sections published (ibid., pl. XII) seem to show that the system of walls is *later* than the earliest activities on the site in the MB II period.

[3] See Kenyon, op. cit. (above p. 203, n. 5), p. 19.

[4] G. E. Wright, *Schechem*, N.Y., 1965, p. 63.

[5] R. de Vaux, *RB* 69, 1962, pp. 237 ff.

[6] W. G. Dever, H. D. Lance, G. E. Wright, *Gezer I*, Jerusalem, 1970, p. 42.

[7] See good analyses by Kenyon, op. cit. (above p. 203, n. 5), pp. 27 ff.

[8] See the comprehensive summary by the excavators, Ruth Amiran and A. Eytan, in the *Enc. of Arch. Exc. in the Holy Land*, pp. 589 ff.

Ta'anach. A gap in MB IIA. First fortifications in a late phase of the MB IIB–C.[1]

Beth-Zur. Practically no MB IIA. First fortified in MB IIB.[2]

Now we can return to the problems of Tell Beit Mirsim and Megiddo —the only apparent exceptions:

Tell Beit Mirsim. The cause of some of the uncertainty regarding the nature of the MB IIA cities, is undoubtedly Tell Beit Mirsim, in which Albright ascribed the huge, vertical city-wall (G) and the inner addition (F), to Strata G–F (MB IIA). A close examination, however, of the excavation plan,[3] shows quite plainly that the houses of G are virtually cut by the city-wall, and their orientation disregards the course of the wall.[4] Furthermore, I am convinced, that even the F houses are *prior* to the wall and its addition, since some of them, too, run in a different orientation, while in many others, the foundations of the city-wall are *higher* than theirs.[5] In fact, even Albright noticed the contrast between the magnitude of the defences and the 'poverty of the place at this [strata G–F—*Y.Y.*] time'.[6]

It seems that Albright's first impression was the correct one: 'Inside the city-wall we were also at first *misled* [my italics—*Y.Y.*] by the fact that E and D walls were built against the F reconstruction.'[7] One should remember, also, that the E stratum consists in fact of *three phases*, although later, for convenient reasons, one refers mainly to E1 and E2. The conclusion is, therefore, that G–F were poor, unwalled settlements, while the city's fortifications—ascribed to G–F—were first erected in the early phases of E, i.e. in the MB IIB.

Megiddo. Having seen that Tell Beit Mirsim was not fortified in the MB IIA period, we come now to Megiddo, seemingly the only MB IIA defended city in Palestine. While such a situation could theoretically have existed at Megiddo because of its exceptionally important position, the archaeological data seems to cast doubt on it.

It is impossible, within the frame of the present discussion, to go into the complicated and fragmentary picture presented by the excavators in *Megiddo II*. I would like, nevertheless, to put forward my views that as far as the fortifications shown on the plans of Area BB are concerned, I tend to agree with much of Kenyon's view,[8] that the city-wall attributed by the excavators to Stratum XIIIA, is in fact later (i.e. MB IIB)

---

[1] P. W. Lapp, *BASOR* 195, 1969, p. 4.

[2] R. W. Funk, in *AASOR* 38, 1968, pp. 4 ff.

[3] *AASOR* 17, 1938, Pl. 49.

[4] The non-alignment of the G houses to the city-wall was stressed also by Kenyon (op. cit. above, p. 203, n. 5, p. 30) and by my student A. Eytan in an M.A. seminar paper.

[5] I hope to publish elsewhere the detailed evidence.

[6] *AASOR*, 17, p. 23, § 32.   [7] Ibid., p. 20.

[8] K. M. Kenyon, *Levant*, 1, 1969, pp. 25 ff. This possibility seems to me much more convincing, stratigraphically, than the suggestions of Dunayevsky and Kempinsky, supported by Mazar (*IEJ* 18, 1968, p. 72, n. 16). On the other hand, it seems to me that Dunayevsky and Kempinsky are right in attributing the three temples to the EB.

and thus the whole of the preceding MB II cities (XIV–XIII, with additional phases) were unwalled. I would like to go one step further, and suggest that the famous Stratum XIIIA gate in Area AA,[1] does not belong to the MB IIA period, but rather to the Early Bronze![2] The gate—with its bent passage and stepped approach—is different from the MB II gates all over the country. On the other hand, the stepped approach resembles the EB gate at Tell el Far'ah (North), and the buttresses of the approach wall are similar to those of EB Troy gates. Moreover, one should remember that even the excavators were not sure in ascribing the gate to XIII. This number simply denotes that the gate was found under XII.[3]

The general picture attained of Palestine in the MB IIA period is therefore of a series of unwalled settlements on most of the well-known sites in the country. At the beginning of the MB IIB, these settlements are turned, slowly but surely, into fortified cities. Thus this process resembles strongly the much earlier situation in the EB I period, which heralded the fortified cities of the EB II, as well as the very beginning of the Iron Age—with its poor settlements preceding the fortified cities of the later phases.

It seems to me that the tendency of some scholars to magnify the size, nature, and duration of the MB IIA period was prompted by the fact that the MB IIA corresponds, timewise, to the XIIth Dynasty in Egypt and by the discovery of statues of Egyptian dignitaries in some MB IIA cities. However, if we look at the situation from a different view-point, it seems that some of the apparent difficulties will disappear. Palestine at this period, as far as Egypt was concerned, was the source of agricultural supplies, including cattle.[4] For this purpose Egyptian procurement personnel were stationed at key settlements and only in cases of rebellion of the local inhabitants and refusal to comply with the Egyptian demands were punitive missions sent by Egypt. Thus, too much, it seems, was made of the expedition recorded by Khu-Sebek[5] to Schechem. In fact it is the 'country of Schechem,' and not the city which is mentioned, and the incident recorded, shows that it was a skirmish with some bands, rather than an assault on a fortified city: 'Then I smote an Asiatic.'

To sum up, it seems to me that the latest find at Hazor confirms also the data from other sites: In MB IIA (the beginning of which was in the first half of the nineteenth century B.C.), and at the very beginning of the MB IIB, most of the sites are either unwalled, or as yet non-existent. The true MB IIB is indeed the period in which the large fortified cities of the MB II begin to appear. It is in this period that the second urban revolution took place.

---

[1] *Megiddo II*, Fig. 378.

[2] Kenyon (op. cit., p. 205, n. 8, p. 55) attributes the gate 'probably early in MB II [i.e. MB IIB—*Y.Y.*] or possibly MB I' [i.e. MB IIA—*Y.Y.*]. Such a possibility has previously been suggested by Kenyon herself (op. cit., p. 203, n. 5, p. 23).

[3] *Megiddo II*, p. 6.   [4] Cf. also Mazar, *IEJ* 18, 1968, p. 73, n. 18.   [5] *ANET*, p. 230.

§ 3. *Mari Letter A. 1270*

After the present book had passed the proof stage, this letter
(A. 1270) was published by G. Dossin, in *Revue d'Assyriologie*, 64, 1970,
pp. 97 ff. The relevant passage (to be found on the reverse of the above-
mentioned tablet) has now been translated into English by A. Malamat,
with important historical and geographical commentary (*IEJ* 21, 1971,
pp. 34 ff.). Because of the importance of the text, Malamat's translation
is reproduced hereunder:

        10 minas tin (for) Sumu-Erah
        at Muzunnum
20   8 ⅓ minas tin (for) Wari-taldu
        at Laish (Layišim/Lawišim)
        30 minas tin (for) Ibni-Adad, King of Hazor
        Comptroller: Add[. . .   ] at Hazazar
        for the first time;
25   20 minas tin (for) Amud-pī-El,
        20 minas tin (for) Ibni-Adad,
        [for the] second time;
        [X] minas tin for the Caphtorite,
        1[+? minas] tin for the dragomen,
30   [X minas tin for] the Carian (?),
        [at Ug]arit;
        20 (?) [minas tin for Ib]ni-Adad for the third time;
        - - - -

            · · ·

INDEX (PEOPLE AND PLACES)

(Prepared by Mrs. Orly Ophrat)

'Abdi Tirshi ('Abdi-Tirši), 8, 9.
Abel-beth-maacah, 12.
'Abi-Milki, 8, 9.
Abydos, 126.
Achshaph, 6.
Ahab, 113, 115, 147, 164–78 passim, 200.
Aharoni, Y., 11, 23–4, 86, 131–2, 135, 150, 190.
'Aiâb, 9.
Alalakh, 8, 9, 60, 87, 90–1, 101, 104, 124.
Albright, W. F., 2, 5, 7–8, 10–11, 28, 31, 39, 74, 107, 130, 153, 205.
Alkim, B., 90.
Alt, A., 4, 10, 131.
Amen-em-Opet, 7.
Amenophis II, 7.
Amenophis III, 19, 28.
Amiran, R., 23–4, 35, 121, 130–1, 133, 190, 204.
Amman, 98–100.
Ammi-Ṣaduqa, 83.
Amurru, 5.
Anatolia, 47, 90, 104.
Andrae, W., 97.
Arad, 86, 201.
Arrapḫa, 4.
Arslan-Tash, 182.
Artzi, P., 31.
Ashkelon, 6.
Ashtaroth, 8–9.
Asia, 126.
Asshur, 97–8.
Assyria, 5, 12.
Ayeleth Ha-Shahar, Kibbutz, 23, 25, 194, 196.

Ba'al Ḥammon, 73.
Babylon, 4, 6.
Baḫdi-Lim, 3–4.
Barag, D., 195.
Baraq, 108.
Barnett, R. D., 182, 190.
Batyevsky, M., 26.
Beer-Sheva, 168.
Beisan (see also Beth-Shean), 15, 19, 28.
Ben-Hadad, 143, 200.
Ben-Tor, A., 26, 120.
Bethel, 11.
Beth-Shean (see also Beisan), 105, 201.
Beth-Shemesh, 168.
Beth-Zur, 205.
Biran, A., 19, 56, 107, 132.
Birot, M., 6.
Boaz, 89.

Böhl, L., 31, 107.
Boling, R. G., 99.
Bottéro, J., 6–8.
du Buisson, du Mesnil, 51.

Campbell, E. F. Jr., 7, 99–100, 107.
Canaan, 5, 8, 10.
Carchemish, 6, 51, 53, 106.
Carthage, 73.
Crete, 31.

Damascus, 15.
Dan (see also Laish, Tell Dan), 2, 107.
David, 153.
Deborah, 10, 108, 131–2, 134.
Demetrius, 12, 197.
Dever, W. D., 121, 148, 150, 178, 204.
Djahy, 6.
Dossin, G., 5, 207.
Dothan, M., 23–4.
Dothan, T., 23–4, 75, 157, 165.
Dunayevsky, I., 23–6, 54, 58, 63, 75, 89, 96, 135, 165, 184, 205.

Egypt, 4, 206.
Eitan (Eytan), A., 26, 204–5.
Ekallatum, 4.
El-Amarna, 7, 45, 198, 200–1.
Ellis, R. S., 94.
Emar, 6.
Epstein, C., 23–4.
Esdraelon Valley (see also Jezreel, Valley of), 10.
Eshnuna, 4, 6, 100.

Frankfort, H., 94, 104, 140.
Fritz, V., 10.
Funk, R. W., 205.
Furumark, A., 41, 46, 108.

Galilee, 9, 10–12, 14, 15, 120, 131, 200.
Galling, K., 73.
Garstang, J., 14–15, 18–21, 27–8, 42, 46, 51, 58, 91, 110, 112, 114, 116, 118, 136, 167–8, 196.
Gerizim, Mount, 99–100.
Gezer, 11, 59, 135, 147–50, 154–5, 172, 178, 201, 204.
Gibeon, 172.
Gilead, 12.
Gimil-Sin, 100.
Goetze, A., 107.
Gofna, R., 203.
Golénischeff, W., 6.

Gray, J., 74.
Greenberg, M., 7–8.
Gt̠i, 1, 5.
Guy, P. L. O., 150, 158–9, 196.
Ḫabiru, 7–9.
Hadad, 95, 146.
Hagia Triada, 31.
Haifa, 164.
Ḥalab, 4.
Haller, A., 97–8.
Hammurabi, 2, 4, 107.
Hankey, V., 33, 41.
Harosheth of the Gentiles, 10.
Hathor, 45.
Hattušiliš I, 90.
Hazor: Ha-ṣú-ra, 3, 8, 201; Ḫa-ṣú-ra-a, 3;
   Ḫa-ṣú-ra-ya^ki, 3, 6; ḥd̠r, 6, 7; ḥd̠wiз̌i
   (ḥd̠wiз̌), 1; ḥd̠⟨w⟩r, 6, 7.
Heber the Kenite, 10.
Helck, W., 2.
Hendâj, 13.
Hennessy, J. B., 98, 120.
Hofri, B., 26.
Ḥori, 7.
H-t-m, 6.
Hûleh: Basin, 15; Lake, 12–13, 15; Plain, 14.

Ibni-Adad (see also Yabni-Hadad), 5.
ib̠з-hdd, 2.
Idri-mi, 91.
Ijon, 12.
^mIš-me-^dAdad, 31.
^mIš-me-Ilam^lam, 31.
Israel, 1, 9, 11–12, 23, 178.
Ištar, 83.

Jabin (see also Yabin), 9–11, 132, 134.
Jachin, 89.
Jael, 10.
Janoah, 12.
Jenin, 164.
Jericho, 28, 56, 120, 123, 202, 204.
Jeroboam II, 113, 200.
Jerusalem, 86, 147.
Jezreel, Valley of (see also Esdraelon Valley),
   132.
Jordan, cis-, 9.
Joshua, 9–11, 27–8.
Josephus, 12–13.

Kaplan, J., 203.
Kaptara, 5.
Karana, 4.
Kedesh, 12–13.
Kempinsky, A., 25, 54, 205.
Kenyon, K. M., 45, 56, 108, 141–2, 161,
   203–6.
Kertes, G., 26.
Khu-Sebek, 206.
Kibbutz Ayeleth Ha-Shahar, see Ayeleth
   Ha-Shahar.
^matKi-na-aḫ-na, 8.

Kinnereth, 6.
Kirkbride, D., 203.
Kitchen, K. A., 7.
Klir, G., 26.
Knudtzon, J. A., 7.
Kokhavi, M., 204.
Kupper, J. R., 5.

Lachish, 11, 32, 40, 42, 105.
Laish (see also Dan, Tell Dan), 2, 5.
Lamon, R. S., 150, 160, 162–4.
Lance, H. D., 150, 204.
Landsberger, B., 82–3, 107.
Lapp, P. W., 39, 61, 120, 127, 205.
Loud, G., 150, 159.

Ma'ayan Barukh, 121.
Macalister, R. A. S., 147–8.
Makhbiram, 181–2, 186.
Malamat, A., 4–6, 10–11, 31, 107–8, 207.
Mari, 2–3, 5–6, 8, 31, 41, 106–7, 198, 200–1.
May, H. G., 133, 150, 171.
Mazar, A., 26.
Mazar, B., 2, 5, 7, 11, 26, 107–8, 131, 203,
   205–6.
Megiddo, 6, 11, 15, 32, 78, 103, 135, 147–8,
   150–65, 172–3, 178, 203–5.
Menahem, 200.
Men-Kheperw-Re (see also Thutmosis IV),
   46.
Menzel, E., 26.
Mercer, S. A. B., 7, 9.
Merhav, R., 104.
Mesha, 178.
Mesopotamia, 3, 5, 66, 98, 100.
Mirgissa, 2.
Mishrefeh, el (see also Qatna), 4.
Moortgat, A., 98.
Moscati, S., 73.

Nahariyah, 105.
Naphtali, 12.
Naumann, R., 89.
Negbi, O., 82, 133.
Negev, 120.
Nergal, 83.
Nimrud, 182, 190.
Noth, M., 2, 131.

Ohata, K., 204.
Omri, 113, 164.
Oppenheim, A. L., 4.
Orthmann, W., 90.
Ory, J., 204.
Osiris, 126.

Palestine, 1–3, 7, 15, 30–1, 39, 50, 60–1, 69,
   82–3, 86, 90, 94, 100, 105–6, 120, 130–1,
   179, 196, 203–6.
Parker, B., 94.
Parr, P. J., 57, 203.
Parrot, A., 104.
Pekah (Peqaḥ), 12, 185, 190.

Perrot, J., 23–4.
Pohl, A., 5.
Porter, J. L., 13.
Posener, M. G., 1–2.
Pritchard, J. B., 150.
Ptah, 126.

Qatna (see also Mishrefeh, el), 2, 4–5, 51, 60, 106–7.

Rameses II, 7, 198.
Rameses III, 7, 152, 162.
Rameses VI, 152.
Ras el 'Ain, 204.
Rosh-Pinnah, 26.
Rothschild, J. A. de, 23.
Rowton, M. B., 107–8, 131.

Samaria, 161, 171–2, 182.
Samochontis (see also Semechonitis), Lake, 13.
Samsu-ditana, 83.
Sanders, J. A., 73.
Schaeffer, C. F. A., 31.
Schumacher, G., 150, 157.
Semechonitis (see also Samochontis), Lake, 12.
Sethi I, 7, 108.
Shamshi-Adad I, 5, 98, 107–8.
Shechem, 56, 78, 103, 105, 206.
Shiloh, Y., 26, 202.
Shimron, 6.
Shipton, G. M., 150.
Shishak, 150, 160.
Sidon, 15.
Simons, J., 6–7.
Sin, 73.
Sin-Shamash ('double temple'), 97.
Sisera, 10, 132.
Smith, S., 107.
Solomon, 9, 11, 18–19, 21–2, 26, 113, 135, 141, 147–8, 150–3, 155, 158, 160–4.
Stern, E., 24, 196.
Syria, 3, 27, 57, 82, 90, 104.

Ta'anach (Ta'anakh), 6, 61, 127, 205.
Tadmor, H., 82–3, 107, 124.
Tananir, 99–100.
Täubler, E., 7.
Tell Abu Hawâm, 168.
Tell Beit Mirsim, 202–5.
Tell Dan (see also Dan, Laish), 51, 56, 132, 203.

Tell el 'Ajjul, 204.
Tell el Amarna, see El-Amarna.
Tell el Far'ah (North), 204, 206.
Tell el-Qedah, 13–15, 17–18, 21–4, 26, 201.
Tell es-Sa'idiyeh, 168.
Tell Hesy, 120.
Tell Mardikh, 51, 64, 106.
Tell Nagilah, 204.
Tell Poleg, 203.
Tell Waggâs (see also Wadi el-Waggâs), 13.
Tell Zeror, 204.
Thebes, 126.
Thotmes III (see also Thutmosis), 28.
Thureau-Dangin, F., 9.
Thutmosis III (see also Thotmes), 6, 32, 198, 200.
Thutmosis IV (see also Men-Kheperw-Re), 45.
Tiglath-Pileser III, 9, 12, 113, 115, 191, 198.
Tilmen Hüyük, 90.
Tyre, 8, 195.

Ugarit, 5, 50.
Uzziah, 113, 181, 198.

de Vaux, R., 204.
Vercoutter, J., 2.

Wadi el-Waggâs (see also Tell Waggâs), 13, 15, 17, 172.
Waggâs, 13.
Weidner, E. F., 107.
Weippert, M., 7, 10–11, 131.
Welter, G., 99.
Wilson, J. A., 7, 126.
Wiseman, D. J., 8.
Woolley, C. L., 51, 53, 79, 91, 104, 124.
Wright, G. E., 56, 78, 87, 99, 100, 150, 153, 204.
Wright, G. R. H., 98–100.

Yabin (see also Jabin), 5.
Yabni-Hadad (see also Ibni-Adad), 5.
Yadin, Y., 36, 51, 57, 148, 178.
Yamḫad, 2, 4, 6.
Yarim-Lim, 104.
Yasmaḫ-Adad, 5.
Yavne-yam, 203.
Yeivin, S., 10.
Ykmt-'mw, 2.

Zimri-Lim, 3, 6.
Zinjirli, 90, 140, 155.

PLATE I

a. Aerial view. Looking north. Foreground—the Tell of the Upper City. Above—the enclosure of the Lower City.

b. Aerial view. Looking south. The bottle-shaped Tell of the Upper City (right—Area B). Foreground—southern part of Lower City (right—Area C and earthen rampart).

PLATE II

a. Area C. Looking west. Above—earthen rampart. Most of the buildings shown are of LB periods. The MB II strata—bottom left.

b. Area F. Aerial view, looking west. Big altar—centre left.

PLATE III

a. Area D. Looking south-west. Tripods above rock-hewn cisterns. Buildings of MB II and LB periods.

b. Area 210. Strata 4–1A (MB II–LB III).

PLATE IV

a. Area A. The 'Big Trench'. Looking south. Section through the MB II brick-wall.

b. Area G. Looking south. The MB II stone glacis and moat.

PLATE V

a. Area A. Looking south-east. The MB II palatial building. Below left—The Early Bronze strata. Above—the pillared building of Stratum VIII (9th century B.C.).

b. Area F. A section of the MB II underground rock-hewn tunnel 8108.

c. Area F. Rock-hewn cave 8207. MB II.

PLATE VI

a. Area C. Looking north-west. The MB II strata.

b. Area 210. Burials in jars. Left—Stratum 3 (T1); right—Stratum 4 (T3–T4). MB IIB–C.

PLATE VII

a. Area K. Looking south-west. The city-gate at the commencement of excavations.

b. Area K. Looking south-west. Eastern face of southern half of the gate. Stratum 3—MB IIC.

PLATE VIII

a. Area K. Looking south-west. The revetment wall of the gate approach. MB IIC (B?).

b. Area K. Looking north-west. Section along gate's passageway. Paving (1A–B) covered by ashes and brick debris from final destruction.

PLATE IX

a. Area P. Looking west. The two-roomed western tower of the city-gate. MB II, with some LB additions.

b. Area P. Looking south-west. The terraced stone foundations of the brick wall between the city-gate and the earthen rampart. MB IIB.

PLATE X

a. Area H. The clay liver-model. Stratum 2 (LB I).

b. Area F. Burial 8112 (Stratum 2—LB I) inside drainage-channel of the Stratum 3 (MB IIC) 'Double Temple'.

c. Area H. The bronze plaque. Stratum 2 (LB I).

PLATE XI

a. Area C. Looking south-west. A general view of the ıʙ–ᴀ strata (LB II–III). Building 6225 (below) and 6063.

b. Area C. Looking north-west. Room 6217 with nest of pithoi. Note upper potter's wheel at bottom left. Stratum ıʙ (LB II).

PLATE XII

a. Area F. Looking north-west. Burial-cave 8144 with hundreds of LB II (1B) vessels.

b. Mycenaean IIIA vessels from above burial (14th century B.C.).

c. Two Cypriote 'Bucchero' ware juglets from the same burial (14th century B.C.).

PLATE XIII

Area C. Looking west. Section through western earthen rampart (MB IIB), and 'Stelae Temple'
(IA–LB III), at bottom of rampart.

PLATE XIV

a. Area C. Looking north-west. The niche of the 'Stelae Temple' as found (head of statue was found at bottom). IA–LB III (13th century B.C.).

b. Area A. Looking west. Stelae and offering bowl, in front of the ruined LB I 'Long Temple' (LB III)—Stratum XIII (13th century B.C.).

PLATE XV

b. Area C. The clay mask shown in a, left.

a. Area C. Potter's workshop (locus 6225), with potter's wheel and clay mask. Stratum IB (14th century B.C.).

c. Area C. A bronze silver-plated cult-standard. Stratum IB (IA?) 14th–13th century B.C.

d. Area D. A clay mask similar to that from Area C. 14th–13th centuries B.C.

PLATE XVI

a. Area H. The 'Orthostats Temple'. Looking south-east. The 'Holy of Holies' (2113) in its Stratum IA (13th century B.C.) phase.

b. As above. Looking east. 'Holy of Holies' 2123 of Stratum IB. Above earth bulk, pillar and base of Stratum IA.

PLATE XVII

a. Area H. The 'Orthostats Temple', looking north. Bottom, porch 2128 with two bases of pillars, Stratum IA. Lion shown in following pictures was found under a heap of stones at bottom left.

b. Area H. 'Lion orthostat' as buried under heap of stones (see also above, *a*).

PLATE XVIII

a. Area H. The big lion orthostat. Originally of LB I period, buried in LB II or LB III.

b. Area C. The small lion orthostat, found in secondary use in the IA (LB III) phase of the 'Stelae Temple'. Originally LB I.

c. Area A. The 'lioness orthostat', found broken in debris of Stratum XIII.

PLATE XIX

a. Area H. Vessels in 'Holy of Holies', as found in Stratum IA. Note the incense-altar, the basin, two libation-tables, and basalt krater near four-handled pot.

b. Area H. The incense-altar with the 'four-pointed star', within the circle, the emblem of the Temple's deity.

c. Area A. A clay bull's head, with circle and four-pointed star on foreground. Found in Stratum IXB.

PLATE XX

b. Area H. Orthostats Temple. A bronze bull (5 cm. in length) found in the 'Holy of Holies' of the Temple, Stratum IA.

a. Area H. The deity statue with its bull base, found broken in front of the Orthostats Temple. Note the emblem of the deity (circle and four-pointed star) on pendant.

c. A Mycenaean IIIB clay bull figurine, found in Stratum IA of the Orthostats Temple.

d. Area H. A cylinder seal showing a deity with winged 'solar disc', found in Stratum IA of 'Holy of Holies'. (An heirloom from earlier strata?)

PLATE XXI

a. Area C. Three views of the deity statue of the Stelae Temple. Note the deity's emblem: inverted crescent.

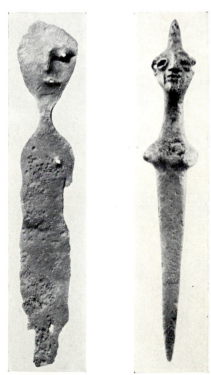

b. Area H. A seated figure (a king?) found in the burnt layer of Stratum 1A; the 'Holy of Holies' of the Orthostats Temple. Height of statue: 18 cm.

c. Area H. 'The Picasso figurine' from Stratum 2 (LB I) Bronze, 5 cm.

Area H. Peg, bronze figurine. Stratum 1A; 11·5 cm.

PLATE XXII

a. Area A. Looking west. The orthostats entrance to the 'Long Temple', Stratum XV–LB I.

b. Area A. Looking west. The vaulted corridor to the water reservoir. LB.

PLATE XXIII

Area A. Aerial view, looking south at end of 1958 season. Solomonic city-gate and casemate-wall (Strata X–IX) below. MB and LB buildings at the centre and pillared building (Stratum VIII) and the Stratum VI courtyard building, above.

PLATE XXIV

a. Area A. Looking south-west. Oven made of upper part of upturned store jar. Stratum XII (12th century B.C.).

b. Area B. Cult-place of Stratum XI. Jar with bronze votives (11th century B.C.)

c. Area B. A bronze deity figurine and a lugged axe blade, from *b*, left.

PLATE XXV

a. Area A. Aerial view, looking south-east. Solomonic city-gate and casemate-wall (bottom and left) and pillared building (Stratum VIII) and courtyard building (Stratum VI) above.

c. Detail of *b*, left.

b. Area M. Looking south-east. Bottom—corner of casemate-wall (Stratum X) turning west (right), and joint of solid wall (Stratum VIII) to the left. Above—Area A.

PLATE XXVI

a. Area A. Looking south-west. The northern row of pillars of the pillared building (Stratum VIII) as excavated by Garstang.

b. The pillared building (Stratum VIII). Looking south-east, at the end of the 1956 season.

PLATE XXVII

a. Area A. Looking south-east. The two northern halls of the pillared building (Stratum VIII). Note the rectangular depressions in the floor and compare the following picture.

b. The same as above, after the removal of the Stratum VIII floor. The building's Solomonic (Strata X–IX) plan corresponds to the form of the depressions.

PLATE XXVIII

a. Area B. Aerial view (looking south-west) of the citadel (top centre) of Stratum VIII, the ancillary administrative buildings—right and left of Stratum VIII–V, and the partially filled casemate-wall (left).

b. Area B. A Proto-Aeolic capital of the citadel of Stratum VIII.

PLATE XXIX

Area L. The water-system as seen from the air at the end of the dig. Note the casemate-wall (Stratum X) on right; the 'four-roomed' administrative building (Strata VIII–V) top, right, and the 'entrance-structure' to the vertical shaft— top centre.

PLATE XXX

Area L. The water-system, looking west. The rock-hewn shaft and the entrance to the tunnel.

PLATE XXXI

Area L. The water-system, looking west into the tunnel, from its entrance, showing the debris as found.

PLATE XXXII

a. Area L. The water-system, looking west. The water at the end of the tunnel. The wooden planks support the ceiling to prevent collapse, during the excavations.

b. As above, showing the top basalt steps, at the bottom of the rock-hewn stairs in the tunnel.

PLATE XXXIII

a. Area A. Looking south-east. The courtyard building (2a) of Stratum VI. Note the tilted pillars resulting from an earthquake.

b. Area A. Looking east. The destruction of Stratum V. (Room 4 in building 1.)

PLATE XXXIV

a. Area G. Looking south-east. Building 10037c (Stratum VI), with the stone staircase leading to upper floor or roof.

b. Area G. Looking south (from outside city). The postern gate with stone blocking of Stratum Vₐ.

c. The same; looking north. The brick blocking as seen from inside city.

PLATE XXXV

a. Area D. A sherd (2·5 cm. wide) with proto-Canaanite inscription: [ʽ]lt?

b. Area B. A fragment of a stele with hieroglyphic inscription. Unstratified. For decipherment see p. 126, n. 1.

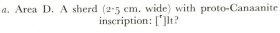

c. Area B. Stratum Vᴀ. Outer face of a bowl with a Hebrew inscription. The second word is קדש = *Holy*. The same inscription is incised also on the rim.

d. Area B. Stratum Vᴀ. A Hebrew inscription on the shoulder of a jar: לפקח סמדר = *belonging to Pekah. Semadar* (wine of tender grapes).

e. Area A. Stratum VI. A Hebrew inscription on a shoulder of a jar: למכברם = *belonging to Makhbiram.*

f. Area A. Stratum VI. A Hebrew inscription painted on a jar: ירבעם בן אלמ = *Jeroboam, Son of Elm(athàn?)*.

PLATE XXXVI

a. Area A. Stratum VI. Three sides of a carved bone handle.

b. Area A. Stratum VI. Three views of an ivory cosmetic spoon.